PORTRAITS

OF

ILLUSTRIOUS PERSONAGES

OF

GREAT BRITAIN.

ENGRAVED

FROM AUTHENTIC PICTURES IN THE GALLERIES OF THE NOBILITY, AND THE
PUBLIC COLLECTIONS OF THE COUNTRY.

WITH

Biographical and Historical Memoirs

OF THEIR LIVES AND ACTIONS.

BY EDMUND LODGE, ESQ., F.S.A.

IN TEN VOLUMES.

VOL. III.

LONDON:
WILLIAM SMITH, 113, FLEET STREET.
MDCCCXL.

LONDON:
BRADBURY AND EVANS, PRINTERS, WHITEFRIARS.

CONTENTS.

VOLUME III.

CONTENTS.

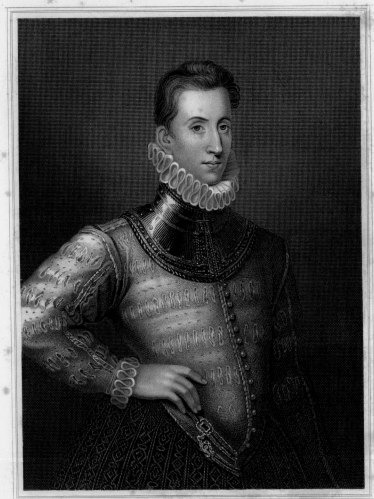

Engraved by H.Robinson.

SIR PHILIP SIDNEY.

OB. 1586.

FROM THE ORIGINAL OF SIR ANT? MORE, IN THE COLLECTION OF

HIS GRACE THE DUKE OF BEDFORD.

William Smith, 1, Bouverie Street, London.

SIR PHILIP SIDNEY.

—◆—

BIOGRAPHY, like painting, derives a main interest from the contrast of strong lights and shadows. The glowing serenity of Italian skies, and the constant verdure of our own plains, delight us in nature, but on the canvass we look for tempestuous clouds, and rocky precipices, to break the uniformity of milder beauties; and, however necessary it may be that the judgment should be assured of the truth of the representation, yet, at all events, the fancy must be gratified. So it is with the reality and the picture of human life. The virtues which adorned the living man are faint ornaments on his posthumous story, without the usual opposition of instances of infirmity and extravagance. Whether it be an envy of perfection, a hasty prejudice which may have induced us to suppose that it cannot exist in the human character, or a just experience of its extreme rarity, that renders the portrait displeasing, unnatural, or at best insipid; or whether, under the influence of the secret principle of selfishness, virtue, in losing its power of conferring benefits, may not seem to have lost most of its beauty, are questions not to be solved; the fact, however, is incontrovertible.

Under the pressure of these reflections, and of others nearly as discouraging, I sit down to write some account of the life of SIR

1

PHILIP SIDNEY, whose character displays almost unvaried excellence ; whose splendour of talents, and purity of mind, were, if possible, exceeded by the simplicity and the kindness of his heart ; whose short, but matchless, career was closed by a death in which the highest military glory was even more than rivalled, not by those degrees of consolation usually derived from religion and patience, but by the piety of a saint, and the constancy of a stoic : a life too which has so frequently been the theme of the biographer ; of which all public facts are probably already recorded, and on which all terms of panegyric seem to have been exhausted.

Sir Philip Sidney was born on the twenty-ninth of November, 1554. His family was of high antiquity, Sir William Sidney, his lineal ancestor, a native of Anjou, having accompanied Henry the Second from thence, and afterwards waited on that Prince as one of his Chamberlains. From this courtly origin the Sidneys retired suddenly into privacy, and settled themselves in Surrey and Sussex, where they remained for nearly four hundred years in the character of country gentlemen, till Nicholas Sidney, who was twelfth in descent from Sir William, married Anne, daughter of Sir William Brandon, and aunt and co-heir to Charles Brandon, Duke of Suffolk, a match which gave him a sort of family connection to Henry the Eighth, and probably drew him to the court. William, his only son, became successively an esquire of the body, a chamberlain, steward, and gentleman of the privy chamber, to that Prince, whom he afterwards repeatedly served with distinguished credit both in his fleets and armies, and from whom he received the honour of knighthood. To this Sir William, who is thus especially spoken of, because he may be esteemed the principal founder of the subsequent splendour of his family, Henry granted, in 1547, several manors and lands which had lately fallen to the crown by the attainder of Sir Ralph Vane, particularly the honour and park of Penshurst in Kent. He too left an only son, Sir Henry Sidney, the dear friend of King Edward the Sixth, who died in his arms, one of Elizabeth's well-chosen knights of the garter, the celebrated governor of Ireland, and President of Wales ; a wise

2

statesman, a true patriot, and a most honourable and beneficent gentleman. Of his three sons, by Mary, eldest daughter of the great and miserable John Dudley, Duke of Northumberland, the first was our Sir Philip Sidney.

With such zeal has every scattered fragment relative to this admirable person been preserved, that the circumstances of his very infancy would form a collection more extensive than the whole history of many a long and eminent life. "Of his youth," says Sir Fulke Greville, one of his school-fellows, and his first biographer, "I will report no other than this; that though I lived with him, and knew him from a child, yet I never knew him other than a man; with such a steadiness of mind, lovely and familiar gravity, as carried grace and reverence above greater years; his talk ever of knowledge, and his very play tending to enrich his mind, so as even his teachers found something in him to observe and learn, above that which they had usually read or taught." In order that he might be near his family, which resided at Ludlow Castle during Sir Henry's Presidency of Wales, he was placed at a school in the town of Shrewsbury, and seems to have been at no other; yet we find him, at the age of twelve years, writing to his father, not only in Latin, but in French, and doubtless with correctness at least, since no censure is uttered on his epistles by his father, from whom we have the fact. It is communicated in a letter to him from Sir Henry, so excellent in every point of consideration, and more particularly as it should seem to have been the very mould in which the son's future character was cast, that I cannot help regretting that its great length, not to mention that it has lately been published by Dr. Zouch, should render it unfit to form a part of the present sketch.

He was removed to Christchurch in the University of Oxford in 1569, and placed under the care of Dr. Thomas Thornton, (who became through his means a Canon of that house), assisted by Robert Dorsett, afterwards Dean of Chester. Dr. Thornton was the gratuitous preceptor of Camden, and introduced him to Sidney, who became afterwards one of his most earnest patrons: and that

3

faithful historian, who so well and so early knew him, has told us that " he was born into the world to shew unto his age a sample of ancient virtues." Sidney studied also for some time at Cambridge, and there confirmed that fast friendship with Greville which had commenced at their school, and which the latter, with a warmth which the lapse of more than forty surviving years had not impaired, so emphatically commemorates on his own tomb, in the collegiate church of Warwick, by this inscription—" Fulke Greville, servant to Queen Elizabeth, counsellor to King James, and friend to Sir Philip Sidney."

He concluded his academical studies at seventeen years of age, and on the twenty-sixth of May, 1572, departed for France with Edward Clinton, Earl of Lincoln, and Admiral, then appointed by Elizabeth her ambassador extraordinary. His uncle Leicester, who probably cared little for talents in which cunning had no place, gave him on that occasion a letter to Sir Francis Walsingham, then resident minister at Paris, in which he says " he is young and rawe, and no doubt shall find those countries, and the demeanours of the people, somewhat straunge to him, in which respect your good advice and counsell shall greatlie behove him," &c. He was received with great distinction. Charles the Ninth appointed him a gentleman of his bedchamber, and he became familiarly known to Henry, King of Navarre, and is said to have been highly esteemed by that great and amiable Prince. Charles's favour to him, it is true, had been considered but as a feature of the plan of that evil hour to lull the protestants into a false security during the preparations for the diabolical massacre of St. Bartholomew, which burst forth on the twenty-second of August, within a fortnight after he had been admitted into his office. Sidney, on that dreadful occasion, sheltered himself in the house of Walsingham, and quitted Paris as soon as the storm had subsided.

After a circuitous journey through Lorrain, by Strasburgh, and Heidelburgh, he rested for a time at Frankfort, where he became acquainted with the celebrated Hubert Languet, then resident minister there for the Elector of Saxony; a man who to the profoundest erudition joined the most intimate knowledge of the history, the laws, the political systems, and the manners of modern Europe; and whose eminent qualifications received their last polish from an upright heart, and a benign temper. At an age when men usually retire to the society of the friends of their youth, and the flatterers of their opinions, this sage selected the youthful Sidney, not only as his pupil, but as the companion of his leisure, and the depository of his confidence. "That day on which I first beheld him with my eyes," says Languet, "shone propitious to me." They passed together most part of the three years which Sidney devoted to his travels, and, when absent from each other, corresponded incessantly by letters. Languet's epistles have been more than once published, and amply prove the truth of these remarks; nor are Sidney's testimonials of gratitude and affection to him unrecorded.

Having halted long at Vienna, he travelled through Hungary, and passed into Italy, where he resided chiefly at Venice and Padua, and, without visiting Rome, which, it is said, no doubt truly, that he afterwards much regretted, he returned to England about May, 1575, and immediately after, then little more than twenty-one years of age, was appointed ambassador to the Emperor Rodolph. The professed object of the mission was mere condolence on the death of that Prince's father; but Sidney had secret instructions to negociate a union of the protestant states against the Pope and Philip of Spain; and the subsequent success of the measure has been ascribed to his arguments and address. While transacting these affairs he became acquainted with William, the first Prince of Orange, and with Don John of Austria; and those heroes, perhaps in every other instance uniformly opposed to each other, united, not only in their tribute of applause, but in an actual friendship with him. William, in particular, held a constant correspondence with him on the public affairs of Europe, and designated him as "one of the ripest and greatest counsellors of state of that day in Europe."

Sidney returned from his embassy in 1577, and passed the eight succeeding years undistinguished by any public appointment. His spirit was too high for the court, and his integrity too stubborn for the cabinet. Elizabeth, who always expected implicit submission, could not long have endured such a servant; yet he occasionally advised her with the utmost freedom, and she received his counsel with gentleness. Of this we have a remarkable instance in his letter to her, written at great length, in 1579, against the proposed match with the Duke of Alençon, after of Anjou, which may be found in the Cabala, and in Collins's Sidney Papers, and which Hume has pronounced to be written "with an unusual elegance of expression, as well as force of reasoning." Sir Fulke Greville calls him "an exact image of quiet and action, happily united in him, and seldom well divided in others;" activity, however, was the ruling feature in the mechanism of his nature, while the keenest sensibility reigned in his heart. Perhaps, too, if we may venture to suppose that Sidney had a fault, those mixed dispositions produced in him their usual effect, an impatience and petulance of temper which the general grandeur of his mind was calculated rather to aggravate than to soften. Hence in this his time of leisure, he fell into some excesses, which in an ordinary person, so much is human judgment swayed by the character of its subject, might perhaps rather have challenged credit than censure. Such were his quarrels with the Earls of Ormond and Oxford, the one too worthy, the other too contemptible, to be the object of such a man's resentment. Ormond had been suspected by Sidney of having endeavoured to prejudice the Queen against his father, and had therefore been purposely affronted by him; but the Earl nobly said (as appears by a letter in Collins's Papers to Sir Henry Sidney), "that he would accept no quarrel from a gentleman who was bound by nature to defend his father's cause, and who was otherwise furnished with so many virtues as he knew Mr. Philip to be." We are not told, however, that Sidney was satisfied. Oxford was a brute and a madman; insulted him at a tennis-court, without a cause, and with the utmost vulgarity of manners and language:

yet, so angry was Sidney, that the privy council, finding their endeavours to prevent a duel would be ineffectual, were obliged to solicit Elizabeth to interpose her authority. Her argument on this occasion, for with him she condescended to argue, is too curious to be omitted. "She laid before him," says Sir Fulke Greville, "the difference in degree between earls and gentlemen; the respect inferiors owed to their superiors; and the necessity in princes to maintain their own creations, as degrees descending between the people's licentiousness and the anointed sovereignty of crowns; and how the gentleman's neglect of the nobility taught the peasant to insult both." Sidney combated this royal reasoning with freedom and firmness, but submitted. He retired, however, for many months, much disgusted, into the country; and, in that season of quiet, thus forced upon him, is supposed to have composed his Arcadia. These things happened in 1580; but the strongest and most blameable instance of his intemperance is to be found in a letter from him, on the 31st of May, 1578, to Mr. Edward Molineux, a gentleman of ancient family, and secretary to his father, whom he had hastily, and it seems unjustly, suspected of a breach of confidence. Let it speak for itself, and, saving us the pain of remarking further on it, allow us to take leave of the sole imperfection of Sidney's character.

"MR. MOLINEUX,

"Few woordes are best. My lettres to my father have come to the eys of some; neither can I condemne any but you for it. If it be so, yow have plaide the very knave with me, and so I will make yow know, if I have good proofe of it: but that for so muche as is past; for that is to come, I assure yow before God, that if ever I knowe you do so muche as reede any lettre I wryte to my father, without his commandement, or my consente, I will thruste my dagger into yow; and truste to it, for I speake it in earnest. In the mean tyme farewell.

"By me,
"PHILIPPE SIDNEY."

About this time he represented the county of Kent in Parliament, where he frequently was actively engaged in the public business. He sat in 1581 on a most select committee for the devising new laws against the Pope and his adherents. In the same year the proposals for the French marriage were earnestly renewed; the Duke of Anjou visited Elizabeth; and, after three months' ineffectual suit, was through her wisdom or folly, finally, but pompously dismissed. Sidney was appointed one of the splendid train which attended him to Antwerp, and we find him, soon after his return, soliciting for employment. "The Queen," says he, in a letter to Lord Burghley, of the twenty-seventh of January, 1582, " at my L. of Warwick's request, hathe bene moved to join me in his office of ordinance; and, as I learn, her Majestie yields gratious heering unto it. My suit is your L. will favour and furdre it, which I truly affirme unto your L. I much more desyre for the being busied in a thing of som serviceable experience than for any other comoditie, which is but small that can arise from it." His request was unsuccessful, and it was perhaps owing to this disappointment that he devoted the whole of the next year to literary leisure, one result of which is said to have been his " Defence of Poesy." In 1583 he married Frances, the only surviving daughter of Sir Francis Walsingham, by whom, two years afterwards, he had an only child, Elizabeth, who became the wife of Roger Manners, Earl of Rutland; and on the thirteenth of January in that year was knighted at Windsor, as a qualification for his serving as proxy for John, Prince Palatine of the Rhine, at an installation of the order of the Garter.

It is strange that almost immediately after his disinterested marriage to a young woman of exquisite beauty and accomplishments, he should have laid a plan to accompany Drake, in his second voyage, all the great objects of which it was agreed should be committed to his management. The whole had been devised and matured with the utmost secrecy, and it should seem that he was actually on board when a peremptory mandate arrived from the Queen to stay him. A speculation, the extravagance of which was perhaps equal to its honour, awaited his return. He was invited to enrol himself among the candidates for the crown of Poland, vacant in 1585 by the death of Stephen Bathori; and this historical fact affords a stronger general proof of the fame of his transcendant character than all the united testimonies even of his contemporaries. That a young man, sprung from a family not yet ennobled; unemployed, save in a solitary embassy, by his own sovereign; passing perhaps the most part of his time in literary seclusion; should have been solicited even to be certainly unsuccessful in so glorious a race, would be utterly incredible, were it not absolutely proved. Here Elizabeth's prohibition again interfered : "She refused," says Naunton, "to further his advancement, not only out of emulation, but out of fear to lose the jewel of her times." She became, however, now convinced that this mighty spirit must have a larger scope for action. Sidney was sworn of the Privy Council, and, on the seventh of November in the same year appointed Governor of Flushing, one of the most important of the towns then pledged to Elizabeth for the payment and support of her auxiliary troops, and General of the Horse, under his uncle Leicester, who was Commander-in-Chief of the English forces in the Low Countries. On the eighteenth of that month he arrived at Flushing, and, as it were by an act of mere volition, instantly assumed, together with his command, all the qualifications which it required. His original letters, preserved in our great national repository, abundantly prove that he was the ablest general in the field, and the wisest military counsellor in that service : of his bravery it is unnecessary to speak. I insert one of them addressed to Sir Francis Walsingham, and hitherto unpublished ; not with the particular view of making that proof, but to give perhaps the strongest possible instance of the wonderful variety, as well as of the power of his rich mind : to exhibit the same Sidney whose pen had so lately been dedicated to the soft and sweet relaxation of poesy and pastoral romance, now writing from his tent, amid the din of war, with the stern simplicity, and shortbreathed impatience, of an old soldier. The letter, indeed, is in many other respects of singular curiosity. The view which it imperfectly gives us of his earnest zeal for the protestant cause, of Elizabeth's feelings towards him, and of the wretched provision made at home for the campaign, are all highly interesting.

"RIGHT HONORABLE,

"I receave dyvers letters from you, full of the discomfort which I see, and am sorry to see, y^t yow daily meet with at home; and I think, such is ye goodwil it pleaseth you to bear me, y^t my part of ye trouble is something y^t troubles yow; but I beseech yow let it not. I had before cast my count of danger, want, and disgrace: and, before God, Sir, it is trew in my hart, the love of ye caws doth so far over ballance them all, y^t, with God's grace, thei shall never make me weery of my resolution. If her Ma^{ti} wear the fountain, I wold fear, considering what I daily fynd, y^t we should wax dry; but she is but a means whom God useth, and I know not whether I am deceaved, but I am faithfully persuaded, y^t if she shold wthdraw herself, other springes wold ryse to help this action: for methinkes I see ye great work indeed in hand against the abusers of the world, wherein it is no greater fault to have confidence in man's power, then it is too hastily to despair of God's work. I think a wyse and constant man ought never to greeve whyle he doth plaie, as a man may sai, his own part truly, though others be out; but if himself leav his hold becaws other marriners will be ydle, he will hardly forgive himself his own fault. For me, I can not promis of my own cource, no, not of the . . . becaws I know there is a eyer power y^t must uphold me, or else I shall fall; but certainly I trust I shall not by other men's wantes be drawne from myself; therefore, good Sir, to whome for my particular I am more bownd then to all men besydes, be not troubled with my troubles, for I have seen the worst, in my judgement, beforehand, and wors then y^t can not bee.

"If the Queene pai not her souldiours she must loos her garrisons; ther is no dout thereof; but no man living shall be hable to sai the fault is in me. What releefe I can do them I will. I

10

will spare no danger, if occasion serves. I am sure no creature shall be hable to lay injustice to my charge ; and, for furdre doutes, truly I stand not uppon them. I have written by Adams to the council plainli, and thereof lett them determin. It hath been a costly beginning unto me this war, by reason I had nothing proportioned unto it ; my servantes unexperienced, and myself every way unfurnished ; but hereafter, if the war continew, I shall pas much better thorow with it. For Bergem up Zome, I delighted in it, I confess, becaws it was neer the enemy ; but especially, having a very fair hows in it, and an excellent air, I destenied it for my wyfe ; but, fynding how yow deal there, and y^t ill paiment in my absence thens might bring foorth som mischeef, and considering how apt the Queen is to interpret every thing to my disadvantage, I have resigned it to my Lord Willowghby, my very frend, and indeed a vaillant and frank gentleman, and fit for y^t place ; therefore I pray yow know that so much of my regality is faln.

" I understand I am called very ambitious and prowd at home, but certainly if thei know my hart thei woold not altogether so judg me. I wrote to yow a letter by Will, my Lord of Lester's jesting plaier, enclosed in a letter to my wyfe, and I never had answer thereof. It contained something to my Lord of Lester, and council y^t som wai might be taken to stai my lady there. I, since, dyvers tymes have writt to know whether you had receaved them, but yow never answered me y^t point. I since find y^t the knave deliver'd the letters to my Lady of Lester, but whether she sent them yow or no I know not, but earnestly desyre to do, becaws I dout there is more interpreted thereof. Mr. Erington is with me at Flushing, and therefore I think myself at the more rest, having a man of his reputation ; but I assure yow, Sir, in good earnest, I fynd Burlas another manner of a man than he is taken for, or I expected. I would to God, Burne had obtained his suit. He is ernest, but somewhat discomposed with consideration of his estate. Turner is good for nothing, and worst for ye sownd of ye hackbutes. We shall have a sore warr uppon us this sommer, wherein if appointment had been kept, and these disgraces forborn, wch have greatly weakened us, we had been victorious. I can sai no more at this tyme, but prai for your long and happy lyfe. At Utrecht, this 24th of March, 1586.

" Your humble son,

" PH. SIDNEY.

" I know not what to sai to my wyve's coming till you resolve better; for if yow run a strange cource, I may take such a one heere as will not be fitt for anye of the feminin gender. I prai yow make much of Nichol Gery. I have been vyldlie deceaved for armures or horsemen; if yow cold speedily spare me any out of your armury, I will send them yow back as soon as my own be finished. There was never so good a father find a more troublesom son. Send Sir William Pelham, good Sir, and let him have Clerke's place, for we need no clerkes, and it is most necessary to have such a one in the counsell."

On the fifth of May, following the date of this letter, he lost his father, and on the ninth of August, his mother. Providence thus mercifully spared them the dreadful trial which was fast approaching. Sir Philip having highly distinguished himself in many actions of various fortune, commanding on the twenty-fourth of September a detachment of the army, met accidentally a convoy of the enemy, on its way to Zutphen, a strong town of Guelderland, which they were then besieging. He attacked it with a very inferior force, and an engagement of uncommon fury ensued, in which having had one horse shot under him, and being remounted, he received a musket shot a little above the left knee, which shattered the bone, and passed upwards towards the body. As they were bearing him from the field of battle towards the camp (for the anecdote, though already so often told, cannot be too often repeated,) he became faint and thirsty from excess of bleeding, and asked for water, which he was about to drink, when observing the eye of a dying soldier fixed on the glass, he resigned it to him, saying " Thy necessity is yet greater than mine." He was carried to Arnheim, and variously tortured by a multitude of surgeons and physicians for three weeks. Amputation, or the extraction of the ball, would have saved his inestimable life, but they were unwilling to practise the one, and knew not how to perform the other. In the short intervals which he spared during his confinement from severe exercises of piety he wrote verses on his wound, and made his will at uncommon length, and with the most scrupulous attention. Of that instrument, which is inserted, with some mistakes, in Collins's Sidney Papers, Sir Fulke Greville most justly says, " This will of his, will ever remain for a witness to the world that those sweet and large, even dying, affections in him, could no more be contracted with the narrowness of pain, grief, or sickness, than any sparkle of our immortality can be privately buried in the shadow of death." It is dated the last day of September, 1586, and on the seventeenth of October he added a codicil, with many tokens of regard to intimate friends. A small but interesting fact disclosed by that codicil, has hitherto escaped the notice of his biographers. It ends with these words; "I give to my good friends, Sir George Digby and Sir Henry Goodier, each a ring of . . . ." His dictation was interrupted by death.

Thus ended a life, doubtless of great designs, but of few incidents. The jealousy and timidity of Elizabeth denied to Sir Philip Sidney any share in her state confidence; excluded him from a cabinet which he would have enlightened by his counsels, and purified by the example of his honour and integrity; and devoted him to an honourable banishment, and a premature death. Such a man should have had such a master as Henry the Fourth of France, and a concord of all that was wise, and virtuous, and amiable, might have gone far towards gaining the empire of Europe, by winning the hearts of its people. But he was consigned to almost private life, and a strict observer of his mind and heart would have been his best biographer. Most of the inestimable story which such a one might have preserved for our delight and our instruction is lost for ever. Sir Fulke Greville, who however entirely loved him, wanted the talent, or the feeling, or both, which might have excited and enabled him to record innumerable effusions of goodness, and wisdom, and genius, imbibed by himself, even at the fountain head : but his book, which has been the chief groundwork for subsequent writers, contains little but meagre facts and vapid eulogium. Those who would study then with precision the detail of Sidney's character must seek it in his writings, and I regret that the proposed limits of the present publication are too confined to allow of disquisition to that effect. I shall conclude, however, by enumerating them, adding a very few remarks.

We do not find that any of his works were published while he lived. The Arcadia, which has been translated into most of the living tongues, and so frequently reprinted, first appeared in 1591 ; as did "Astrophel and Stella," a long series of Sonnets and Songs, intended, as is said, to express his passion for the fair Lady Rich. "The Defence of Poesy," a critical rhapsody, full of classical intelligence and acute observation, was first printed in 1595 ; these only of his works were published singly. Other of his Sonnets, a poem called "A Remedy for Love," and "The Lady of May," a masque, have been subjoined to different editions of the Arcadia. In a volume published in 1600, and now lately reprinted, with the title of "England's Helicon, or a Collection of Songs," are many from his pen. His answer to that furious volume of vengeance against his uncle, well known by the title of "Leicester's Commonwealth," remained in manuscript so late as 1746, when Collins inserted it in his fine publication of the Sidney Papers. There are a few other pieces, both in verse and prose, which, having been perhaps falsely ascribed to him, I forbear to mention.

Notwithstanding all that we have heard of Sir Philip Sidney's early fondness for literature, I am inclined to think that, had he been placed in his proper sphere, we might never have known him as an author. The character of his talents, the form of his education, the habits of his early society, and his own earnest inclination, combined to qualify him for a statesman of the first order. Disappointed in his favourite views, his activity probably sought relief in literary exercise, and hence we find more of the mind than of the heart, more judgment than fancy, in the productions

14

of his pen. He fled to the muse, perhaps, rather for refuge than enjoyment, and courted her more in the spirit of a friend than of a lover ; but the warmth of the attachment was sufficient to produce a flame which was always bright and pure, and which, if it did not dazzle, at least never failed to enlighten. His works in general may be characterised as the choicest fruits of universal study, and unbounded recollection, selected by a mind which while it possessed equal measures of the most powerful vigour, and the most refined delicacy, was ruled by the highest sentiments of religious, moral, and social duty. He was deficient in originality, but the splendour of his virtues and of his talents awed criticism to silence, or charmed it into unqualified approbation ; till a writer, confessedly at the head of his own most agreeable class, stood boldly forward, not to start that objection, but to deny nearly all which the united suffrages of Europe had for two centuries implicitly agreed to grant. Lord Orford, in his sketch of the life of Sir Fulke Greville, calls Sir Philip Sidney "an astonishing object of temporary admiration ;" discovers his Arcadia to be " a tedious, lamentable, pedantic, pastoral romance ;" and insults the sublimity of his exit by ascribing it to " the rashness of a volunteer." But the noble writer delighted in biographical paradoxes, and perhaps in controverting received opinions and high authorities. It was natural enough for the champion of Richard the Third to turn his weapons against Sir Philip Sidney, as well as to endeavour to pull down the character of Lord Falkland, from the height on which it had been placed by the glowing pen of the immortal Clarendon. But a truce with such specks of criticism. Let them who are able and willing to judge for themselves, turn to the Defence of Poesy for the prodigious extent and variety of Sidney's studies, and for his judicious application of the results of them : let them contemplate even in the very first pages of the Arcadia, the readiness and playfulness of his wit, and in the whole, innumerable scattered proofs of his speculative and practical wisdom ; let them compare his style, both in verse and prose, with those of contemporary authors ; and they will turn, with a senti-

15

ment almost amounting to anger, from a solitary judgment founded in caprice, and uttered at least with indiscretion.

However imprudent it may be to place in the same view with my own observations a passage so finely conceived, and so exquisitely expressed, I cannot conclude, without citing in justification of some of the opinions which I have presumed here to give, the words of an admirable living critic. "Sidney," says he, in comparing his poetical talents with those of Lord Buckhurst, "displays more of the artifices, and less of the inspiration of Poetry. His command of language, and the variety of his ideas are conspicuous. His mind exhibits an astonishing fund of acquired wealth; but images themselves never seem to overcome him with all the power of actual presence. The ingenuity of his faculties supplies him with a lively substitute; but it is not vivid, like the reality."

Engraved by W. T. Fry.

MARY, QUEEN OF SCOTS.

OB. 1587.

FROM THE ORIGINAL IN THE COLLECTION OF

THE RIGHT HON.^{BLE} THE EARL OF MORTON.

Published Dec.r 1 1836, by Harding & Lepard, Pall Mall East.

MARY STUART,

QUEEN OF SCOTLAND.

THE writer of these memoirs having formerly been the humble instrument of discovering and promulgating many very curious particulars of Mary's eventful story, it might perhaps be expected that he should be more inclined, and even better qualified, than many others, now to treat of it somewhat at large; neither of those motives however, were he sensible of such, could tempt him to assume the task. All the stores of history and tradition, of public records and private collections, have been already ransacked; argument and reasonable conjecture have been exhausted; the fields even of imagination and fancy have been traversed in search of bright or hideous visions to enhance the charms of her person and her wit, and to aggravate the horror of her sufferings. Nay, while in the fear of saying too much I am thus apologising for saying so little, appears a complete " Life of Mary, Queen of Scots," from the ever employed and ever instructive pen of Mr. George Chalmers, who has once more journeyed over the whole of this interesting ground, and seems to have left no stone unturned which might by possibility have concealed any novel object of his research. The whole result is surely now before the public. It comprehends a tale which the heart has eagerly accepted from all the passions, and fixed irrevocably in the memory. To repeat it would be impertinent; to enlarge it, till new discoveries shall be made, is impossible.

The only object then of the few following lines is to give some account of the picture an engraving from which accompanies them. The numerous portraits hitherto ascribed to this Princess

1

are as various and as dissimilar as the circumstances of her life, or the features of her character, agreeing only in the single fact of representing her as eminently beautiful. No strong internal presumption, no inveterate tradition, tends to distinguish the authenticity of any one of them : the several professed resemblances of her countenance have excited almost as much doubt and controversy as the disputed points of her history ; and thus a genuine likeness of this celebrated lady may be reckoned among the first of the elegant and tasteful desiderata of the present age. How far the beautiful specimen of two arts which is before us may tend to decide the question must rest in a great measure on the degree of credit that may be esteemed due to a report which has been regularly handed down in the family of the noble owner of the picture, and which must necessarily be here prefaced by the brief recital of a small portion of Mary's history.

In the year 1567, which is well known to have been distinguished, fatally for her reputation, by the murder of her husband, and her marriage to the infamous Bothwell, the most powerful among the nobility of Scotland associated for the declared purposes of separating her from that wretch, and protecting the person of the young Prince, her son. With the usual fate of such combinations, they went much further ; they made their Queen a captive ; led her triumphantly through the army with which they had strengthened themselves ; and, having imprisoned her closely in the Castle of Lochleven, deposed her, and crowned her son. The owner of the castle was a Douglas, nearly related to the celebrated Earl of Morton, the most considerable person of the confederates, and who had been commissioned by them to accept her surrender. Here she remained nearly twelve months. At length, after the failure of various plans to liberate her, formed by those who still remained true to her interest, she accomplished it herself, by gaining over George Douglas, brother of her keeper. On this young man, under the age of twenty, and already a slave to that beauty the magic of which no one could wholly resist,

2

she employed all the graces of mind and manners with which nature and art had so abundantly furnished her, and, to leave no passion of his heart unassailed which might be rendered subservient to her view, is said to have tempted his ambition by giving him hopes that he might obtain her hand. When she had completed her charm, she besought him to aid her escape. He instantly complied, for who could have hesitated? and, by means which, however curious and interesting, it is not to the present purpose to recapitulate, restored her to freedom.

The picture which has furnished the plate before us has been preserved with the greatest care from time immemorial in the mansion of Dalmahoy, the principal seat in Scotland of the Earl of Morton; on the upper part of it is inscribed, with a modesty of assertion which tends to favour the report of its originality, " Mary, Queen of Scots, said to have been painted during her confinement in Lochleven Castle;" and the noble Earl who at present possesses it, has enhanced the value of his permission to place an engraving from it among the chief ornaments of this work, by condescending to state that according to an invariable tradition in his lordship's family, it was once the property of George Douglas, the liberator of Mary, and that it passed from him, together with other curious relics of that unhappy Princess, to his eminent relation, James, fourth Earl of Morton, who has been mentioned above, in whose posterity it has remained to the present day.

From the same picture also professes to have been engraved a plate which supplies the frontispiece to the first volume of Mr. Chalmers's new work, and its striking dissimilitude to the portrait here presented renders some reluctant remarks on it highly necessary in this place. It is scarcely too much to say that neither the features, nor the general character of countenance, given in the two engravings, bear even the slightest resemblance to each other, and this variance between two copies taken from the same original, which is allowed to possess stronger claims to

3

authenticity than any other painting, is the more distressing, as it was hoped that the engraving before us would have done much towards putting to rest the long disputed question as to Mary's features, and the skill and talents of the painter who copied the original, together with a clear opinion of its correctness, after actual comparison with the painting, expressed by the noble Earl who possesses the picture, may be received as pledges for its exact fidelity. Having thus established the claim of the engraving here presented, to be considered as the genuine representation of Mary's portrait, the failure in that of Mr. Chalmers's alone remains to be accounted for.

That gentleman discloses to us in his preface a new and most extraordinary discovery by which he has been enabled, with the aid of an artist, of whom he expresses an high opinion, to produce, de novo, a correct portrait of Mary; and one of the most singular features of the invention is that the distracting variety of those which have hitherto individually pretended to originality constitutes the very source which gives undoubted authenticity to his. Having spoken of those perplexities of which no one before had known how to take the advantage, Mr. Chalmers says, " in this state of uncertainty with regard to the person of the Scottish Queen, I employed a very ingenious artist to paint that celebrated Queen from such sketches, pictures, and other materials, as might be laid before his intelligent eyes: at the same time I presumed to think that her features might be settled by ascertaining the facts relating to her person like other matters of history." In other words, that the artist was to copy from one picture a pair of eyes, justified by the authority of Melvil; a nose from another, corroborated by the report of Keith; from a coin, a smile which had been cursed by Knox; and from a figure on a tomb, a frown which Buchanan had recorded to have been levelled at him; and the like; and from the combination of these pictorial and historical tesseræ Mr. Chalmers's hopes were at length fulfilled by the acquisition of a portrait which, to use his own words, " has been very generally admired for its truth, and its elegance." From this picture was engraved the plate which is prefixed to the second volume of his work.

Now, to speak seriously, Mr. Chalmers, whose kindness and candour I know too well to expect his displeasure at these remarks, has left, fortunately for us, to the idle and the careless those lighter studies which employ the mind without fatigue, and gratify the fancy without informing the understanding. A votary to history, his affection for it has led him to give too large a credit to its descriptive powers, while a negligence of the more delicate and less important theory of the human face divine has left him at liberty to suppose the impossibility, that a mere junction of features, however correctly each may have been individually represented and copied, should produce what we commonly call a likeness. The artist who could propose or encourage such a suggestion merits not so mild a judgment.

To conclude, the fact seems to be that the picture which assumes to have been so whimsically composed (vol. 2.) was ill copied from that which is stated to be a copy from the Douglas picture, (vol. 1.) to which it has scarcely any resemblance (except in the dress, in which the artist condescendingly tells us in Mr. Chalmers's preface, he " did not chuse to make any fanciful alteration") or vice versa: in short, that the artist judged it necessary to produce somehow an evident agreement between the two. It need only be added that the sole view of these observations is to record a caveat against any inference adverse to the authenticity of the portrait here presented, which might possibly be drawn from a careless comparison of it with either of the two engravings in Mr. Chalmers's history of Mary; and this is rendered the more necessary by an anticipation of the respect which will undoubtedly and justly be paid to that work. A jealousy of fair reputation, and a regard to weighty interests, equally excusable, have demanded this explanation.

ROBERT DUDLEY, EARL OF LEICESTER.

OB. 1588.

FROM THE ORIGINAL, IN THE COLLECTION OF

THE MOST NOBLE, THE MARQUIS OF SALISBURY.

London, Published Dec. 1.1836, by Harding & Lepard, Pall Mall East.

ROBERT DUDLEY,

EARL OF LEICESTER.

THIS mighty Peer, whose history will ever remain a memorial of the injustice and the folly, as well as of the unbounded power, of his Sovereign, was the fifth son of the equally mighty, but less fortunate, John Dudley, Duke of Northumberland, by Jane, daughter of Sir Henry Guldeford. The father's greatness shot forth with the rapidity and the splendour of a vast meteor, and was as suddenly lost in darkness: the son's, planet-like, rose somewhat more slowly, and traversed its hemisphere in a more regular obedience to the power, from which it derived its motion and its brilliancy. It obeyed however no other power, for Leicester offended against all laws, both divine and human. He seems not to have possessed a single virtue, nor was he highly distinguished by the qualities of his understanding; but the unlimited favour of Elizabeth, which for many years rendered him perhaps the most powerful subject in the world, invested him with a factitious importance, while, on his part, by a degree of hypocrisy so daring that it rather confounded than deceived the minds of men, he contrived to avoid open censure. Even flattery however seems to have been ashamed to raise her voice for him while he lived, and the calm and patient research of after times, with all its habitual respect for the memory of the illustrious dead, has busied itself in vain to find a single bright spot on his character.

He was born in or about the year 1532. His father, who surrounded the person of Edward the sixth with his offspring, procured for him in 1551 the post of one of the six Gentlemen of

1

the Bedchamber, and about the same time that of master of the King's buck-hounds. Edward, with the common readiness of youth, accepted him as a familiar companion, and evinced towards him a partiality bordering on favouritism. On the discomfiture of the feeble attempt to place his sister-in-law, Jane Grey, on the Throne, and the accession of Mary, he was imprisoned in the Tower, merely, as it should seem, because he was his father's son, for history furnishes us with no trace of his active participation in that design. He was indicted, however, of high treason, and prudently pleading guilty, received sentence of death, apparently as a matter of form, and, soon after, a pardon, and was liberated on the eighteenth of October, 1554. Mary indeed immediately took him in some measure into her favour; and we find in Strype's Memorials that after her marriage to Philip he attached himself particularly to that Prince, and was chosen " to carry messages between the King and Queen, riding post on such occasions, and neglecting nothing that might ingratiate himself with either of them." It was at the intercession of Philip, as all historians agree, that such of the prisoners for Jane's forlorn cause as escaped with life were set at liberty; nor is it less certain that the rigours of Elizabeth's captivity were softened through his influence. It may be very probably conjectured, though it has hitherto escaped the observation of historical speculatists, that Dudley was the secret instrument of correspondence between the King and that Princess, and that the dawn of her enormous subsequent favour towards him may be very reasonably ascribed to the impression made on her youthful heart, in a season of danger and misfortune, by a young man who possessed every natural and artificial quali-fication to win feminine affection.

She appointed him, immediately on her accession, to the distin-guished office of Master of the Horse, and shortly after, on the fourth of June, 1559, he was installed a Knight of the Garter, and sworn of the Privy Council. These great preferments were presently followed by grants of estates to an immense value, among which we find his celebrated manor and castle of Kenilworth, in Warwickshire; nor was the Crown the sole source of his growing power and wealth, for numerous public bodies, particularly of the ecclesiastical order, in the hope of securing to their respective interests the vast influence which he evidently possessed over the mind of the Queen, elected him to their stewardships, and other municipal offices, which, not to mention the sums which he annually derived from them, extended his authority into almost every part of the realm. That such an extravagance of good fortune should have excited envy and competition might reasonably be expected, but few ever ventured to appear in open rivalry towards him. Thomas Radclyffe, Earl of Sussex, perhaps the most virtuous and high-spirited, and certainly one of the wisest, of Elizabeth's servants, openly opposed himself from public motives to the secret design which Dudley undoubtedly entertained of becoming her husband, and was joined by Henry Fitzalan, Earl of Arundel, who had with less reserve aspired to that proud distinction: the rest submitted with despair, or sullen patience, to a power which seemed impregnable by the attacks of faction or the machinations of intrigue; even Burghley, esteemed as he was for his sagacity and probity, condescended to profess for the favourite an esteem which he could not have felt. Elizabeth, as though for the express purpose of giving a colour to his arrogant view of partaking her bed, now proved to himself and to the world that she thought him worthy of a royal spouse, by proposing him in form as a husband to the young Queen of Scots, by whom she knew he would be rejected. Thus he stood in the Court of his mistress, when on the twenty-eighth of September, 1564, she raised him to the dignity of Baron of Denbigh, and on the following day to the Earldom of Leicester, and towards the end of that year the University of Oxford elected him their Chancellor. He accompanied Elizabeth soon after in a visit to that learned body, and was received with a respect and deference perhaps never before conceded to any of her subjects, and which in fact could not properly have been due to any one beneath the rank of her consort.

3

In the mean time however the Queen, by a treaty of marriage with the Archduke Charles of Austria, which bore every mark of sincerity, cast a lasting damp on his proud hopes. Leicester had so far presumed on her partiality as to oppose the negotiation, not only in argument with herself and her Council, but even publicly, and was rebuked by her with a severity which, while it convinced him of the vanity of his splendid pretensions, left him no room to doubt that self love, and a resolution to preserve her independence, were the ruling features of her character. His disappointment was confined to the frustration of this single view, for in all other matters her favour and his influence remained unimpaired; and, now at leisure to pursue a more ordinary track of ambition, he sought, with the aid of a most profound dissimulation, to maintain the possession of them : nor was this cautuion unnecessary, for the repulse which he had lately experienced from the Queen had disclosed to him enemies perhaps before unsuspected, and encouraged his rivals to a more open show of competition. Among the latter was Thomas Howard, fourth Duke of Norfolk, a nobleman not only invested with the utmost importance that splendour of descent, immense wealth, and no very distant kindred to Elizabeth, could bestow, but one of the few of her subjects whom a party in her Court and Council had flattered with the hope of gaining her hand. Leicester determined on the ruin of a man thus in every way hateful to him ; and, as it could be accomplished only by treachery, insinuated himself into the confidence of the Duke, who was distinguished by the generosity and simplicity of his character. Norfolk communicated to him the plan which he had formed for a marriage with the Queen of Scots, with all his weighty dependencies ; was directed in every step towards it by his counsel, and when it approached to fruition was betrayed by him to Elizabeth; who indeed it may be reasonably suspected had employed him from the beginning for that purpose.

These detestable facts have been fully proved against him; but it is to the last degree difficult, not to say impossible, such were the depth of his artifices, and the dead secrecy of his instruments,

4

to obtain clear historical evidence of the most remarkable features of his conduct in public measures, and towards public servants. His agency was felt, but not seen ; or if those who were bound by his spells sometimes obtained a glimpse of the enchanter, he was presently again shrouded in utter darkness. Much however has been proved, and more inferred from circumstances. Having overthrown the Duke of Norfolk, he conceived about the same time a bitter hatred against the Queen of Scots, and Burghley, who had been the intimate and confidential friend of that unfortunate nobleman. It was probably the offspring of fear, for there can be little doubt that each of them possessed damning proofs of his late treachery. The rigours of Mary's tedious captivity, the strange vacillations of Elizabeth's policy regarding her, and her tragical end, may be most reasonably ascribed to his influence over the worst passions of his infatuated mistress ; yet he found means to impress on the mind of Mary a persuasion that he commiserated her sufferings, and she more than once appealed to his pity. His reiterated insinuations against Cecil were however always unsuccessful. Elizabeth regarded that great minister with feelings directly opposite to those of fear and anger, and all her selfishness was awakened to protect him. Leicester at length ventured to quit for a moment the strong-hold of his accustomed obscurity, and allowed the faction of which he was the acknowledged head to frame a regular accusation of Burghley to the Privy Council, but the plan was discovered to the Queen before it was fully matured, and the favourite was once more reprimanded by her. Original letters from him to the Treasurer, written at this precise period, stuffed with the most fulsome flattery, and professions of the warmest friendship, are still extant.

He is said to have appeased his vengeance by the sacrifice of Sir Nicholas Throgmorton, a bold and busy politician, who, after having been deeply concerned in the negotiations between Mary and the Duke of Norfolk, unexpectedly quitted Leicester's party, and attached himself to Burghley. He died very suddenly in the Earl's house as it was industriously reported, of a pleurisy, after partaking of a supper to which Leicester had invited him, but little doubt was entertained that he had been taken off by poison, and the malice with which the favourite presently afterwards pursued his family almost established the fact. That Leicester dealt in that horrible method of assassination cannot be reasonably controverted, however we may be inclined to question some particular charges of that nature among the many which have been made against him. The honourable and amiable Walter Devereux, Earl of Essex, to whom, both for public and private causes, he was a determined enemy, and whose gallant services in Ireland he had cruelly thwarted and depreciated, perished in that country with a clear impression on his mind, corroborated by the opinion of all who happened to be then about him, that his death had been so procured. The Countess of Lennox, (the mode of whose royal descent presented an obstacle to the possible inheritance of the Crown, derived from George Duke of Clarence, by Leicester's kinsman and favourite the Earl of Huntingdon, a speculation which he much cherished,) died, with strong symptoms of poison, presently after having received a visit from him. Nay, it has been generally reported, though probably untruly, that he retained in his establishment two persons, an Italian and a Jew, who were adepts in the diabolical art of preparing the means for such sacrifices; but the very exaggerations of the general charge on his memory tend to prove that it must have been in some degree well founded.

Yet this iniquitous man, not less odious in his private life, as we shall presently see, than disgraceful to the Queen and her Court; an enemy and torment to her ministers; the prime patron of the Puritans, whom she secretly regarded perhaps with more terror than the Papists; not only maintained his ground, but gradually rose in the estimation of Elizabeth to the last hour of his life. She seemed even anxious to publish to the world the distinction in which she held him. Her celebrated visit to him at his mansion of Kenilworth, in July 1575, was protracted to the length of nineteen days, an honour never on any other occasion granted by her to a subject. In June 1577, she so far forgot herself as to write thus to the Earl and Countess of Shrewsbury—" Our very good cousins—Being given to understand from our cousin of Leicester how honourably he was not only lately received by you, our cousin the Countess, at Chatsworth, and his diet by you both discharged at Buxtons, but also presented with a very rare present, we should do him great wrong, holding him in that place of favour we do, in case we should not let you understand in how thankful sort we accept the same at both your hands, not as done unto him but to our own self, reputing him as another self; and therefore ye may assure yourselves that we, taking upon us the debt not as his but our own, will take care accordingly to discharge the same in such honourable sort as so well deserving creditors as ye shall never have cause to think ye have met with an ungrateful debtor." Numerous instances of this extravagant folly might be cited, and indeed Leicester's arrogance and presumption under such temptations form the most defensible part of his character. The degrading exposure of her motive however was yet to come—at this period he once more asked her hand, and was once more refused. Enraged at the disappointment, he instantly married, without making any communication to her of his intention ; and Elizabeth, in utter contempt not only of the delicacy of her sex and the dignity of her station, but of all principles of law and justice which could bear any relation to the case, tore him from the arms of his bride, and imprisoned him in a little fortress which then stood in the park at Greenwich. This transport of angry jealousy however soon subsided. Leicester was released, and restored to full favour, and is said to have consoled himself for his short disgrace with schemes for the assassination of Simier, an agent from the Duke of Anjou, who was then in London, negotiating for the projected marriage of that Prince to Elizabeth, and whom he suspected to have apprised her of his own secret nuptials.

This treaty, which had been for a while suspended, was renewed in 1581, when a more honourable embassy arrived from the

7

French Court, and Leicester, who had now thought fit to assume the character of an advocate for the proposed union, was named among those who were appointed to confer with the commissioners. Anjou soon followed; but the strange caprice of Elizabeth on this occasion, which forms a remarkable and well known feature in the history of the time, finally disgusted him so highly, that, after three months' residence in her court, he suddenly embarked in the beginning of the succeeding year for the Low Countries, the government of which he had lately accepted. She indulged Leicester with the triumph of convoying thither his illustrious and rejected rival, and in this visit he probably laid the groundwork for that proud appointment to which, by the joint act of herself and those States, he was soon after nominated. He returned to a Court and Council agitated by the discovery of some designs lately projected by the friends of the unhappy Mary, and yet more by doubts and suspicions. He seized the opportunity of displaying his loyalty, and of indulging his hatred of the royal prisoner, by proposing to the nobility and gentry a bond of association by which they should engage themselves to pursue, even unto death, those who might form any plan against the life, or crown, or dignity, of Elizabeth. Mary was in fact the secret object of this widely extended menace, but the terror which it inspired having for a time paralysed the efforts of her adherents, he became impatient of her existence, and boldly moved the Queen that she should be taken off by poison. Elizabeth, nothing loth, undoubtedly proposed it to her ministers, for it is historically proved that Walsingham, practised and even hackneyed as he was in a sort of treachery legalized by the fatal necessity of States, protested against so heinous a measure, and insisted that she should not be put to death without at least the forms of judicial enquiry.

It was just at this period that a deadly invective, under the title of "Leicester's Commonwealth," or at least so entitled in subsequent editions, issued from the press in Flanders, and was presently dispersed in vast abundance throughout England, and indeed in

8

most of the nations of Europe. It consisted of a circumstantial relation of all the crimes and faults which had been at any time laid to the charge of the favourite, delivered with the utmost artifice of affected candour and simplicity, and intermixed with political reflections, tending to prove that every cause of complaint which existed in England might be traced to his malign influence. No publication ever before obtained so sudden and extensive a circulation. It was read with the utmost avidity; and the ridiculous efforts for its suppression made by Elizabeth, whose policy where Leicester was concerned always gave way to her passions, served but to excite to the highest pitch the curiosity of her subjects. She compelled her Council to address letters to the lieutenants of counties, and other public functionaries, charging them to prohibit the perusal of the pamphlet, and to punish severely the dispersers of it; and, not content with this degree of folly, made them insert a declaration (to use their own words) that " her Majesty testified in her conscience before God that she knew in assured certainty the books and libels published against the Earl to be most scandalous, and such as none but an incarnate devil himself could dream to be true." Her subservient Council, most of the members of which utterly detested him, outran their mistress in vehement assertions of his innocence—assertions which they knew to be false, and of the truth of which, had they been otherwise than false, no evidence could possibly have been obtained. There is indeed little reason to doubt any of the allegations of this celebrated libel. Sir Philip Sidney, who was Leicester's nephew, sat down, in all the pride and heat of youth and full consciousness of talent, to refute them, and almost wholly failed. Despairing of success, and perhaps at length deterred from attempting it in such a cause by that fine moral feeling which distinguished him, he laid his work aside, after considerable progress, the fruit of which remained unpublished till the appearance, of late years, of the Sidney Papers.

In the following year, 1585, the United Provinces, yet unable to establish their independence, reiterated a request formerly made to Elizabeth, to become their sovereign. Anxious at once to avoid the jealous imputation of an ambitious desire of extending her dominion to curb the power of Spain, and to aid the Protestant cause, she refused the offer, but readily agreed to furnish them with a powerful aid of troops and money. Leicester solicited, and instantly obtained, the command of this expedition, and was received, on his landing at Flushing, of which his nephew Sidney had been previously appointed Governor, with all the respect due to a Viceroy, which character, in contradiction to his instructions, he instantly assumed. The States, eager to persuade Philip the second that Elizabeth exercised a virtual sovereignty over them, invested the Earl by a solemn act with supreme authority, which he readily accepted, and, amidst the gorgeous festivities prepared to celebrate his exaltation, letters arrived from her, both to himself and to the States, in a tone of unexampled fury.— " We little thought," said she to Leicester, " that one whom we had raised out of the dust, and prosecuted with such singular favour above all others, would with so great contempt have slighted and broken our commands in a matter of so great consequence, and so highly concerning us and our honour," &c. This was worthy of the daughter of Henry the eighth, but the weakness of Elizabeth presently succeeded. Leicester returned a submissive explanation, and was instantly restored to full favour, nor does it appear even that the appointment which had produced this ebullition of capricious wrath was revoked. His service however in the Low Countries was marked by misfortune and disgrace. Totally deficient in military experience, he found himself opposed to the Prince of Parma, one of the first generals of the age, and a politician also of no mean fame ; and his admirable nephew, whose advice had aided him in the council, and whose example had invigorated him in the field, fell a sacrifice to the intemperance of his valour before the walls of Zutphen. The States became envious of his authority, and thwarted the measures of his government, already weak and inefficient, and he increased their jealousy by striving to ingratiate himself with the people. He returned

10

to England, disgusted but unwillingly; the faction which he had formed prevailed on the States again to solicit his presence, and on the twenty-fifth of June, 1587, he landed in Zealand, with new levies. Fresh discords however arising, Elizabeth, with his concurrence, finally recalled him in the succeeding November, and shielded him by her authority against a regular charge of mal-administration in the Low Countries, which had been prepared before his arrival, and was now preferred to the Privy Council by a party of his enemies, headed by the Lord Buckhurst, whom the Queen had lately sent thither to learn the true state of affairs, and who was rewarded for his pains by a vote of censure and an imprisonment of several months.

Leicester had now reached the highest pinnacle of favour and power. Elizabeth could refuse him nothing, and her ministers, even Burghley himself, seem to have trembled at his nod. All the most important commands, civil and military, in the nation, were in the hands of his relations or friends; to the offices already held by himself she had very lately added those of Steward of her Household, and Chief Justice of the forests south of Trent; and in the summer of 1588, placed him at the head of the army which she had raised to resist the expected Spanish invasion. She thus concluded her speech to these troops, when she reviewed them at Tilbury—" Rather than any dishonour shall grow by me, I myself will take up arms; I myself will be your general, judge, and rewarder of every one of your virtues in the field. I know already by your forwardness that you have deserved rewards and crowns; and I do assure you, on the word of a prince, they shall be duly paid you. In the mean time, my lieutenant general shall be in my stead, than whom never prince commanded a more noble and worthy subject." In this moment, such is the insatiable thirst of ambition, he solicited Elizabeth to appoint him to the office, not less unusual than enormously powerful and dignified, of Lieutenant, or Vicegerent, of her Kingdoms of England and Ireland, and even this, tenacious as she was of her royal authority, she readily conceded to him. It is said that a patent for this mighty

11

appointment was ready for the Great Seal, when Burghley, and her Chancellor Hatton, ventured to remonstrate with her, and so far succeeded as to obtain leave to suspend for some days that gratification. In the mean time Leicester left London for a short sojournment at Kenilworth castle, and on his way thither stopped at his house of Cornbury, in Oxfordshire, where he was seized by a rapid fever, and expired on the fourth of September, 1588.

From the foregoing sketch I have hitherto excluded any particulars of the domestic life of this most remarkable person. They will be found, singularly enough, considering the cast of his character, to be little concerned with his public story, the chain of which they would therefore but have served to disconnect. All parts of his conduct however, morally viewed, were in horrible harmony, for the man was as abominably wicked as the statesman and courtier.

Leicester, at the age of eighteen, married Anne, or Amy, daughter and heir of Sir John Robsart, a gentleman of Norfolk, distinguished by antiquity, indeed splendour, of descent, and by his great possessions in that county. They were wedded, as Edward the sixth, in whose presence the nuptials were solemnized, states in his journal, on the fourth of June, 1550, and lived together, with what degree of cordiality we are not informed, for ten years, but had no children. It is scarcely to be doubted that he caused this lady to be assassinated, and the circumstances of the time, as well as of the case itself, tend to press on his memory this dreadful charge perhaps more heavily than any other of the same character. Her death occurred on the eighth of September, 1560, at the very period when the lofty hope of obtaining the hand of his sovereign may be clearly presumed to have reigned with the strongest sway in his overheated mind. He sent her, with what avowed motives does not appear, to the solitary manor-house of Cumnor, in Berkshire, a village not far from Oxford, inhabited by one of his train, named Anthony Forster. Thither she was shortly followed by Sir Richard Verney, another of his retainers, and a few days after, these persons having sent all her servants to

12

Abingdon fair, and no one being with her but themselves, she died in consequence, as they reported, of a fall down a staircase. But "the inhabitants of Cumnor," says Aubrey, in whose history of Berkshire all that could be collected on the subject is minutely detailed, "will tell you there that she was conveyed from her usual chamber where she lay to another, where the bed's head of the chamber stood close to a privy postern door, where they in the night came, and stifled her in her bed; bruised her head very much; broke her neck; and at length flung her down stairs; thereby believing the world would have thought it a mischance, and so have blinded their villainy." Nor was this plan of violence adopted till after they had vainly attempted to destroy her by poison, through the unconscious aid of Dr. Bailey, then professor of Physic in the University of Oxford, who had resisted their earnest importunity to make a medicine for her, when he knew she was in perfect health, suspecting, from his observation of circumstances, as he afterwards declared, that they intended to add to it some deadly drug, and trembling for his own safety. The disfigured corpse was hurried to the earth without a coroner's inquest; and to such a height did the pity and resentment of the neighbouring families arise, that they employed the pen of Thomas Lever, a prebendary of Coventry, to write to the Secretaries of State, intreating that a strict enquiry should be made into the true cause of the lady's death, but the application had no effect. The strongest inference however of Leicester's guilt in this case is to be drawn from a string of reasons, noted down by Cecil himself, why the Queen should not make him her husband, one of which is—"that he is infamed by the death of his wife."— The effect of such a remark, made by such a person, and for such a purpose, wants little of the force of positive evidence.

The relaxations of such a man as Leicester are commonly sought in the gratification of mere appetite, and such were his. After a variety of amorous intrigues, not worthy of recollection, he became more than usually attached to Douglas, daughter of William Howard first Lord Effingham, and widow of John, Lord

13

Sheffield. Vulgar report, presuming on the known enormities of his life, proclaimed that he had disposed of her husband by those infernal secret means, so frequently ascribed to him in other cases. Be this as it might, it is certain that he married her, or deceived her into a pretended marriage, immediately after the death of Lord Sheffield. By this Lady he had a son, with whose future story, remarkable as it was rendered by the dispositions unhappily and infamously made by the father, this memoir has no concern, and a daughter. He stipulated with the unfortunate Douglas that their marriage should be kept profoundly secret; the children were debarred from any intercourse with their mother; and the Earl, having some years after determined to marry another, compelled her by threats, by promises, and at length, by attempts on her life, to make a most effectual, though tacit, renunciation of all marital claims on him, by publicly taking to her husband Sir Edward Stafford. These nefarious circumstances were disclosed, shortly before the death of Elizabeth, in the prosecution of a suit in the Star Chamber instituted to establish the legitimacy, and consequent right of inheritance, of her son; and on this occasion Douglas, after having proved by the testimony of many respectable witnesses her marriage to the deceased Earl, declared on oath the foul proceedings by which she had been forced to throw herself into the arms and on the protection of Stafford; concluding with a relation of the means which Leicester had previously used to take her off by poison, under the operation of which she swore that her hair and her nails had fallen off; that her constitution had been ruined; and that she had narrowly escaped with life.

The object for whom he abandoned this miserable lady was Lettice, daughter of Sir Francis Knollys, and relict of Walter Devereux, Earl of Essex. The already strong suspicion that Leicester had caused by the same diabolical means the death of that nobleman, to which some slight allusion has already been made, was aggravated to the utmost by the indecent haste with which he wedded the widow, with whom there was no doubt that he had for some time before maintained a guilty intercourse. This was the marriage which so highly excited the displeasure of Elizabeth, and which she unremittingly resented towards the Countess by an insulting neglect, in spite of all the instances of the young Essex, her son, who succeeded his uncle in the Queen's extravagant favour. Leicester had by this lady, one son, Robert; who died in childhood four years before his father. She survived the Earl for nearly half a century; and persecuted with tedious and ruinous suits his son by Lady Sheffield, whose legitimacy Leicester, with a folly equal to his injustice, had sometimes affirmed and sometimes denied, and to whom he had bequeathed his princely castle and domain of Kenilworth, of which the unfortunate gentleman was at last in a manner defrauded by the Crown in the succeeding reign.

Such, on the whole, was Elizabeth's most distinguished favourite. History, to its lamentable discredit, invariably asserts, in the same breath, his wickedness and the wisdom of his royal patroness—one or the other of those assertions must be false.

Engraved by H.T. Ryall.

AMBROSE DUDLEY, EARL OF WARWICK.

OB. 1590.

FROM THE ORIGINAL, IN THE COLLECTION OF

THE MOST NOBLE THE MARQUIS OF SALISBURY.

London, Published Dec.r 1, 1826, by Harding & Lepard, Pall Mall East.

AMBROSE DUDLEY,

EARL OF WARWICK.

———◆———

EMINENCE of consanguinity, rather than any special merit or fame of his own, beyond the quiet and unassuming recommendation of an unblemished moral character, has preserved the memory of this nobleman from a neglect perhaps approaching to oblivion. A son, and at length heir, of the mighty Duke of Northumberland; a brother of that paragon of royal favour and of wickedness, Leicester, and of the innocent and ill fated consort of Jane Grey; claimed, as it were, in their right some degree of distinction, and history has probably preserved all that could have been collected of his story. He was the fourth, but at length eldest surviving son of his father, by Jane, daughter of Sir Henry Guldeford, and was born in the year 1530, or 1531.

He is said to have manifested at an early age a passion for military fame. It is certain that he was in the expedition commanded by his father in 1549 against the Norfolk rebels, and not improbable that he owed the honour of knighthood, which he received on the seventeenth of November in that year, to some instances of that wild gallantry which in those days was esteemed the prime qualification for a soldier. He returned to the insipid life of a courtier, and we hear of him only as a partaker in tournaments and banquets till the arrest of the Duke, his father, with whom of course he had engaged in the support of Jane Grey's weak and unwilling pretensions to the Crown in July 1553. He was attainted, and received sentence of death, together with his

1

brothers, John, Robert, and Henry, and they were confined in the Tower of London till the eighteenth of October in the succeeding year, when Mary granted him a pardon for life, permitted him to come to Court, and received him into some degree of favour. Philip, her consort, for reasons not clearly assigned, became the patron of the crest-fallen remains of the House of Dudley. Ambrose volunteered into the Spanish army, in the Low Countries, and distinguished himself in the summer of 1557 at the celebrated battle of St. Quintin, and his younger brother, Henry, who accompanied him in the same character, fell during the siege of that place. Mary, at the King's intercession, now dispelled the cloud in which the extravagant ambition of Northumberland had involved his progeny, and in the conclusion of that year, this young nobleman, together with his surviving brother Robert, afterwards Earl of Leicester, were fully restored by an act of Parliament.

The stupendous influence of that brother, which marked even the commencement of the reign of Elizabeth, presently secured a large share of her favour to Ambrose. He obtained a royal grant of estates in Leicestershire in her first year, and in the next she appointed him Master of the Ordnance for life. These boons were presently followed by the restoration of some of his father's dignities ; on the twenty-fifth of December, 1561, he was created Baron of Kingston Lisle in the county of Berks, and on the following day Earl of Warwick. It was just at this period that the great contest began in France between the Papists and the Huguenots which afterwards obtained the denomination of the war of the League. The reformers solicited the aid of Elizabeth, and offered to place in her hands one of the most considerable ports in Normandy, which they besought her to garrison with English troops. She consented, not only readily but eagerly, and Havre de Grace, generally called Newhaven by the historical writers of that time, was given up to her ; Warwick was nominated to the command, with the title of the Queen's Lieutenant in the province ; and on the twenty-ninth of October, 1562, landed at Havre, with three thousand soldiers, and was with much ceremony sworn into his office.

In this command, the only arduous public service in which we find him, his conduct, equally distinguished by fidelity, prudence, and courage, amply proved his ability for the most important military undertakings. The effects of his vigilance and activity were felt in every part of Normandy, from whence, by the aid of repeated excursions from his stronghold, he had enabled the Protestants almost wholly to expel their enemies, when he found himself suddenly abandoned by them, and discovered that they had treacherously agreed on certain terms with the Leaguers, and even engaged themselves to turn their arms against him. He now shut himself up in his garrison, having previously dismissed the French of both persuasions, and was presently invested by a powerful army, under the command of the Constable de Montmorency. Terrible hardships and calamities ensued. The spring and summer passed almost without rain; the French cut the aqueducts which supplied the town; and the soldiers were obliged to boil their miserable sustenance in sea-water, which was frequently too their only beverage. An epidemic distemper, which carried off great numbers, succeeded. At length Warwick, after having sustained with uncommon perseverance a siege not less obstinate than his defence, surrendered in the autumn of 1563, but not till he had received the Queen's especial command, and effected a most honourable capitulation. During the treaty, having appeared without his armour on the ramparts to speak to a distinguished French officer, a villain fired at him from beneath, and wounded him in the leg with a poisoned bullet, a misfortune the consequences of which during the remainder of his life probably rendered retirement almost necessary to him, and prevented his accepting favours and distinctions which he seems so well to have merited. He was elected a Knight of the Garter in 1562, and invested at Havre with the ensigns of the Order.

In 1568, he was appointed one of the commissioners for the inquiry into the great matter of the Queen of Scots, on her arrival

3

AMBROSE DUDLEY,

in England; in 1569, on the occasion of the rebellion of the Earls
of Northumberland and Westmoreland, himself and the Lord
Clinton were appointed, jointly and severally, the Queen's
Lieutenants in the north, and the suppression of it was chiefly
owing to his care and vigilance; and in the succeeding year
Elizabeth conferred on him the dignified office, or rather title, of
Chief Butler of England. In 1570 he was sworn of the Privy
Council, and included in the number of Peers appointed by the
royal commission for the trial of the Duke of Norfolk; and this,
with the exception of his having been similarly employed on the
trial, as it was called, of the Queen of Scots, is the last notice to
be found of his interference in any matter of the State. After
the conclusion of the sitting, Mary addressed herself to him as to
one for whom she felt a regard, and in whom she placed some
confidence. Of Elizabeth's esteem for him, or of her inclination
at least to persuade him how highly she esteemed him, a fair
judgment may be formed from the following postcript, in her own
hand-writing, to a letter from her privy Council, written to him
during the siege of Havre.

"My dear Warwick,
      If your honour and my desire could accord with
the loss of the needfullest finger I keep, God so help me in my
utmost need as I would gladly lose that one joint for your safe
abode with me; but since I cannot that I would, I will do that I
may; and will rather drink in an ashen cup than you or your's
should not be succoured both by sea and land, yea, and that with
all speed possible; and let this my scribbling hand witness it
unto them all.
                                    Yours, as my own,
                                              E. R.

Warwick is said to have understood and patronised the commercial and manufacturing interests of his country. Certain it
is that he was much engaged in a design projected by some

4

London merchants for opening the trade to Barbary, which at length proved unsuccessful; and that in 1585 he obtained from the Queen an exclusive licence for two years for the exporting woollen cloths thither by some of them who had suffered the heaviest losses; but no farther inference can be drawn from those circumstances than that he himself was a party in their speculations, a condescension by no means rare among the nobility towards the conclusion of the reign of Elizabeth. Of the fact that he was a person of most unblemished conduct both in public and private life, there can be no possible doubt. His character stands wholly unimpeached: even in that volume of virulent censure on the rest of his family, known by the title of " Leicester's Commonwealth," his name is never mentioned disrespectfully: In the few notices of him with which history furnishes us it is always accompanied by praise, and his popular appellation was " the good Earl of Warwick." Towards the conclusion of his life the misery of the incurable wound which he had received at Havre gradually increased, and at length became intolerable, and threatened mortification. In an unsigned letter to George, sixth Earl of Shrewsbury, of the fourth of February, 1589-90, the writer says—" My Lo. of Warwick is like to go. His offices are already nere bestowed. Grafton" (doubtless the royal honour of Grafton which we are not elsewhere informed was held by him) " upon the Lo. Chancellor; Butlerage, upon the Lo. of Buckehurst; for the M^r.ship of the Ordynaunce my Lorde Graye and Sir John Parratt stryve." Mr. Thomas Markham, in a detail of court news to the same nobleman, of the seventeenth of that month writes—" on Wednesdaye was sennight, as I am suer your L. hath hard, my Lord of Warwyk had his leg cutt off, since which tyme he hath amendid, but not so faste as I wolld wyshe." On the twentieth he expired at the house of his brother-in-law, the Earl of Bedford, in Bloomsbury, and was buried at Warwick, where a curious altar tomb was erected to his memory by his widow.

This nobleman was thrice married; first to Anne, daughter

and heir of William Whorwood, Attorney General in the reign of Henry the eighth, by whom he had his only child, John, who died an infant before 1552. His second Lady was Elizabeth daughter of Sir Gilbert Talboys, and sister and sole heir to George, last Lord Talboys. He married, thirdly, Anne, daughter of Francis Russel Earl of Bedford.

SIR FRANCIS WALSINGHAM.

OB. 1590.

FROM THE ORIGINAL IN THE COLLECTION OF

HIS GRACE, THE DUKE OF DORSET.

London, Published Dec.r 1,1836, by Harding & Lepard, Pall Mall East.

SIR FRANCIS WALSINGHAM.

THE life of Walsingham, reputed one of the first statesmen of his time, affords but scanty materials to the biographer. Continually devoted, from an early age, to public affairs, the character of the man was almost absorbed in that of the minister; while, on the other hand, the mysterious secrecy with which he moved, invisibly, as it were, in his service of the State, conceals from us most of the particulars of that great agency which we know he exercised. It may be fairly said of him, without either compliment or insult to his memory, that he was an illustrious spy; but it must be added, that he is said to have been in private life an honest and kind-hearted man. He certainly was a wise and faithful public servant.

He descended from a very ancient and respectable family in Norfolk, said to have derived its surname from the town of Walsingham, a junior branch of which migrated into Kent about the time of Henry the sixth, and was the third and youngest son of William Walsingham, of Scadbury, in the parish of Chislehurst, by Joyce, daughter of Edmund Denny, of Cheshunt, in Hertfordshire. He was bred in his father's house, under a private tutor, and afterwards studied for a time in King's College, in Cambridge, from whence he went, very young, to seek a more enlarged education on the continent. The persecution raised by Mary induced him to remain abroad till her death, for his family were zealous protestants, and he was earnestly attached to that persuasion. He had thus abundant leisure for the employment of a most acute mind, naturally, if it may be so said, directed to the observation of the characters of nations and of individuals, of courts and of councils, of manners, customs, and political systems. He returned

1

therefore, soon after the accession of Elizabeth, a self-made statesman, with the additional advantage of a perfect knowledge of most of the European languages, for he had always the reputation of being the first linguist of his time. Thus qualified, he fell in the way of Secretary Cecil, afterwards the celebrated Lord Burghley, who, presently discerning the true character of his talents, retained him with eagerness, and made him, almost immediately, a principal agent in such affairs, as peculiarly required activity and secrecy. Thus the management of Elizabeth's concerns at the Court of France was implicitly committed to his charge, at a time when they required the most refined diplomatic skill; while a dreadful civil war was raging in that country, and its Cabinet distinguished by a policy equally acute and perfidious.

Having remained there many years, he returned, for a short time, to aid the deliberations of Elizabeth's ministers on the great question of the French marriage, to which he seems to have been then really inclined; and in August, 1570, was sent again to Paris, professedly to negotiate on that subject, but, in fact, rather to agitate others of the highest importance. A very fine collection of his dispatches during that mission fell into the hands of Sir Dudley Digges, and were published in 1655, under the title of " The Compleat Ambassador." Those letters exhibit the perhaps unparalleled combination in one and the same mind of the most enlarged understanding, and the minutest cunning. Such were his wisdom and his address, that he contrived, while he treated of a proposal which might seem to have no chance of success but in mutual good faith, and perfect amity, to embarrass Charles the ninth to the utmost by fomenting the insurrection of the Huguenots; to thwart the great designs of the House of Austria, by laying the foundation of the war in the Low Countries; and, after having passed three years in the prosecution of these opposite plans, to leave an honourable character behind him in a Court whose favourite interests he had constantly and successfully endeavoured to injure. He returned in April, 1573, and

2

was received by Elizabeth with the highest grace and approbation.

Very shortly after his arrival he was nominated one of the principal Secretaries of State. Gilbert Lord Talbot writes to his father, George, Earl of Shrewsbury, on the eleventh of May, 1573, " Mr. Walsingham is this day come hither to the Courte : It is thought he shall be made Secretary : Sir Thomas Smythe and he, both together shall exercise that office." They were accordingly appointed ; but the superintendance of all matters of extraordinary delicacy and secrecy in their department was committed to Walsingham alone, and he seems to have referred them all to one principle of management. Espionage, to use a word which is now almost English, and for which our language affords no synonyme, had been reduced by him to a system of precise regularity. Lloyd, making a nice distinction, states the number of persons employed by him in foreign Courts to have been fifty-three agents, and eighteen spies. " He had the wonderful art," says the author of the Life of Lord Bolingbroke, almost copying after the same Lloyd, without acknowledging the obligation, " of weaving plots, in which busy people were so intangled that they could never escape ; but were sometimes spared upon submission, sometimes hanged for examples." Lloyd, again, tells us that he would " cherish a plot for some years together ; admitting the conspirators to his, and the Queen's, presence familiarly, but dogging them out watchfully ;" and that " his spies waited on some men every hour for three years."

In 1578 he was sent for a short time, accompanied by Lord Cobham, to the Netherlands, to treat, with little sincerity, of a peace between the new republic and the King of Spain ; and in 1581 was again appointed Ambassador to the Court of France. The Duke of Anjou, since the accession of his brother, Henry the third, had renewed with earnestness his solicitations for the hand of Elizabeth, who, on her part, from a policy which has never been clearly understood, or from a caprice yet more unaccount-

able, had met his advances with a warmth and freedom ill suited
to the dignity of an independent Queen, or to the prudence of a
woman at the age of forty-five. The Duke had been thus tempted
to visit her Court, in the declared character of a lover; had been
received by her with unbecoming tokens of affection; and soon
after repelled with coldness and disdain. The professed objects of
Walsingham's mission was to negotiate, previously to the proposed
marriage, an offensive and defensive league, but the real view
was either to reconcile those contrarieties, or to involve them in
deeper mystery. He was dispatched in 1583 on an embassy,
equally faithless, to the young King of Scotland, afterwards our
James the first. Sir James Melvil, a plain honest man, who was
naturally prejudiced in Walsingham's favour, as well because
they had been acquainted, and had travelled together, in their
youth, as that one part of the Secretary's instructions was to
detach the King from a party which Melvil disliked, gives a large
and remarkable account in his memoirs of this minister's intercourse with James. "His Majesty," says Melvil, "appointed four
of the Council, and himself, to reason with Sir Francis, and to
sound what he would be at; but he refused to deal with any but
with his Majesty, who heard him again." He flattered James's
vanity with the highest praise of his wisdom and erudition, and
fully persuaded Melvil that he had visited Scotland with the
purest intention of serving that Prince. "The King marvelled,"
concludes Sir James, " that the Chief Secretary of England,
burthened with so many great affairs, sickly, and aged, should
have enterprized so painful a voyage without any purpose; for it
could not be perceived what was his errand, save only that he gave
his Majesty good counsel." It is not surprising that even
Walsingham should have failed to accomplish the object of this
embassy, inasmuch as he had to contend, not with politics, but
with passions. His secret instructions doubtless had been to
detach James from his favourite, the Earl of Arran; and to place
him again in the hands of the very noblemen who had just before

4

held him in a degrading captivity, and even threatened his life, in that mysterious outrage distinguished in Scottish history by the name of " The Raid of Ruthven," Elizabeth's participation in which was more than suspected.

He returned from thus attempting to cajole the son, to take a frightful share in the odious measures of Elizabeth against the mother. Patriotism and loyalty, however enthusiastic, could furnish no apology for the fraud and treachery with which he surrounded the unhappy Mary in her prison. The exquisite refinement, and endless variety, of his designs to entrap her savoured more of a natural taste for deception than of zeal for the public service. He seems indeed in many instances to have purposely delayed the fruition of his artifices for the mere delight of changing or repeating them. In the remarkable case of what is usually called " Babington's conspiracy," Ballard, a priest, who was the original mover of the design, was continually attended, from the very dawn of it, by Maude, one of Walsingham's spies. Maude first affected to aid him in England; then passed over with him into France, to tamper with the Spanish Ambassador, and others, and returned with him; assisted largely in debauching Babington, and several other young men of good families, and in constructing the whole machinery of the plot, in constant intelligence always with his master. In the mean time, another, named Giffard, insinuated himself into the society of some who were in the confidence of the Queen of Scots, and undertook to manage a correspondence between her and the conspirators, in which every letter written by her, as well as their answers, were delivered first to Walsingham, by whom they were opened, deciphered, copied, re-sealed, and forged additions occasionally made to them, and then dispatched to their several destinations. Walsingham at length condescended to become intimate with Babington, purposely to prostitute his own personal agency in this base tragedy; and, having occupied himself for six months in drawing his net every hour nearer and nearer to the unsuspecting victims, was at last compelled to close it over them by positive orders from Elizabeth, dictated by her fears. " Thus far," says Camden, who gives a most interesting and circumstantial detail of the whole, " had Walsingham spun the thread alone, without acquainting the rest of the Queen's Council; and longer would he have drawn it, but the Queen would not suffer it, lest, as she said herself, by not heeding and preventing the danger while she might, she might seem rather to tempt God than to trust in God."

But a charge of a blacker nature rests heavily on the memory of Walsingham. In a long letter in the Harleian Collection, addressed by him, and his Co-Secretary, Davison, within the period of which I have just now spoken, to Sir Amias Powlett, and Sir Drue Drury, by whom Mary was then held in close custody, are these terrific passages—" We find, by speech lately uttered by her Majesty, that she doth note in you both a lack of that care and zeal for her service that she looketh for at your hands, in that you have not in all this time, of yourselves, without other provocation, found out some way to shorten the **** ** that Queen, considering the great peril she is hourly subject to so long as the said Queen shall live; wherein, besides a kind of lack of love to her, she noteth greatly that you have not that care of your own particular safeties, or rather of the preservation of religion, and the public good and prosperity of your country, that reason and policy commandeth; especially having so good a warrant and ground for the satisfaction of your consciences towards God, and the discharge of your credit and reputation towards the world, as the oath of the association, which you both have so solemnly taken and vowed; especially the matter where-with she standeth charged being so clearly and manifestly proved against her. And therefore she taketh it most unkindly that men professing that love towards her that you do, should, in a kind of sort for lack of the discharge of your duty, cast the burthen upon her, knowing, as you do, her indisposition to shed blood, especially of one of that sex and quality, and so near to her in blood as the said Queen is. These respects we find do greatly trouble her Majesty, who we assure you hath sundry times protested that, if the regard of the danger of her good subjects, and faithful servants, did not more move her than her own peril, she would never be drawn to assent to the shedding of her blood, &c."

Great pains have been taken to discredit the authenticity of this letter, but it is difficult to conceive with what view such a document could have been forged; for the character of Elizabeth, who so soon after publickly stained herself with the blood of that miserable Princess, could scarcely have suffered further deterioration by such a charge. Besides, were it proper to argue the point in this place, evidence nearly positive might be produced that Elizabeth had at other times given private orders that she should be put to death, in the event of the occurrence of certain circumstances; but we have here no business with the letter, except as an additional proof of Walsingham's habitual abandonment of every principle of justice, humanity, and honour, to the will of a sanguinary tyrant. Mary, on her trial, challenged him as her bitterest and most treacherous enemy. Camden informs us that she said, alluding to the charges against her with regard to Babington's plot, " that it was an easy thing to counterfeit the cyphers and characters of others, as a young man did very lately in France, who gave himself out to be her son's base brother; and that she was afraid this was done by Walsingham, to bring her to her end; who, as she had heard, had practised both against her life, and her son's."

The detail of Walsingham's secret machinations would fill a volume. Perhaps the most remarkable was that by which he managed for a considerable time to prevent the fitting out of that famous expedition called the Spanish Armada. He had obtained intelligence from Madrid that Philip, had informed his ministers that he had written to Rome, to disclose to the Pope, the secret object of his great preparations by sea and land, and to beg his Holiness's blessing on the enterprise; and that he should conceal his views from them till the return of the courier. Walsingham, so far informed, employed a Venetian priest, one of his resident spies at Rome, to gain a copy of the King of Spain's letter. The priest corrupted a gentleman of the Pope's bedchamber, who took the key of his Holiness's cabinet out of his pocket while he slept; transcribed the letter; and returned the key. Hence Walsingham discovered that Philip had negotiated to raise the money to equip his fleet by bills on Genoa, and he contrived, through the aid of Sutton, the famous founder of the Charter-House, as it is said, and other eminent English merchants at Genoa, that nearly all those bills should be protested, and by that artifice impeded the sailing of the fleet for more than twelve months.

Walsingham, like several others of Elizabeth's most faithful servants, received few solid marks of her favour. He never held any public office, in addition to his laborious and unprofitable Secretaryship, except that of Chancellor of the Duchy of Lancaster, which was not conferred on him till about 1587, late in his life, and he afterwards obtained the Order of the Garter. He lived and died miserably poor; for, such was his zeal, and such his mistress's baseness, that he lavished great sums from his own purse on the public service, and was never repaid. Camden says that "he watched the practices of the papists with so great an expense that he lessened his estate by that means, and brought himself so far in debt that he was buried privately, by night, in St. Paul's Church, without any manner of funeral ceremony." This is truly stated, for in his will I find this passage—" I desire that my body may be buried without any such extraordinary ceremonies as usually appertain to a man serving in my place, in respect of the greatness of my debts, and the mean state I shall leave my wife, and heir, in; charging both my executor and overseers, to see this duly accomplished, according to the special trust and confidence I repose in them." He bequeaths to that heir, his only surviving child, no more than an annuity of one hundred pounds, and orders his " lands in Lincolnshire" to be sold for the payment of his debts. He died on the sixth of April, 1590, of a local complaint, not understood by the surgeons of that day; or rather, as Camden with much probability tells us, by the violence of the medicines which were administered to him; having been twice married; first, to Anne, daughter of Sir George Barnes, an Alderman of London, who died childless; secondly to Ursula, daughter of Henry St. Barbe, of Somersetshire, and widow of Richard Worsley, who brought him two daughters, Frances, and Mary, the latter of whom died unmarried in June, 1580. Frances was thrice splendidly wedded: first, to the memorable Sir Philip Sidney; secondly, to Robert Devereux, Earl of Essex; and thirdly, to Richard de Burgh, Earl of Clanricarde; by each of whom she left issue.

Sir Francis Walsingham founded a Divinity Lecture at Oxford, and acknowledged his affection to King's College in Cambridge, by bestowing on it a library. A book which appeared not long after his death, and which has frequently been reprinted, intituled " Arcana Aulica, or Walsingham's Manual of Prudential Maxims," has usually been reputed the work of his pen; but was more probably a compilation by some confidential person about him.

Engraved by W.H. Mote.

SIR CHRISTOPHER HATTON.

OB. 1591.

FROM THE ORIGINAL OF KETEL, IN THE COLLECTION OF

THE RIGHT HON^BLE VISCOUNT DILLON.

London, Published July 1, 1831, by Harding & Lepard, Pall Mall East.

SIR CHRISTOPHER HATTON.

WE know but enough of this gentleman's history to make us wish for more. His elevation to the first place in the cabinet, and to the supreme seat in the administration of justice, coupled with the fantastic singularity of the incongruous and uncon nected steps by which he ascended, throw about his legend an air of romance, while our utter ignorance of the motives which induced Elizabeth thus greatly and strangely to distinguish him, involve it in suitable mystery. It is scarcely less extraordinary that these circumstances should not have excited the curiosity of the historians and pamphleteers of the succeeding century, or, if they did enquire into them, that they should have withheld from us the fruit of their researches, recording only the silly and incre- dible tale that he danced himself into his preferments. This remarkable silence on a point of history so likely to provoke discussion, induces a suspicion that it arose from fear, or pru- dence, or delicacy. Hatton was one of the handsomest and most accomplished men of his time, and the conduct of Elizabeth had already betrayed, in more than one instance, the extravagances into which personal predilections, of a nature not easy to be de- fined, were capable of leading her. These are facts of such noto- riety, that the supposition of an additional instance of similar weakness will not be deemed a libel on the memory of the virgin Queen. That Hatton was an object of this anomalous partiality seems highly probable, and, had his character been marked by the ambition of Leicester, or the rashness of Essex, the ground of his

1

good fortune would perhaps have been not less evident than theirs.

He descended from a junior line of the very ancient house of Hatton of Hatton in Cheshire, which migrated into Northamptonshire, and was the third and youngest son of William Hatton, of Holdenby, by Alice, daughter of Laurence Saunders, of Horringworth, both in that county. He was born in 1539, or in the succeeding year, and, after having been carefully instructed in his father's house, was entered a gentleman commoner of St. Mary Hall, in Oxford, where he probably remained not long, as he quitted the university without having taken a degree, and enrolled himself in the society of the Inner Temple. It has been said that he was placed there not to study the law with a view of qualifying himself for the profession, but to give him the advantages of a familiar intercourse with men who joined to deep learning an extensive knowledge of the world, and of the arts of social prudence. This report was probably invented for the sake of increasing the wonder excited by his final promotion; though thus much is certain, that we hear nothing of his practice in any of the courts, nor indeed have we any direct intelligence that he was ever called to the bar. It is amply recorded however that he joined at least in the sports of his fellow students, for it was at one of those romantic entertainments which at that time the Inns of Court frequently presented to royalty, that he first attracted the notice of the Queen. " Sir Christopher Hatton," as Naunton somewhat obscurely says, "came into the court as Sir John Perrott's opposite ; as Perrott was used to say, ' by the galliard,' for he came thither as a private gentleman of the Inns of Court, in a masque ; and, for his activity and person, which was tall and proportionable, taken into her favour." Honest Camden, with more plainness, tells us that, "being young, and of a comely tallness of body, and amiable countenance, he got into such favour with the Queen," &c.

He was presently admitted into her band of gentlemen pensioners, at that time composed of fifty young men of the best

2

families in the kingdom, and was soon after placed among the gentlemen of her privy chamber; then appointed captain of her body guard, and vice-chamberlain of her household, about the time of his promotion to which latter office he was knighted, and sworn of the privy council. In 1586 Elizabeth granted to him and his heirs the Island of Purbeck, in Dorsetshire, and in the same year named him as one of her commissioners for the trial, or rather for the conviction, of the Queen of Scots. It is said that Mary was persuaded chiefly by his reasoning to submit to their jurisdiction, and Camden has preserved the speech which for that purpose he addressed to her, and which exhibits little either of eloquence or argument. "You are accused," he said, "but not condemned, to have conspired the destruction of our lady and Queen anointed. You say you are a Queen: be it so; however in such a crime as this the royal dignity itself is not exempted from answering, either by the civil or canon law, nor by the law of nations nor of nature; for if such kind of offences might be committed without punishment, all justice would stagger, yea fall to the ground. If you be innocent, you wrong your reputation in avoiding trial. You protest yourself to be innocent, but Queen Elizabeth thinketh otherwise, and that not without ground, and is heartily sorry for the same. To examine therefore your inno-cency, she hath appointed commissioners, honourable persons, prudent and upright men, who are ready to hear you according to equity, with favour, and will rejoice with all their hearts if you shall clear yourself of what you are charged with. Believe me, the Queen herself will be transported with joy, who affirmed to me, at my coming from her, that never anything befel her that troubled her more than that you should be charged with such misdemeanours. Wherefore lay aside the bootless claim of privilege from your royal dignity, which now can be of no use unto you; appear to your trial, and shew your innocency; lest by avoiding trial you draw upon yourself a suspicion, and stain your reputation with an eternal blot and aspersion."

On the twenty-third of April, 1587, to the astonishment of the country, he was appointed Lord High Chancellor, unluckily succeeding in that great office Bromley, a lawyer of the highest fame ; and on the twenty-third of May, in the succeeding year, as though to crown properly the heterogeneous graces which had been already bestowed on him, was installed a Knight of the Garter. Camden, the only writer who has affected to account for his appointment to the Great Seal, informs us, rather improbably, that "he was advanced to it by the Court arts of some, that by his absence from Court, and the troublesome discharge of so great a place, which they thought him not to be able to undergo, his favour with the Queen might flag and grow less." He was received, naturally enough, in the Chancery Court with cold and silent disdain, and it is even said that the barristers for a time declined to plead before him ; but the sweetness of his temper, and the general urbanity of his manners, soon overcame those difficulties, while the earnestness and honesty with which he evidently applied the whole force of a powerful mind to qualify himself for his high office, gradually attracted to him the esteem of the public. "He executed," says the historian just now quoted, "the place with the greatest state and splendour of any that we ever saw, and what he wanted in knowledge of the law he laboured to make good by equity and justice." He is said to have introduced several good rules into the practice of his court, and to have at length acquired, by the wisdom of his decrees, and by the moderation, impartiality, and independence, of his conduct on the bench, an eminent share of popularity. Anthony Wood asserts that he composed several pieces on legal subjects, none of which however are extant, except one, which has been plausibly attributed to him, entituled "a treatise concerning Statutes, or Acts of Parliament, and the Exposition thereof," which was not printed till 1677.

Sir Robert Naunton, again with some obscurity, thus concludes the very short notices which he has left us of Hatton. "He was a gentleman that, besides the graces of his person and dancing, had also the adjectaments of a strong and subtle capacity : one that could soon learn the discipline and garb both of the times and court. The truth is he had a large proportion of gifts and endowments, but too much of the season of envy, and he was a mere vegetable of the court, that sprung up at night, and sunk again at his noon." Does Naunton mean that Hatton was envious, or that he was the object of envy in others?

With relation to one, of the character of whose mind, and of the extent of whose talents and accomplishments so little has been handed down to us, it is fortunate to be able to form some opinion from the familiar effusions of his own pen. In the great treasure of epistolary remains of the eminent men of his time, Hatton's letters are of rarest occurrence. No apology then will be necessary for illustrating this unavoidably imperfect sketch with two of them; the one, without date, to Elizabeth, from a rough draft in the Harleian MSS., and hitherto unpublished; the other, now reprinted from the Cecil Papers, to the gallant and unfortunate Robert Devereux, Earl of Essex. The first is indorsed —"S^r. Ch^r. Hatton, Vicechamberlaine to the Queene, upon some words of the Queene, his protestacion of his owne innocence."

"If the woundes of the thought wear not most dangerous of all wthout speedy dressing I shold not now troble yor. Ma^{ty}. wth. the lynes of my co'playnt; and if whatsoever came from you wear not ether very gracious or greevous to me what you sayd wold not synke so deepely in my bosome. My profession hath been, is, and ever shalbe, to your Ma^{ty}. all duty wthin order, all reverent love wthout mesure, & all trothe wthout blame; insomuch as when I shall not be fownde soche as to yor. Highness Cæsar sought to have hys wife to himselfe, not onely wthout synne, but also not to be suspected, I wish my spright devyded from my body as his spowse was from his bedde; and therfore, upon yesternight's wordes, I am driven to say to yor. Ma^{ty}. ether to satisfye wronge conceyts, or to answer false reports, that if the speech you used of yor. Turke did ever passe my penne or lippes to any creature owt of yor. Highnes' hearing, but to my L. of Burghley, wth. whom

5

I have talked bothe of the man & the matter, I desyre no lesse condemnation than as a traytor, & no more pardon than hys ponyshment; and, further, if ever I ether spake or sent to the embassad. of France, Spayne, or Scotland, or have accompanied, to my knowledge, any that conferres wth. them, I doe renownce all good from yor. Ma^{ty}. in erthe, & all grace from God in heaven; wch. assurans if yor. H. thinke not sufficyent, upon the knees of my harte I hu'bly crave at yor. Ma^{ty's}. handes, not so much for my satisfaction as yor own suerty, make the perfitest triall heareof; for if upon soch occasions it shall please yor. Ma^{ty}. to syfte the chaffe from the wheate, the corne of yor. co'monwealth wolde be more pure, & myxt graines wolde lesse infect the synnowes of yor. suerty, wch. God most strengthen, to yor. Ma^{ty's}. best & longest preservation."

His letter to Essex, then commanding the English troops at the siege of Rouen, in which his brother, Walter, had lately fallen, forms a striking contrast to the bombastic piece which, in conformity to her own taste, he addressed to the Queen, and may perhaps be justly considered as an example of the best epistolary composition of the time.

"My very good Lord,

"Next after my thankes for yor. honorable l^{res}., I will assure yor. Lo^p. that, for my part, I have not failed to use the best endeavors I cold for the effecting of yor. desire in remaininge ther for some longer tyme, but wthall I must advertise you that her Ma^{ty}. hath been drawn therunto wth. exceeding hardenes, & the chefe reason that maketh her sticke in it is for that she doubteth yor. Lo^p. doth not sufficiently consider the dishonor that ariseth unto her by the King's ether dalliance or want of regard, having not used the forces sent so friendly to his aid from so great a Prince, and under the conduct of so great a personage, in some employment of more importance all this while: wherefore, by her Ma^{ty's}. co'mandement, and also for the unfaigned good wyll I bear yor. L^p., I am very earnestly to advise you that you have gret care for the accomplishement of her Highnes' instrucc'ons effectually, and according to her intenc'ons, in those thinges wherin you are to deale wth. the Kinge."

" Further my good Lord, lett me be bolde to warne you of a matter that many of yor. frendes here gretely feare, namely, that the late accident of yor. noble brother, who hathe so valiantly & honorably spent his lyfe in his Prince's & countrey's service, draw you not, through griefe or passion, to hasard yo^rselfe over venturously. Yo^r. Lo^p. best knoweth that true valour consisteth rather in constant performinge of that wch. hathe been advisedly forethought than in an aptnes or readines of thrusting yor. p'son indifferently into every daunger. You have many waies, & many tymes, made sufficient proof of yor. valientnes : No man doubteth but that you have enough, if you have not overmuche : and therfore, both in regard of the services her Ma^{ty}. expecteth to receve from you, and in respect of the greife that would growe to the whole realme by the losse of one of that honorable birth, & that worthe wch. is sufficiently knowen (as greater hathe not beene for any that hathe beene borne therin these many & many yeeres) I must, even before Almighty God, praye & require yor. Lo^p. to have that cercumspectnes of yo^rselfe wch. is fitt for a generall of yor. sorte. Lastly my Lo., I hope you doubt not of the good disposic'ons I bear towards yor. Lo^p., nor that out of the same ther ariseth & remaineth in me a desire to doe yor. Lo^p. all the service that shalbe in my pore abilitie to p^rforme, & therfore I shall not neede to spende many wordes in that behalf; but, wth. my earnest prayers for yor. good succes in all yor. honorable actions, &, after, for yor. safe returne, to the comfort of yor. frendes & wellwillers here, I leave yor. Lo^p. to God's most holy and m'cifull protecc'on. From London, the 5th of October, 1591.

" Yo^r. good L^{p's} most assured and true frende,

" Ch^R. Hatton."

The faithful historian, already so frequently quoted, records that " he was a man of a pious nature, and of opinion that in matters of religion neither fire nor sword was to be used ; a great reliever of the poor; and of singular bounty and munificence to students and learned men, for which reason those of Oxford chose him Chancellor of their University." He succeeded the favourite Leicester in that dignified office in September, 1588. He is said in his earlier days to have sacrificed occasionally to the muse, of which however no proof is extant, except in the tragedy of Tancred and Ghismunda, which was the joint production of five students of the Inner Temple; was acted by some members of that society before the Queen in 1568; and printed in 1592. To the fourth act is subscribed "Composuit Ch^r. Hatton."

His death, which happened on the twentieth of November, 1591, has been ascribed in great measure to the harshness and suddenness with which Elizabeth demanded the instant payment of a great sum in his hands, arising from the collection of first fruits and tenths. " He had hopes," says Camden, " in regard of the favour he was in with her, she would have forgiven him; but she could not, having once cast him down with a harsh word, raise him up again, though she visited him, and endeavoured to comfort him." He was buried in St. Paul's Cathedral, and, having died a bachelor, bequeathed his fortune to his nephew, Sir William Newport of Harringham, in Warwickshire, with remainder to Christopher, son and heir of John Hatton, his nearest kinsman of the male line. Sir William Newport, who assumed the surname of Hatton, died childless, and Christopher succeeded accordingly; his son and heir, of the same name, was created in 1643 Baron Hatton, of Kirby, in Northamptonshire: and the heir male of that son in 1682 obtained the title of Viscount; both which became extinct about 1770.

Engraved by J. Cochran.

CARDINAL ALLEN.

OB. 1594.

FROM THE ORIGINAL IN THE POSSESSION OF

BROWNE MOSTYN ESQ.RE

PROOF

London, Published Dec.r 1, 1836, by Harding & Lepard, Pall Mall East.

WILLIAM ALLEN,

CARDINAL.

THE face and the character of this remarkable person have hitherto been almost equally unknown. While he lived, and for several years after his death, to have possessed his portrait might have been deemed misprision of treason, and to have spoken favourably even of the slightest act of his life would certainly have been considered as a high misdemeanour. He was perhaps the most formidable enemy to the reformed faith, and the ablest apologist for the Romish church, that England ever produced, for he was armed at all points, either for attack or defence, and indefatigable in the prosecution of each. He was generally learned, but in sacred and ecclesiastical history profoundly; and while he reasoned with equal acuteness, boldness, and eloquence, used that urbanity of expression, so uncommon in the polemics of his time, which polishes, while it sharpens, the weapons of argument, and disarms an adversary, at least of personal enmity. He exercised in fact, though without the name, the office of vice-gerent to the Pope for the affairs of his church in England; and in that character opposed, with a most honest zeal, the progress of a system which the most part of Europe then considered as a frightful schism, and which was at that time indebted for its support perhaps more to the vigilance and severity of Elizabeth's government than to the affection of its professors. But that system had already become firmly interwoven with the civil polity of England, and the most dangerous enemy to a state is he

1

who would wound it through the shield of its religious establishment. Elizabeth, therefore, would have acted but with strict justice had she put Cardinal Allen to death, as she certainly would, could she have got him into her power; and he would have been, as justly, canonized.

He descended from two respectable, and rather ancient, families, for he was the second son of John Allen, the elder line of whose house had been long seated at Brockhouse, in Staffordshire, by Jennet, daughter of a Lyster, of Westby in Yorkshire. He was born at Rossall, in the latter county, about the year 1532, and became a student of Oriel College in 1547, where he was so distinguished for his talents, and for the rapidity and success of his studies, that he was within three years afterwards unanimously elected a fellow of that house; and before he had reached the age of twenty-five, was chosen Principal of St. Mary's Hall, and one of the Proctors of the University. About 1558, he was appointed a Canon of York, but was scarcely fixed there when the death of Queen Mary blasted all his hopes of further preferment in his own country. He continued, however, in England till 1560, when he retired to Louvain, and fixed his residence for a time in the famous theological college there, which, since the accession of Elizabeth, had become the favourite place of refuge for those of the English Catholic divines who had the highest reputation for learning and zeal. But the passive devotions of a mere pious asylum were ill suited to the disposition of one who seemed to exist but for the service of his church: he returned, under the pretence of seeking relief in his native air from a lingering illness, and settled in Lancashire, where his endeavours to reclaim the wanderers from his profession became soon so notorious that the magistrates chased him from that county. He went then into Oxfordshire, where he not only followed the same course, but published treatises in the English language, which he had printed at Louvain,—" In Defence of the lawful Power and Authority of the Priesthood to remit sins;" " Of the Confession of Sins to God's Ministers;" and a third,

2

intituled, " The Church's Meaning concerning Indulgences, commonly called Popes' Pardons." Such a visitor could not long be permitted to remain near the University. He removed, doubtless under compulsion, into the neighbourhood of Norwich, where he dwelt chiefly in the house of the Duke of Norfolk, and, having composed there a strenuous defence of his church, under the title of " Certain brief Reasons concerning Catholic Faith, " returned once more to Oxford, and boldly took up his residence there. His attempts, though with unabated zeal, were now more secretly practised. He ceased to publish his opinions, and contented himself with endeavouring to gain individual proselytes by the acuteness of his arguments, and the charms of his conversation. An experiment of that kind, in which he had fully succeeded, drew down on him the vehement resentment of the relations of his convert, who happened to be zealous reformers. They prosecuted him with the utmost vengeance ; he found means to escape from the consequences ; and quitted England, never again to return.

He fled to Flanders, and, after having resided for some time in a monastery in the city of Mechlin, removed about 1568 to Douay, where an academy had been some years before established, which had acquired considerable reputation. On that foundation he raised the college which after many vicissitudes yet subsisted there in much fame at the commencement of the accursed French revolution, when its peaceful inmates were dispersed, and it became first a military hospital, and, since, a manufactory. To this seminary, which was declaredly devoted to the reception of learned English Romanists who had fled their country for religion's sake, he gave a regular collegiate form, and procured from the Pope a yearly stipend for its maintenance. He was now appointed a Canon of the archiepiscopal church of Cambray, and, soon after, of that of Rheims, in France, where he prevailed on the great family of Guise to erect another college for the same purpose, to which he removed the members of his house at Douay, during the distraction which for a time agitated the

3

Netherlands. He commenced also a similar foundation at Rome, and two in Spain. All these were devoted to the education of English youth, and every sort of learning was cultivated in them to the utmost perfection of the time; but the grand and secret object of the teachers was to instruct their pupils in the religious and civil doctrines of the church of Rome; to inspire them with the most zealous and implicit veneration towards all its institutions; and so to qualify them to become, when they should return to their own country, the most effectual of all missionaries.

In spite of the personal application and activity which these objects necessarily required, it should seem that his pen too was almost incessantly employed, as well in a continual correspondence with his friends and abettors in England, as in the composition of multifarious publications which he disseminated throughout Europe with the utmost industry. Elizabeth, who held her brother Sovereigns and their councils in contempt, was awed by the talents, the perseverance, and, perhaps most of all, by the sincerity of this man. He fought against her, or, in other words, against that system of faith of which she was then the life and soul, as well in the field as in the closet; for while he opposed himself, with exquisite power of argument, to her most eminent divines, and used the sweetest persuasion to those whom he hoped to convert, the catholic soldiers and mariners of England, as well as those of Spain, went into battle with treatises in their hands which he had written for their use, and adapted to their capacities. Thus he prevailed on Sir William Stanley, and Rowland York, who commanded a body of thirteen hundred men in the Low Countries, to surrender to the Spaniards, in 1587, the strong fortress of Deventer, and other places, with their garrisons; and, immediately after, printed a letter, intituled, " Epistola de Deventriæ Ditione," together with a translation into English, in which he highly commended their treachery, and incited others to imitate it. So too, in the following year, upon the sailing of the Spanish Armada, he published " A Declaration of the Sentence of Sixtus the Fifth," by which that Pope had given plenary indulgence and pardon of all sins, to those who would assist in depriving Elizabeth of her kingdom; to which was added a supplement, most energetically conceived and written, with the title of "An Admonition to the Nobility and People of England." Elizabeth herself bore testimony to the weight and importance of this book by dispatching a minister to the Prince of Parma, Governor of the Low Countries for the King of Spain, specially to expostulate with him on the publication of it.

For these eminent services to his church, he was at length, on the twenty-eighth of July, 1587, created a Cardinal Priest, and in 1589, consecrated Archbishop of Mechlin, to which latter dignity the King of Spain added the gift of a rich abbey in Naples. The utter failure of the great Spanish naval expedition, on which the Roman Catholics had founded such mighty hopes, seems to have broken his spirit. He retired to Rome immediately after that event, "under a great disappointment," says Camden, "and at length tired out with the heats and dissensions of the English fugitives, both scholars and gentlemen." That historian, zealous as he was for the reformed faith, and writing under the influence almost naturally produced by his servitude to Elizabeth, speaks of Allen with less asperity than might have been expected; while Anthony Wood, more independent, though perhaps not unjustly suspected of some leaning to the Romish church, having very fairly stated the invectives of several authors against him, adds—"Let writers say what they please, certain it is that he was an active man, and of great parts, and high prudence: that he was religious, and zealous in his profession: restless till he had performed what he had undertaken: that he was very affable, genteel, and winning, and that his person was handsome and proper; which, with an innate gravity, commanded respect from those that came near, or had to do with him." His taste in literary composition was admirable. Of his Latin little need be said. The age in which he lived was ornamented by many distinguished writers in that language, and it would have been strange indeed had not such a man appeared in the foremost rank: but his English style was incomparable. At once dignified and simple; clear and concise; choice in terms, without the slightest affectation; and full of an impassioned liveliness, which riveted the attention even to his gravest disquisitions; it stood then wholly unrivalled, and would even now furnish no unworthy model. Such however is the weakness, and it is almost blameless, of human prejudice, that the merits of the writer were condemned to share in the abomination of his doctrines, and that an example, which might have anticipated the gradual progress of nearly a century in the improvement of English prose, was rejected because he who set it was a rebel and a Papist.

Cardinal Allen wrote, in addition to the works already mentioned, "A Defence of the Doctrine of Catholics concerning Purgatory, 1565;" "An Apology, and true Declaration, of the Institution and Endeavours of the two English Colleges, in Rome and at Rheims, 1581;" "Apologia pro Sacerdotibus Societatis Jesu, et Seminariorum Alumnis, contra Edicta Regiæ," which I have never seen, and of which the book mentioned before it was probably a translation; "Concertatio Ecclesiæ Catholicæ;" and "Piissima Admonitio et Consolatio verè Christiana ad Afflictos Catholicos Angliæ;" the three last named tracts printed in one volume, 1583; and "A true, sincere, and modest Defence of the English Catholics that suffer for their Faith both at home and abroad, against a scandalous Libel intituled, the Execution of Justice in England," without date, of which a translation into Latin was published in 1584.

This very eminent person died at Rome on the 6th of October 1594, and was buried in the chapel of the English College there.

Engraved by J. Cochran.

SIR FRANCIS DRAKE.

OB. 1596.

FROM THE ORIGINAL, IN THE COLLECTION OF

THE MOST NOBLE THE MARQUIS OF LOTHIAN.

London, Published Dec.r 1.1836. by Harding & Lepard, Pall Mall East.

SIR FRANCIS DRAKE.

THE narrative of a life for the materials of which no better source could exist than the journal and log-book of a naval commander, and in the absence too of those very authorities, may seem to promise very little of general interest. Drake was a seaman from his cradle, and applied to his profession talents which might have rendered him eminent in any character with such undeviating perseverance that we never find him for an instant in another: yet so dear is that character to Englishmen, that they will dwell with delight on the insulated detail of his expeditions; on discoveries insignificant in the sight of modern navigators, and on tactics which have become obsolete; on motives which have long ceased to actuate our national policy, and on results of the benefit of which we are no longer sensible.

His birth, as might be expected, was mean. In a pedigree of the descendants of his brother Thomas, the inheritor of his wealth, recorded in the Visitation of Devonshire made in 1620, he is simply stated to have been a son of " Robert Drake of that county," and the name even of his mother does not appear. Camden however has left us some particulars of his origin, which, in spite of an anachronism or two that have not escaped the vigilance of antiquarian zeal, may be depended on, especially as he informs us that they were communicated to him by Drake himself. His father, as we learn from this respectable authority, had embraced the Protestant persuasion, and having been threatened with prosecution under the terrible law of the Six Articles, fled his country and wandered into Kent. " There," continues Camden, " after the death of Henry the eighth, he got a place among the seamen in the King's navy, to read prayers to them, and soon after he was ordained deacon, and made vicar of the church of Upnor, upon the river Medway, where the royal navy usually rides: but, by reason of his poverty, he put his son apprentice to the master of a bark, his neighbour, who held him closely to his business, by which he made him an able seaman, his bark being employed in coasting along the shore, and sometimes in carrying merchandise into Zealand and France. The youth, being painful and diligent, so pleased the old man by his industry, that, being a bachelor, at his death he bequeathed his bark unto him by his last will." It is said, but with some uncertainty, that he was born in the town of Tavistock, in 1545.

In his early manhood he became purser of a merchant ship trading to Spain, and two years after made a voyage to Guinea, probably in the same capacity. About this time he attracted the notice of his countryman, and, as some have reported, his kinsman, Sir John Hawkins, and was in 1567 appointed by that celebrated navigator captain of a ship named the Judith, in which he accompanied Hawkins to South America, and eminently distinguished himself in the more glorious than fortunate exploits in the Gulf of Mexico, which were the issue of that expedition. Drake lost in it the whole of that little which he had saved in his more humble employments, but he returned with a reputation which presently attracted public attention, and with a knowledge of the wealth, and an experience of the naval warfare and resources of Spain in those parts, which enabled him to form the most promising plans for his future prosperity. He determined to invite the resolute, the needy, and the avaricious, to join him in an expedition thither, and represented to them, with a power of persuasion with which he is said to have been eminently gifted, the vast acquisitions that might be expected, and the clear probability of success. The bait was taken with an eagerness at least equal to his hopes, and in 1570, and the following year, he made two voyages, the former with two ships, the latter with one; and in these trips, though his private view in undertaking

2

them extended not beyond mere experiment which he could not
have prosecuted without assistance, he managed with such sagacity as to encourage those who had adventured with him by an
ample return; to render himself independent; and to prevent in
a great measure any suspicion in the Spaniards of the extent of
the designs which he secretly meditated against them.

In 1573, however, they were somewhat disclosed. On the
twenty-fourth of March in that year he sailed from Plymouth, in
a ship named the Pascha, accompanied by another in which he
had performed his two former voyages, called the Swan, in which
he placed one of his brothers, John Drake. On board these vessels, which were of very moderate burthen, he had no more than
seventy-three men and boys; yet with this slender force he
stormed on the twenty-second of the following July, the town of
Nombre de Dios, in the Isthmus of Darien, and soon after seized
that of Venta Cruz, where he obtained a considerable booty; but
the most important result of these acquisitions was the establishment of a friendly intercourse with some rulers of the natives, by
the aid of whose intelligence he intercepted a convoy of plate, as
it was the custom then to call it, of such enormous bulk that he
abandoned the silver from mere inability to convey it, and
brought only the gold to his ships. It is needless to say that he
returned with immense wealth; and the fidelity and exactness,
with which he allotted to his partners their respective shares in
his good fortune, contributed equally with it to raise his fame.
The people, in the mean time, in their hatred to Spain, which
Elizabeth used every artifice to chafe, viewed the success of his
piracies, for they were nothing less, with rapture. Enriched
himself, beyond all the occasions of even splendid domestic life,
he now gave way to a laudable ambition to shine in public service,
and to recommend himself effectually to a court and government
in which much of the ancient love of warlike gallantry yet subsisted, fitted out at his own charge, three frigates, with which he
sailed to Ireland, to serve as a volunteer against the rebels, in

aid of the land forces under the command of Walter, Earl of Essex. Stowe, without reciting the particulars of his conduct, informs us that he performed many glorious actions there. His stay however in Ireland was short, and on the premature death of that nobleman he returned; but the secret object of his excursion was fully obtained, for he acquired, probably through the recommendation of the amiable Essex, the patronage of Sir Christopher Hatton, by whom he was soon after introduced to Elizabeth.

Drake, in his last American voyage, had formed an imperfect outline of the enterprize which has immortalized his name. " He had descried," says Camden, " from some mountains the South Sea. Hereupon," continues the historian, " the man being inflamed with ambition of glory, and hopes of wealth, was so vehemently transported with desire to navigate that sea, that, falling down upon his knees, he implored the divine assistance that he might at some time or other sail thither, and make a perfect discovery of the same; and hereunto he bound himself with a vow. From that time forward his mind was pricked continually to perform that vow." He now besought and obtained the aid and countenance of the Queen to his project for a voyage thither, through the Straits of Magellan, an undertaking to which no Englishman had ever yet aspired. On the fifteenth of November, 1577, he sailed from Plymouth in a ship of one hundred tons, called the Pelican, having under his command the Elizabeth, of eighty tons; the Swan, of fifty; the Marygold, of thirty; and the Christopher of fifteen; embarking in his little fleet no more than one hundred and sixty four men, amply supplied however with all necessary provisions. He concealed from his comrades of all ranks the course that he intended to take, giving out that it was for Alexandria; and, after having been forced by a severe storm to return to the English coast to refit, quitted it finally on the thirteenth of December.

Drake's celebrated voyage is so well known, that it would be impertinent to give here any enlarged detail of it. On the twentieth of August, having previously dismissed, for what reason we are not clearly told, two of the vessels which had accompanied him, he entered the Straits of Magellan, where a terrible storm separated him from the others, and he proceeded alone. On the twenty-fifth of September he quitted the Straits, and sailed, still molested by tempest, to the coast of Chili and Peru, which he skirted, attacking the Spanish settlements, which were wholly defenceless, and, having obtained immense spoil, prepared to return to England. Apprehensive however of the vengeance of the Spaniards, among whom the alarm was now fully spread, he determined to avoid the track by which he had entered the Pacific Ocean, and bent his course to the shores of North America, seeking, with that spirit of enterprize which so eminently distinguished him, a passage to Europe by the north of California. Disappointed in this endeavour, he sailed to the East Indies, and, returning to England by the Cape of good Hope, landed at Plymouth on the third of November, 1580, the first of his countrymen by whom the honour of circumnavigating the whole of the known world had ever been enjoyed.

His arrival in London was hailed by the multitude with the utmost extravagance of approbation, but among the cool and discerning many were disposed to censure his conduct with severity. The policy, as well as the legality, of conniving at the sort of warfare which he had used against the Spaniards was freely questioned. His moral character was arraigned; and he was reported to have sacrificed to the private vengeance of the Earl of Leicester one of his principal officers, Doughty, whom he had charged with mutiny, and caused to be put to death during his voyage. In the mean time he was not without apologists of the better sort, who alledged that his attacks on the Spanish colonies were clearly justifiable under the laws of reprisal, and that Doughty, which seems to have been the fact, was regularly tried and condemned by such a Court Martial as could be formed under the circumstances of the expedition. While these questions were contending with increasing heat, Elizabeth suddenly turned the balance in his favour by the most unequivocal and public marks of her grace. She visited him on board his ship at Deptford ; partook of a splendid banquet which he had provided ; and conferred on him the honour of knighthood, commanding, among many other compliments of the most flattering nature that the vessel in which he had achieved the voyage should be carefully preserved, as a precious memorial of his merit, and of the glory of her realm.

These testimonies of approbation produced in Drake their usual effect on generous and active minds, an ardent desire to signalize himself by further exploits. The rank, however, to which his fame and his immense wealth had now raised him in society forbade the further prosecution of that order of enterprize from which he had derived them, and some years elapsed before Elizabeth's determination to commence offensive hostilities against Spain, enabled her to call his powers into action in her immediate service. At length, in 1585, he received for the first time a royal commission, and was appointed to the command of twenty-one ships of war, with which, having on board eleven thousand soldiers, he sailed in the autumn to the West Indies, and, after having sacked the towns of St. Jago and St. Domingo, passed to the coast of Florida, when he took Carthagena, and destroyed several other settlements of smaller importance. In 1587 he was dispatched with four of the largest ships in the Queen's navy, to which the merchants of London added twenty-six vessels of various burthens, to Spain, and in the Bay of Cadiz dispersed and crippled a fleet which lay there, completely equipped, under orders to proceed to Lisbon, the appointed rendezvous for the grand armada, destroying more than a hundred of their store ships, and several superior vessels. He then returned to Cape St. Vincent, ravaging the coast in his way, and at the mouth of the Tagus ineffectually challenged the Marquis of Santa Cruz, the

Spanish Admiral, to an engagement. Having performed this splendid service, which obliged Philip to defer for a whole year the execution of his great project of invasion, Drake turned his attention for an interval to his old friends the merchants, and, using a discretion not uncommon in those days of imperfect discipline, sailed to the Azores, to intercept a carrack of immense value, of whose coming from the East Indies he had received secret intelligence, which he accomplished, and returned to his country to receive new honours from his Sovereign, and increased homage from her subjects. In the ever memorable service of the following year, Drake, whom Elizabeth had appointed Vice Admiral under Lord Howard of Effingham, had the chief share. His sagacity, his activity, and his undaunted courage, were equally conspicuous in the series of mighty actions which composed it, and the terrible vengeance experienced by the dispersed and flying Armada was inflicted principally by his division of the fleet. Don Pedro de Valdes, a Spanish Admiral, by whom the enterprize had been planned, deemed it an honour to have surrendered to him, and was long entertained by him with a generous hospitality, which proved that Drake was as well versed in the chivalrous courtesies as in the essentials of war. In his success in this glorious victory terminated the unmixed felicity which had hitherto invariably attended him.

The year 1589 was distinguished by the ill-concerted and mismanaged attempt to place Don Antonio on the throne of Portugal. In the expedition destined to that service the fleet was commanded by Sir Francis Drake, and the military, amounting to eleven thousand, by Sir John Norris. Drake had never before in any of his enterprises had a partner, and the main features of his character were such as might be expected to disqualify him for any division of authority. The commanders disagreed in the outset. Drake proposed to sail directly to Lisbon, but Norris insisted that the troops should be landed at Corunna, which the Admiral not only conceded, but promised to conduct the fleet immediately after up the Tagus to the capital. Unforeseen obstacles prevented his keeping his word; Norris loaded him with reproaches; and attributed the utter failure of the plan, which in fact arose from various causes, to Drake's absence. The Admiral was obliged to explain and justify his conduct to the Queen and Council, and was acquitted of all cause of blame, but his high spirit had been wounded by the mere enquiry, and he sought to console it by new views of conquest.

Some years passed, though the war with Spain still subsisted, before an opportunity presented itself. At length he prevailed on Elizabeth once more to send a powerful armament to Spanish America, under the direction of himself, and his old friend and original patron, Sir John Hawkins, and in a great measure at their private expense, the Queen however furnishing some of her stoutest ships. The fleet, consisting of twenty-seven vessels, which had been long detained by Spanish rumours, raised for the purpose of a new plan of invasion, sailed from Plymouth on the twenty-eighth of August, 1595. The plan of the expedition was to destroy Nombre de Dios, the scene of one of Drake's early and most gallant exploits, and then to march the troops, of which two thousand five hundred were embarked, to Panama, to seize the treasure supposed to have lately arrived there from Peru. When they were on the point of departure, Elizabeth apprized them that the Plate fleet had arrived in Spain, with the exception of one rich galleon, which had returned to Porto Rico for some necessary repairs, and which she advised them in the first place to secure. They left England differing in opinion on this question, Hawkins, anxious to follow without delay the Queen's direction, and Drake earnest to commence their operations by a descent on the Island of Teneriffe, which was accordingly made, and proved wholly unsuccessful. They then sailed to Dominica, and in the interval the Spaniards, who had been apprised of the main purposes of the voyage, dispatched a strong convoy for the galleon, which they brought off in safety, and so powerfully reinforced Porto Rico, that the English on their arrival there, were obliged to content themselves with ravaging to little purpose the craft in the harbour, and to retire without having made any impression on the town, nor was their attack on Panama, which was made about Christmas Day, more fortunate. Hawkins, died, as is said, of a broken heart, amidst these reverses, and Drake barely survived them. A settled melancholy, attended by a slow fever, and terminating in a dysentery, the common disease of the country, carried him off on the twenty-eighth of January, 1595, O. S. in the fifty-first, or, according to some, in the fifty-fifth, year of his age.

Little has been said here of the natural character of this eminent person, and some circumstances of his life have been hitherto purposely omitted, for the sake of concluding this sketch with the very words of a writer of the fair sex, who has laid before us, in a late publication of singular merit, the fruits of most laborious and accurate historical research, clothed in the light and easy garb of refined table-talk. " The character of Sir Francis Drake," says this lady, " was remarkable not alone for those constitutional qualities of valour, industry, capacity, and enterprize, which the history of his exploits would necessarily lead us to infer but for virtues founded on principle and reflection, which, render it in a high degree the object of respect and moral approbation. It is true that his aggressions on the Spanish settlements were originally founded on a vague notion of reprisals, equally irreconcilable to public law and private equity ; but with the exception of this error, which may find considerable palliation in the deficient education of the man, the prevalent opinions of the day, and the peculiar animosity against Philip the second cherished in the bosom of every protestant Englishman, the conduct of Drake appears to demand almost unqualified commendation. It was by sobriety, by diligence in the concern of his employers, and by a tried integrity, that he early raised himself from the humble

9

station of an ordinary seaman to the command of a vessel. When placed in authority over others, he shewed himself humane and considerate. His treatment of his prisoners was exemplary; his veracity unimpeached; his private life religiously pure and spotless. In the division of the rich booty which frequently rewarded his valour and his toils, he was liberal towards his crews, and scrupulously just to the owners of his vessels; and in the appropriation of his own share of wealth he displayed that munificence towards the public, of which since the days of Roman glory history has recorded so few examples. With the profits of one of his earliest voyages, in which he captured the town of Venta Cruz, and made prize of a string of mules laden with silver, he fitted out three stout frigates, and sailed with them to Ireland, where he served as a volunteer under Walter Earl of Essex, and performed many brilliant actions. After the capture of a rich Spanish carrack at the Terceras in 1587, he undertook at his own expense to bring to the town of Plymouth, which he represented in Parliament, a supply of spring water, of which necessary article it suffered a great deficiency. This he accomplished by means of a canal or aqueduct above twenty miles in length. Drake incurred some blame in the expedition to Portugal for failing to bring his ships up the river to Lisbon, according to his promise to Sir John Norris, the General; but on explaining the case before the Privy Council on his return, he was entirely acquitted by them; having made it appear that, under all the circumstances, to have carried the ships up the Tagus would have been to expose them to damage, without any benefit to the service. By his enemies this great man was stigmatised as vain and boastful —a slight infirmity in one who had achieved so much by his own unassisted genius, and which the great flow of natural eloquence which he possessed may at once have produced and rendered excuseable."

It has been erroneously asserted that Sir Francis Drake died a bachelor. He married, probably in his middle age, Elizabeth, daughter and heir of Sir George Sydenham, of Combe Sydenham, in Devonshire, who survived him, and re-married to William Courtenay, of Powderham Castle, in the same county. He left however no issue, and his brother Thomas became his heir, and was succeeded by his eldest son, Francis, who was created a Baronet in 1622, and is at present represented by his lineal descendant, Sir Francis Henry Drake, of Buckland Monachorum, in the county of Devon.

11

Engraved by H.T. Ryall.

PHILIP HOWARD, EARL OF ARUNDEL.

OB. 1595.

FROM THE ORIGINAL OF ZUCCHERO, IN THE COLLECTION OF

HIS GRACE THE DUKE OF NORFOLK.

London, Published Dec.ʳ 1,1830, by Harding & Lepard, Pall-Mall East.

PHILIP HOWARD,

EARL OF ARUNDEL.

———◆———

THOMAS, fourth Duke of Norfolk, the first victim of his illustrious House to the jealousy of Elizabeth, took to his first wife Mary, second of the two daughters and coheirs of Henry Fitz-alan, last Earl of Arundel of his family. By this lady he had an only son, whose birth proved fatal to his mother, who had not attained to the age of seventeen; but the child survived, and became the Peer who will be the subject of the present memoir. He was born at Arundel House, in the Strand, on the twenty-eighth of June, 1557, and baptized in the Palace of Whitehall with uncommon distinction, in the presence of the King and Queen; and Philip, who was his godfather, and in compliment to whom he was named, left England for ever on the very day that the ceremony was performed. Notwithstanding this, and other royal flatteries, the Duke, his father, educated him in the protestant profession, which however he quitted at an early age for the religion of his ancestors, and from his sincerity in that mode of faith, and the patience and constancy with which he suffered the calamities which resulted from it, he seems to have fairly merited the title of martyr. The paternal dignities which he would have inherited having been swept away by his father's attainder, he assumed that of Earl of Arundel in right of his mother, the possession of the castle of Arundel (a rare instance in this country, where local honours are almost unknown,) having been solemnly adjudged in Parliament in the eleventh year of

Henry the Sixth to carry with it the Earldom. He was accordingly summoned among the Peers by that title in 1583, and in the same year restored in blood.

He possessed for a time a considerable share of Elizabeth's favour, which he probably owed to his youth, and other personal attractions, for he was, according to an account of him, written long after his death, by a domestic priest to his Countess, and which is still preserved at Norfolk House, "a very tall," or, as we should now say, stout, "man, and somewhat swarthy;" to which Dodd, in his Church History, adds that, "he had an agreeable mixture of sweetness and grandeur in his countenance." The Queen's partialities in this kind were in most cases nearly as fatal to their objects as her resentments, and so it proved in this instance. The Earl had been married at the age of fourteen to Anne, sister and coheir of Thomas, last Lord Dacre of Gillesland, of whom we shall presently give, as her memory well merits, some particulars. Elizabeth, says the manuscript lately quoted, " could not endure her, nor indeed the wife of any other to whom she shewed especial favour, and this distaste of the Queen's led the Earl to neglect his Lady, on which score his maternal grandfather, the old Earl of Arundel, and his aunt, the Lady Lumley, were so displeased that they alienated much of their property to others."

The Earl however was so captivated by the royal grace, that (to use again the words of the manuscript, from which I will observe, once for all, that such of the present memoir as is not of a public nature is chiefly extracted) " he made great feasts at Arundel House for the Ambassadors, Ministers, &c. on Coronation days, and other rejoicing days, and entertained the Queen, and all her Court, at Kenninghall and Norwich, for many days together." At one of these banquets, at Arundel House, Elizabeth herself had the profligate baseness to conceal herself, with Leicester, to overhear a conversation between the Earl and Sir Francis Walsingham and Lord Hundson, whom she had directed to tempt him into discourse on the subject of religion. It was

2

probably soon after this flagrant breach of hospitality that he became suspected of intriguing in favour of the Queen of Scots, and was placed in confinement in his own house, from which Elizabeth offered to release him if he would attend her to chapel, and hear the service of the Reformed Church, which he steadily refused. No matter, however, of specific accusation being yet ripe against him, he was set at liberty; but soon after again apprehended, and committed to the Tower, from whence also he was released for want of evidence against him. These repeated attacks, the jealousy of some great men, and, in particular, of Lord Hundson, who had been his father's page, and owed great obligations to his family; and the outrageous rigour with which the penal statutes against the Papists were then enforced, determined him to quit England, and he withdrew himself into Sussex; where, having been betrayed, as is said, by one of his servants, he was seized as he was about to embark on an obscure part of the coast, near his castle of Arundel, and again committed to the Tower. He was now prosecuted in the Star-Chamber, and condemned to a fine of ten thousand pounds, and imprisonment during the Queen's pleasure, merely on the charges, of entertaining Romish priests in his family; of corresponding with Cardinal Allen; and of meditating to leave the kingdom without the Queen's permission. In support of these accusations scarcely anything like proof was produced.

After four years' confinement, mostly so close as to prevent the possibility of new offence, he was arraigned of high treason, and on the fourteenth of April, 1589, brought to trial in Westminster Hall, where of the whole body of the Peerage only twenty-five appeared to sit in judgment on him. He comported himself with great dignity and firmness. "When called on," says Camden, "to hold up his hand, he raised it very high, saying 'here is as true a man's heart and hand as ever came into this hall.'" In addition to the points which had been alleged against him in the Star-Chamber, he was now accused of conspiring with Cardinal Allen to restore the Catholic faith in England; of having

3

suggested that the Queen was unfit to govern ; and of ordering masses to be said for the success of the Spanish Armada : that he intended to have withdrawn himself out of the realm, to serve with the Duke of Parma against his native country ; and that he had been privy to the measure of issuing the Bull of Pope Pius the fifth, for transferring Elizabeth's Crown to Philip of Spain.

History can scarcely produce another instance of so wretched and so wicked a perversion of judicial proceeding. Of the three witnesses produced against him, Sir Thomas Gerrard, a man of the name of Shelley, and Bennet, a priest, the two former had nothing to say, and the last, having previously declared by a letter to the Earl that his original false information to the Privy Council had been extorted from him by the rack, now spoke only as to the Mass said for the success of the Spanish expedition under the dread of a repetition of torture. To this parole testimony, if it deserve to be so called, was added the production of two emblematical paintings which had been found in the Earl's custody, the one representing a hand throwing a serpent into fire, with the motto " if God is for us who can be against us ?" the other, a lion without claws, inscribed " yet still a lion ;" and of some foreign letters in which he was styled " Duke of Norfolk." In the end no charge of high treason could be substantiated against him except on the ground of his having been reconciled to the Church of Rome, and on that only was he found guilty. His speeches during the trial evinced strong and polished talents. He repelled the partial and desultory attacks of Popham the Attorney-General, by acute observations and prompt and ingenious argument, uttered occasionally with rhetorical elegance. " The Attorney-General," said he, " has managed the letters and confessions produced against me as spiders do flowers, by extracting from them nothing but their poison."

Sentence of death however was passed on him, but Elizabeth had secretly resolved that it should not be executed. He passed the remainder of his unfortunate life in close confinement, unceasingly employing himself in the strictest practice of devotion, and in the exercise of his pen on religious and moral subjects. "One book of Lanspergius," says the manuscript at Norfolk House, "containing an epistle of Jesus Christ to the faithful Soul, he translated out of Latin into English, and caused it to be printed for the furtherance of devotion. He wrote also three treatises on the excellency and utility of virtue, which never came to light, by reason he was obliged to send them away upon fear of a search before they were fully perfected and polished." Two memorials of his pious disposition remain in a secluded apartment in what is called Beauchamp's Tower, in the Tower of London, which was his prison, and whose walls are covered with melancholy devices by the hands of many illustrious state prisoners. We find there the following inscriptions, the former of which has by some accident been omitted in the account of this interesting room published by the Society of Antiquaries in the thirteenth volume of their Archæologia.

"Sicut peccati causa vinciri opprobrium est, ita, e contra, pro Christo custodiæ vincula sustinere maxima gloria est.

"Arundell,
26th of May 1587."

"Quanto plus afflictionis pro Christo in hoc sæculo, tanto plus gloriæ cum Christo in futuro. "Arundell,
June 22, 1587."

He was suddenly taken ill, in August 1592, immediately after eating a roasted teal, the sauce of which was supposed to contain poison ; for the cook who prepared it, and whom he had always suspected, and frequently endeavoured in vain to get removed, came to him when on his death-bed, and earnestly besought forgiveness for some offence, which however he would not disclose. The Earl narrowly escaped for the time with life, and lingered for nearly three years in extreme weakness, but never recovered. Shortly before his departure he petitioned the Queen for permission that his Lady, and some other friends, might visit him ; and she answered, "that if he would but once attend the protestant worship his prayer should be granted, and he should be moreover restored to his honours and estates, and to all the favour that she could show him." He was released from his miseries by the hand of death on Sunday, the nineteenth of October, 1595, and was buried on the following Tuesday in the chapel of the Tower, in the same grave with the Duke his father, where his body remained till the year 1624, when his widow and his son obtained permission to remove it to Arundel, where it was interred in an iron coffin, with an epitaph in Latin, stating the principal points of his persecution, and that he died " non absque veneni suspitione."

The Countess, his wife, possessed considerable talents, and virtues yet more eminent. She was a most earnest and zealous Roman Catholic, and it was probably through her persuasion and example that the Earl, after their reconciliation, became a member of that Church. The instances given of her charity, her humility, and her patience, seem almost romantic. Several original letters from her to her daughter-in-law, Alathea Talbot, Countess of Arundel, are now in the possession of his Grace the Duke of Norfolk, and are composed in the best style of her time, and in a strain of unaffected piety, and natural tenderness, which lets us at once into her true character. Part of an elegiac poem written by her, probably on the premature death of her Lord, remains also in the same custody, and abounds with the imperfect beauties of a strong, but unpolished, poetical fancy. Elizabeth's hatred pursued her even after the death of her husband. His attainder having thrown all his property into the Crown, and left her destitute, the Queen allowed her only eight pounds weekly, which was so ill paid that the Countess was frequently obliged to borrow, in order to procure common necessaries; was prevailed on, with much difficulty, to permit her to live in Arundel House in the Strand, from whence however she was always driven when Elizabeth thought fit to reside in its neighbourhood, in Somerset House; occasionally imprisoned her; often insulted her; and always vilified her.

These noble persons had one son, Thomas, who was restored by King James the First to his father's dignities and estates, and was afterwards the Earl of Arundel so highly distinguished by his admirable collection of works of refined taste and art : and one daughter, Elizabeth, who died unmarried at the age of fifteen years.

Engraved by W. Holl.

JOHN, FIRST LORD MAITLAND, OF THIRLESTANE.

OB. 1595.

FROM THE ORIGINAL, IN THE COLLECTION OF

THE RIGHT HON.ᴮᴸᴱ THE EARL OF LAUDERDALE.

London, Published Decemb.ʳ 1.1830, by Harding & Lepard, Pall Mall East.

JOHN, FIRST LORD MAITLAND,

OF THIRLESTANE.

JOHN MAITLAND, perhaps in all respects the most eminent of a family in which great talents and elegant genius seem to have passed almost with the regularity of hereditary succession, was the second son of Sir Richard Maitland of Lethington, Keeper of the Privy Seal of Scotland, and a Lord of Session, by Mary, daughter of Sir Thomas Cranstoun. He was born, according to some accounts, about the year 1537, though the inscription on his tomb, in stating the age at which he died, fixes his birth to 1545. The latter date, however plausible the authority, is probably incorrect, for it can scarcely be believed that he should have succeeded to those offices of high trust in which we shall presently find him, when he had scarcely attained to years of manhood. He was bred with much care in the study of the law, both in Scotland and on the Continent; and we are told that he had passed some years in fruitless attendance at the Court, when he was provided for by a grant of the Abbey of Kelso, which he afterward exchanged for the Priory of Coldingham, yet the date of the patent by which that exchange was ratified is so early as the seventh of February, 1566. On the twenty-sixth of August, in the following year, on the resignation of his father, the Privy Seal was given to him by the Regent Murray, and on the second of the succeeding June he was appointed a Lord of Session.

It is scarcely necessary to inform the reader of history that Maitland's admission into the ministry occurred at the most

1

critical period of the reign of the celebrated Mary. She was then a prisoner in the Castle of Lochleven, and the questions of her deposition, and the advancement of her infant son to the throne, were under discussion. His elder brother, William, at that time Secretary of State, a sketch of whose life is also given in this work, opposed those measures with the most earnest zeal; and he naturally followed the example of one to whose experience he looked for instruction, and to whom he was bound as well by ties of gratitude as of blood. Younger, however, and less artful, he sank under the vengeance of the contrary party, while that subtle and intriguing politician was left for a time at liberty to pursue his plans. He was deprived of his offices and his benefice, and fled for security to the Castle of Edinburgh, then under the command of Kirkaldy of Grange, a firm and able supporter of Mary's interests, with whom his brother also was at length obliged to seek refuge. Here he remained till that fortress surrendered to the troops of the Earl of Morton, now Regent, when he was sent to the Castle of Tantallon, and early in the following year was removed to a less rigorous custody in the house of Lord Somerville, where he remained a prisoner till the fall of Morton, in 1581, when he was released by an order of the Privy Council.

He came again to the Court with every claim to distinction. His abilities were of the highest class; the character of his mind generous, honourable, and candid; his loyalty pure and disinterested: it had subjected him to an imprisonment of many years, during which he had seen his brother fall a victim to the public principles on which they had mutually acted. James received him with becoming gratitude. On his arrival he was appointed a Senator of the College of Justice, and, on the eighteenth of May, 1584, knighted and placed in the office of Secretary of State, which had been so long and ably held by his brother. He now became in fact first minister of Scotland, for James, whose ripening mind discovered that he had at last obtained a servant at once wise, faithful, and moderate, held him in the most perfect confidence; while the nobility, tired of parties, and unable to subdue the storms which themselves had raised, beheld without jealousy the favour of one in whom they could discover no disposition to mix in their intrigues, or to rival their power. He had, however, enemies. James Stuart, the first, and the most worthless, of the long series of minions by whom the Crown of his master was tarnished, not only conceived a bitter hatred against him, but inspired most of the junior branches of the House of Stuart with the same sentiment. This man, with no apparent recommendation but illegitimate descent from the blood royal, James had promoted, as it should seem by an act of insanity, from the station of Captain of his Guard to that of Lord Chancellor, with an Earldom. His power became, even in a few months, unbounded, and his fall was as sudden. He fled with terror from one of those violent attacks which public vengeance then so often produced in Scotland, aided in this instance by the secret influence of Elizabeth, and would have been scarcely again heard of had he not from his retirement accused the Secretary of being accessary to the death of Mary, and of a design to deliver up the person of the King to the Queen of England. When cited to substantiate the charges, which were universally discredited, he neither appeared nor produced witnesses; and James, having kept the office of Chancellor virtually vacant for a considerable time, in the vain hope that his dastardly favourite might return, at length bestowed it on Maitland. His patent or commission for that post is dated on the thirty-first of May, 1587.

Stuart's accusation had been in fact addressed to the royal and the popular feelings of the moment, and failed for want of the support which he expected from them. Maitland, dispassionate, impartial, and consistent, endeavoured to the last to save the unhappy Mary; but, the fatal blow having been stricken, exerted his utmost powers of persuasion to save his master from the ruinous consequences of an impotent resentment, and succeeded; and on a misconstruction of this wise policy, which to ordinary and heated minds might seem to indicate at least an indifference to her tragical fate, had Stuart hoped to insinuate that he had been a party in accelerating it. The disposition of Maitland indeed was not less pacific than that of James, but the forbearance of the one arose from prudence ; of the other from timidity. The King, therefore, was submissive only to his brother Sovereigns ; the minister moderate towards all. In this spirit he undertook and accomplished the difficult task of reconciling James to the Lords who had been banished to England ; and laboured incessantly, though with incomplete success, to compose the unhappy differences which, from private as well as public causes, agitated the great body of the Scottish nobility. In the same spirit too, though not without a secret affection to puritanism, he strove to persuade the King to let the monstrous insolences of the preachers of that sect to his Crown and person pass with impunity ; advising him, says Spotswood, " to leave them to themselves, for they would render themselves ridiculous by their actings, to the people ; whereas his Majesty, by imprisoning of them for their undutiful speeches and behaviour, rendered them the object of their compassion." It is not surprising that James should have rejected advice at once so odious to his feelings, and of such doubtful policy.

In the memorable year, 1588, he opened the business of the Parliament which James had called to advise him on the great impending designs of Philip of Spain, with a speech so wise and patriotic, that some of the Scottish historians have preserved the substance of it much at large. He deprecated with warmth all correspondence with Philip ; advised that Scotland should be put into the best state of defence ; a faithful amity maintained with Elizabeth ; and that the utmost military force which could be raised, and safely spared, might be sent to England, should she claim such aid. Among those, however, whom he addressed on that occasion were men not only envious of his power, but corrupted by the bribes and promises of Spain, and secretly engaged, should Philip find it convenient to his designs to land a force in Scotland, to do their best to secure a safe passage for it into the adjoining realm. At the head of these was another Stuart, the lately created Earl of Bothwell, a man of an intriguing and restless disposition, and a most determined enemy to Maitland. Combined with the Earls of Huntley, Errol, and Crawfurd, he now laid a plan, if a design so extravagant can be properly so called, to seize the person of the King, or the Chancellor, or both, even in the royal palace. The execution, or rather failure, of this enterprise is very obscurely related by the Scottish writers. We are told that the conspirators, attended by several armed men, gained admission into an apartment in which the King was conferring with Maitland, few others being present. That James, having expressed to Huntley, who headed the party, his surprise at their presence, quitted the room, and was presently after followed by the Chancellor, the intruders remaining inactive. It is declared, however, that some resolute persons then with the King, who were earnest friends to Maitland, threw themselves about his person, and guarded his retreat; and it is probable that from this show of defence the others inferred that their design had been disclosed, and preparations made to receive them. They left the palace seemingly panic-struck; James, after some show of displeasure, pardoned them for the insolence which they had offered; and they retired to meditate a better digested attack.

Nor was this long deferred. In the spring of 1589 the same noblemen, instigated, say the writers of the time, by the Roman Catholic party, assembled in open insurrection at Aberdeen, when they issued a proclamation, asserting "that the King was kept a prisoner by the Chancellor, and forced, against his mind, to use his nobility with that rigour to which he was naturally averse; and requiring all the lieges to concur with them, and assist them to set his person at liberty." James raised some troops, and marched to meet them. They submitted without striking a blow; were arraigned of high treason, and found guilty; and after a short restraint, the King, to flatter the Catholic party, whose protection he sought against the puritans, granted them a free pardon, Maitland, with a policy amiable in appearance, and prudent in fact, having interceded peculiarly for Bothwell.

While these matters were passing, James formed a resolution

5

to offer his hand to the Princess Anne of Denmark, and on his return to his capital imparted it to his Privy Council, and met with a steady opposition. Elizabeth, determined to thwart every treaty of marriage that he might propose, had secretly gained over a majority of that body to her purpose, and it is impossible to remove from the character of the Chancellor a strong suspicion that he had engaged to forward her design. It is evident that James entertained that opinion, for his resentment fell on Maitland alone, and at length arose to such a height, that, having failed in all endeavours to obtain his concurrence, he condescended to employ secret agents to inflame the mob of Edinburgh against the Chancellor, and to induce them to threaten his life, should the marriage be prevented or even delayed. In the mean time his enemies in the Court laboured incessantly in aggravating his offence, and renewing their former accusations; and he seems to have been on the point of ruin, when he extricated himself, apparently by an expedient so simple, and of such doubtful sincerity, that his restoration to favour may be more probably ascribed to the King's habitual regard for him. " The Chancellor," says Melvil, who was no friend to him, " being advertised of his Majesty's discontent and displeasure, caused it to come to his Majesty's ears that he would sail himself, and bring the Queen home with him. He forgot not to anoint the hands of some who were most familiar with his Majesty to interpret this his design so favourably that it made the King forget all by-gones; and by little and little he informed him so well of the said voyage, and the great charges he had bestowed upon a fair and swift-sailing ship, that his Majesty was moved to make the voyage himself, and to sail in the same ship with the Chancellor, with great secresy and short preparation, making no man privy thereto but such as the Chancellor pleased, and such as formerly had all been upon his faction."

They sailed on the twenty-second of October, 1589, and returned not till the twentieth of May. Maitland, who foresaw a storm rising against him at home, availed himself of this long leisure to suggest to James, for his own protection, several novelties in the form of the Scottish government, and in the usages of the Court ; meanwhile his enemies in Scotland were not idle, nor had he been able to conceal from the Queen his aversion to her marriage. Anne, on her arrival, naturally enough attached herself to the party which sought his overthrow ; and the remainder of his life was passed in fruitless endeavours, by alternate menaces and concessions, to avert the reverse of fortune which seemed to await him. A faction was formed against him among the principal nobility, and the Privy Council charged him with abusing the influence which he had possessed over the King in the undue acquisition of important grants of wealth and power to himself, his family, and his adherents. James, still earnestly attached to him, had barely composed this difference with the Council, when his great enemy Bothwell, who had lately escaped from a confinement on the charge of conspiring to compass the King's death by witch-craft, again appeared in arms, and, having published a declaration of his profound loyalty, and that the removal of the Chancellor was the sole object of his enterprise, once more sought the life of that minister in the King's palace and presence. A curious detail of the minute circumstances of this attack, too long to be inserted here, may be found in the Memoirs of Sir James Melvil.

Amidst this warfare on the Chancellor, James raised him to the Peerage : on the eighteenth of May, 1590, he received the title of Baron Maitland of Thirlestane, in Berwickshire. Armed with this proof that he yet enjoyed no small share of royal favour, he seems now first to have courted popularity. He resigned the office of Secretary, his long occupation of which together with the great post of Chancellor had excited much disgust, and soon after prevailed on the King to pass that important statute by which the discipline and jurisdiction of the Kirk were finally legalized and confirmed, in 1592. These conciliations had scarcely been offered when he gave a new offence to the Queen by retaining the pos session of an estate which she claimed as a member of the Abbey of Dunfermline, presented to her by the King on their marriage, though Maitland had possessed the lands in question long before

7

that marriage had been even meditated. She now raised a new faction against him in the Court, and he retired, broken down with vexations and disappointments, as well in his private as public affairs, to the country, where he remained most of the year 1593. At length, willing to make a final effort, he resigned the estate ; was reconciled, and graciously received by her ; and, in endeavouring to ensure her future good-will, unfortunately lent his aid to an intrigue by which she sought to detach the Prince, her son, from the custody of the Earl of Mar, in which, by the single authority and special preference of the King, the infant had been placed. James, suddenly apprised of this scheme, fell into a transport of anger unusual to him. He reprehended the Chancellor with the utmost bitterness ; charged him with treachery and ingratitude ; and left him hopeless of pardon. He now retired, never to return. On arriving at his seat at Lauder, where he had built a magnificent mansion, he was seized by a fatal illness. James relented, and a letter from him, which the Chancellor received on his death-bed, is still extant, and bears a pleasing testimony to the tenderness of the monarch's disposition. He died on the third of October, 1595, seemingly of the too common disease called a broken heart, and was buried at Haddington, under a magnificent tomb, which displays an epitaph in English verse, from the hand of his royal master.

The Chancellor Maitland occasionally relieved his severer studies by poetical composition, some specimens of which have been preserved. A satire written by him, " Aganis Sklanderous Toungis," has been published by Mr. Pinkerton ; and several of his epigrams may be found in " Deliciæ Poetarum Scotorum." He married Jane, only daughter and heir of James, fourth Lord Fleming, (who re-married John Kennedy, fifth Earl of Cassilis) and had issue by her John, who succeeded to his dignity, and was in 1624 created Viscount and Earl of Lauderdale ; and a daughter, Anne, married to Robert Seaton, second Earl of Wintoun.

Engraved by H.T. Ryall.

WILLIAM CECIL, LORD BURGHLEY.

OB. 1598.

FROM THE ORIGINAL OF MARK GERARD, IN THE COLLECTION OF

THE MOST NOBLE THE MARQUIS OF SALISBURY.

London Published July 1, 1833, by Harding & Lepard Pall Mall East.

WILLIAM CECIL,

LORD BURGHLEY.

—◆—

No one can expect in this place a regular and digested detail even of the most prominent facts of this great man's life. The history of his country, and indeed of Europe, teem with the particulars of his political conduct; and though these have been repeatedly condensed, and embodied with much skill and labour, in forms of biography confined exclusively to his story, yet so abundant are the materials, and the theme of such mighty interest, that a life of this minister, combining on an ample scale authentic facts and judicious reasonings, with grace of style, and with that warmth of interest which only a real affection to the subject can bestow, would supply perhaps the most important deficiency in the whole circle of our historical literature. Little more can properly be done here than to collect some fleeting circumstances of his private and domestic conduct : to gather from obscure and neglected sources such as may be obtained of those smaller lights and shadows of character which the affected dignity of history has deemed unworthy of notice.

He descended from an ancient and respectable family of country gentlemen which had long been seated in the county of Hereford, a branch of which removed from thence into Lincolnshire, and settled there, in the neighbourhood of Stamford, on considerable estates, purchased by his grandfather, David Siselt, Sitsilt, or

Cyssell, for thus variously does his name seem to have been spelled by this individual person. Numerous attempts were formerly made to trace the origin of his house to remote antiquity, for Burghley's foible, and perhaps he had no other, was to assume a credit for splendid ancestry, and he spared no pains in endeavouring to establish the justice of his claim. So predominant in him was this disposition, that he could not help beginning an answer which he penned to some malignant libels on Elizabeth and her ministers with a diffuse account of his own family. It may be readily conceived that genealogists and antiquaries were not eager to dispute this point with a prime minister. Verstegan, the first of the latter class in the Treasurer's time, taking an ingenious advantage of the classical aspect of the surname " Cecil," an orthography by the way, which seems to have been first used by Burghley himself, gravely derives him from a patrician stock of ancient Rome; and others, of less note, who preceded and followed Verstegan, have been even more complaisant. Burghley's genealogical researches, however, were not confined to his own views. He loved the study, and probably devoted to it most of the little time that he could snatch from his great avocations. I once possessed many manuscript pedigrees, written entirely by himself, which a nobleman, lineally descended from him, did me the honour some years since to accept at my hands. Several of them had been compiled with the evident view of discovering illustrious alliances with his own blood. Others were miscellaneous, comprising many families of nobility and gentry in various parts of the kingdom with whom he sought not for such connexion.

He was born on the thirteenth of September, 1520, in the house of his grandfather, at Bourne, in Lincolnshire, of which parish his mother, Jane, daughter and heir of William Hickington, was a native. His father, Richard Cecil, was master of the robes to Henry the Eighth. He gained the rudiments of his education at the free school of Grantham, and afterwards at Stamford, and at the age of fifteen went to St. John's College, in Cambridge. The cool and sober mind, and the disposition for almost unremitting

2

application, which distinguished his public life, were equally con-spicuous in his childhood: in his college he rose always at four, and could scarcely be prevailed on to quit his studies during the whole of the day. We are told that he suffered much there from a defluxion on his legs, which was ascribed to his sedentary habit, and was cured with difficulty; but this was probably his first attack of that inveterate gout which so cruelly afflicted his maturer years. His father having destined him to the profession of the law, he was entered of Gray's Inn in his twenty-first year, and, about three months after, married Mary, sister of the celebrated scholar Sir John Cheke. A casual disputation with two priests of the Romish Church on some points of doctrine, and of pontifical authority, is said to have introduced him a little before this period to the notice of Henry, who bestowed on him the reversion of an office in one of the courts of law; and the interest of his brother-in-law, who was preceptor to Edward the Sixth, brought him early in the reign of that Prince into the favour of the Pro-tector. He was appointed Master of Requests, and promoted soon after to the office of Secretary of State; was displaced, with the rest of Somerset's friends, and committed to the Tower, where he remained a prisoner for some months; and not long before the King's death was restored by Dudley, who had discovered in him that cool wisdom of which his own intemperate counsels stood so much in need.

Cecil has been taxed with ingratitude, and indeed treachery, to his great patron Somerset, but the charge, which seems to have been grounded on his sudden acquisition of the favour of Nor-thumberland, acquired little credit. Some suspicion, it is true, to that effect might probably have been built on the cold conso-lation which he offered to the Protector when that great man was tottering on the brink of final ruin. He solicited an inter-view with Cecil, then attached to the faction of Dudley; com-municated to him his apprehensions of the impending blow; and asked his friendly advice. Cecil is said to have contented himself with answering that, " if he were innocent, he might trust to that:

3

if he were otherwise, he could but pity him." This anecdote, if it be genuine, furnishes no presumption of treachery. It savours only of the frigid caution which must necessarily attend him who successfully endeavours to rise amidst a conflict of parties. Pure gratitude belongs, almost exclusively, to the intercourse of private society, and Cecil was a statesman by profession; almost by nature.

Aided by the same useful, however narrow, prudence, he steered with safety through the frightful difficulties which arose on the questionable succession to the Crown upon the death of Edward. When directed by that Prince to prepare the instrument for settling it on Jane Grey, he excused himself with admirable address, and shifted the performance of the office on the judges; and, when it was to be signed by the King, and the Privy Council, contrived, though himself a member of that body, that his name should appear on the face of it only as that of a witness to the royal signature. So, when Northumberland, on the King's demise, called on him to draw the proclamation declaring Jane's accession, and asserting her right to the throne, he excused himself by declining to invade the province of the Attorney and Solicitor General; and, shortly after, when the fortunes of that rash nobleman and his family were becoming desperate, positively denied his request to compose an argument in support of her title, and of the dispositions made by Henry for the exclusion of Mary. Armed with these pleas, from which at the best little could be inferred beyond a mere neutrality, he presented himself to that Princess in the very hour which had finally crushed the hopes of Jane, and was graciously received. He prudently took this opportunity to secure himself by a general pardon.

Reserved, mysterious, and perhaps too selfish, in his political views, he preserved however a noble integrity in his affection to the religious faith in which he had been bred. When Mary, on her accession, offered to continue him in the post of Secretary if he would conform to the Church of Rome, he stedfastly refused. In a manuscript account of his life, professed to have been written by

4

one of his servants, which possesses much internal evidence of authenticity, we are told that he answered the noble emissary who conveyed to him the Queen's pleasure on that occasion, "that he thought himself bound to serve God first, and next the Queen, but if her service should put him out of God's service, he hoped her Majesty would give him leave to chuse an everlasting rather than a momentary service; and, as for the Queen, she had been his so gracious lady, that he would ever serve and pray for her in his heart, and with his body and goods be as ready to serve in her defence as any of her loyal subjects, so she would please to grant him leave to use his conscience to himself, and serve her at large, as a private man, which he chose rather than to be her greatest counsellor." The same authority informs us that he now commenced a correspondence with Elizabeth, in her captivity; communicated to her from time to time all public events in which her interests were concerned; assisted her with his counsels; and thus laid the foundation for that future exalted station in her favour which certainly seems to have rested little less on her personal regard for him than on her conviction of his wisdom and his fidelity.

He was the first person on whom she called for advice, for on the very day of her accession he presented to her minutes of twelve particular matters which required her instant attention, and the first appointment of her reign was to replace him in the office of Secretary. To this, three years after, she added that of Master of the Court of Wards, a post of considerable profit and patronage; on the 25th of February 1570, O. S., created him Baron of Burghley in Lincolnshire; in 1572 gave him the Order of the Garter; and in the autumn of that year he succeeded the old Marquis of Winchester as Lord High Treasurer, and so remained till his death, on the fourth of August 1598, having presided uninterruptedly in the administration of public measures for thirty of the most glorious and happy years that England has ever known.

In every feature of this very eminent person's character we trace some one or more of the qualifications for a great statesman, and in every particular of his public conduct we discover their fruition. He burst forth therefore in his youth upon public observation in the possession, almost intuitively, of those rare faculties which deride the slow march of experience, and scarcely need the protection of power; a fact almost incredible, had we not ourselves of late years witnessed a similar phenomenon. In a remarkable letter of Roger Ascham's, in the year 1550, chiefly on the learning of the English ladies, having spoken largely in the praise of the erudite Mildred Coke, who had then become the second wife of Cecil, he digresses to her husband, at that time in his thirtieth year, and a minister of some years' standing. "It may be doubted," says the translator of Ascham, "whether she is most happy in the possession of this surprising degree of knowledge; or in having had for her preceptor and father Sir Anthony Coke, whose singular erudition caused him to be joined with John Cheke in the office of tutor to the King; or, finally, in having become the wife of William Cecil, lately appointed Secretary of State; a young man indeed, but mature in wisdom, and so deeply skilled both in letters and affairs, and endued with such moderation in the exercise of public offices, that to him would be awarded by the consenting voice of Englishmen the four-fold praise attributed to Pericles by his rival Thucydides—to know all that is fitting; to be able to apply what he knows; to be a lover of his country; and to be superior to money."

Perhaps no better proof of his profound sagacity could be found than in the fact of his having, throughout the unusually protracted term of his administration, enjoyed the uninterrupted confidence and esteem of a Princess whom, if we can for a moment forget our own prejudices and her glory, we shall find little less capricious than her father, and almost as unprincipled. One solitary instance of an apparent suspension of her favour towards him accompanied the ridiculous disavowal of her intention to sign the death warrant of the unhappy Mary, and the infamous sacrifice of Davison, through which she sought to conceal one crime by the commission of another; but this was mere affectation and artifice; he is said to have besought her pardon with a show of the most humble contrition, and received it so speedily that the sincerity of her anger was even at that time doubted.

Burghley, a favourite without the name, was ever an overmatch for the unworthy Leicester, on whom that odious title was always bestowed. The fair fame which followed the one unsought was vainly pursued by the other, and thus will the steady and straightforward step of wisdom and rectitude always outstrip the eager and irregular efforts of cunning and deceit. Flattery seems to have had no share in procuring or maintaining to him the unbounded grace of his mistress, nor can an instance be found of his having used artifice to cultivate that popularity which he so largely enjoyed. He chastened with so just a judgment a naturally high spirit, and an ample consciousness of the dignity of his rank and place, as to obtain the reverence of many, and the esteem of the whole body, of the nobility, with the exception of a very few, the impotency of whose factious endeavours against him served but to increase the splendor of his reputation, and to strengthen the grasp with which he upheld the honour of the Crown, and the interests of the nation. Though Elizabeth is said to have ruled by the dexterous opposition of parties, she ever abstained from involving him in the collision. Indeed there is good reason to suppose that he joined her in the prosecution of this policy, and, by affecting a careless neutrality, increased the vain hopes of faction, and encouraged it to disclose its views. In the long course of his ministry, history records not a single instance of erroneous judgment; of persecution, or even severity, for any public or private cause; of indecorous ambition, or thirst of wealth; of haughty insolence, or mean submission. In a word, moderation, the visible sign of a moral sense critically just, was the guide of all his actions; decorated the purity of his religious faith with charity to its opponents, and tempered the sincere warmth of his affection to the Crown with a due regard to all the civil institutions of the realm; it has been therefore happily said

7

of him, that "he loved to wrap the prerogatives in the laws of the land."

The same fine principle coloured the whole conduct of his private life. Without remarkable fondness or indulgence, he was the kindest husband, father, and master, among the great men of his time; with few professions of regard, a warm friend; a steady enemy, with passive resentment; a cheerful, and even jocose companion, with cautious familiarity; just in all his dealings, without ostentation; magnificent in his establishments, without profusion; tenacious of the powers and privileges of his own high station, and tenderly careful of the rights of others. His two marriages, in both of which he was singularly fortunate, have been already mentioned. It is scarcely necessary to say that the Marquis of Exeter is lineally descended from the first, and the Marquis of Salisbury from the second. His second lady brought him likewise two daughters; Anne, who became the wife of Edward de Vere, eighteenth Earl of Oxford; and Elizabeth, married to William, eldest son of Thomas Lord Wentworth.

Engraved by W.T. Mote.

ROBERT DEVEREUX, EARL OF ESSEX.

OB. 1601.

FROM THE ORIGINAL OF HILLIARD, IN THE COLLECTION OF

THE RIGHT HON.BLE THE EARL OF VERULAM.

London, Published Dec.r 1.1836, by Harding & Lepard, Pall Mall East.

ROBERT DEVEREUX,

EARL OF ESSEX.

———◆———

THAT incomparable Essex, who was the second Earl of his family; the great favourite of Elizabeth, and of England; the admiration and the regret of Europe. In an age certainly inquisitive; at least pretending to exquisite taste and judgment; and peculiarly distinguished by its incessant and various employment of the press; it is astonishing that no regular and detailed celebration should have been dedicated to the memory of this very extraordinary man. We have been gorged, even to disgust, with tedious pieces of unmerited biography, and the actions and motives of plodding statesmen, insignificant courtiers, and rebels who resembled Essex in nothing but in their rank and their punishment, have been sifted and analysed with the most insufferable minuteness; while a thousand inestimable memorials of a character, the exquisite perfections and errors of which were almost peculiar to itself, have been suffered to remain scattered and unconnected on the pages of history, or buried in undisturbed manuscript. How can we account for this omission? Have fear and modesty deterred modern biographers from venturing on a task to perform which worthily the pen must sometimes be dipped in the softest milk of human kindness, and sometimes into the burning fermentation of furious passions; or must we ascribe it to a submission, less excusable, to the depraved taste of a time in which history is chiefly devoted to the discovery of political analogies, and to the suggestion of party arguments? The narrow

I

compass to which these essays are limited prohibits the author from an attempt in which he could have but little chance of success. He must confine himself here to a mere recital of circumstances. But it were earnestly to be wished that some one, in whom delicate feeling is united to acute judgment; who could form a fair estimate of admirable merits and of venial imprudences; who may be qualified by an extensive knowledge of the history of the human heart as well as of his country, would write a life of the Earl of Essex.

He was the son of Walter Devereux, Viscount Hereford, &c., who had been created Earl of Essex by Elizabeth, in 1572, and whose portrait, with a sketch of his life and character, may be found elsewhere in this work. His mother was Lettice, daughter of Sir Francis Knollys, K.G., a relation, at no great distance, to Anne Bullen, the Queen's mother; and Robert, the elder of their two sons, was born at the Earl's seat at Netherwood, in Hereford-shire, on the tenth of November, 1567. His childhood was undistinguished by any promise of more than ordinary parts. We are told indeed by Sir Henry Wotton, who may be said to have studied the history of the family, that his father had formed a very mean judgment of his understanding, and directed his attention therefore chiefly to the improvement of Walter, his younger son. Robert had not attained his tenth year when he succeeded to the honours and estates of his family. His father had committed him to the care of persons of uncommon wisdom and worth. Burghley was his guardian, and the severely virtuous Sussex, in regard of a promise to the Earl on his death-bed, his firm friend. Sir Edward Waterhouse, a man perhaps equal to them in talents, as he certainly was in honour and integrity, personally superintended his affairs, and watched over his conduct with a vigilance which was sweetened, as well as strengthened, by the most earnest affection, for Waterhouse had been entirely beloved and trusted by the deceased Earl, and entered on his charge with a heart overflowing with kindness and gratitude. Towards the end of the year 1578, the young Essex, by the

2

direction of Lord Burghley, became a student of Trinity College, in Cambridge. Whitgift, afterwards Primate, who was then master of that house, undertook the direction of his education, and here the character and powers of his mind were presently unfolded : his obedient application to the severer orders of learning was not less remarked than his attachment to more polite studies, and he was distinguished for an elegance and fluency of composition of which his time afforded few instances. His manners were peculiarly engaging; his temper mild, compliant, and marked by a graceful seriousness which approached to melancholy; his moral conduct stained by no vice, and becomingly tinctured with dignity. He remained in the University till 1582, when he took the degree of Master of Arts, and soon after went into South Wales, where he resided in one of his family mansions, and became, says Wotton, so enamoured of a rural life, that it required much persuasion to withdraw him from his retirement.

In 1584 he came at length to Court, introduced and patronised by his father-in-law, Leicester, who was then in the zenith of his power. It had been strongly rumoured that Leicester caused the late Earl's death by poison. He had married the widowed Countess with indecent haste, and perhaps now sought to lessen the suspicion under which he laboured by thus publicly professing his affection for the son. It has been said that Essex was inclined to reject his proffered friendship; we find, however, that in the succeeding year he accompanied Leicester, then appointed Captain-General in the Low Countries, to Holland, where, though little more than eighteen years old, he received the commission of General of the Horse. He was distinguished in that campaign by his personal bravery, especially in the battle of Zutphen, and on the twenty-seventh of December, 1587, shortly after his return, was suddenly elevated to the dignified post of Master of the Horse. In the following year, when Elizabeth assembled an army to await at the mouth of the Thames the awful attack threatened by Spain; when superior military skill, to direct the

3

bravery of her troops, was perhaps even more important than the wisdom of her ministers to the support of a crown which was then thought by many to totter on her head; she chose this youth to command her horse, and decorated him with that splendid order of knighthood which she had frequently denied to the best and the noblest of her old servants. Thus far he seemed to common observers to have been borne forward on the wing of Leicester's power, or rather till this period had Elizabeth been able to conceal that extravagant partiality which presently after astonished all Europe, and still remains perhaps the most remarkable paradox in English history.

Leicester died in the autumn of that year, and Essex instantly rose to a measure of favour which that extraordinary man, whose influence over the Queen had been so long envied, never enjoyed. It was unsought by himself. It pursued him. It seemed even to molest him, by interrupting the course of his inclinations, and confining his ardent and independent spirit to spheres of action which, though the amplest that a monarch could offer, were too narrow for its rapid and eccentric range. Even so early as the spring of 1589 he fled, unpermitted, from the Court, and sailed to Portugal with Norris and Drake, a volunteer in the expedition then undertaken for the restoration of Don Antonio to the throne of that kingdom. The degree of anger to which Elizabeth was provoked by this extravagant step, and by his disobedience to a previous summons, may be best inferred from the letter by which she commanded his instant return.

" Essex,

" Your sudden and undutiful departure from our presence, and your place of attendance, you may easily conceive how offensive it is, and ought to be, unto us. Our great favours bestowed upon you, without deserts, hath drawn you thus to neglect and forget your duty, for other construction we cannot make of these your strange actions. Not meaning therefore to tolerate this your disordered part, we gave directions to some of our Privy Council, to let you know our express pleasure

4

for your immediate repair hither, which you have not performed, as your duty doth bind you, increasing thereby greatly your former offence, and undutiful behaviour, in departing in such sort without our privity, having so special offices of attendance and charge near our person. We do therefore charge and command you forthwith, upon the receipt of these our letters, all excuses and delay set apart, to make your present and immediate repair unto us, to understand our farther pleasure; whereof see you fail not, as you will be loth to incur our indignation, and will answer for the contrary at your uttermost peril.

"The 15th of April, 1589."

Essex at length presented himself, and these threats were revoked. He returned not to inquiry and punishment, but to renewed grace. The gallantry with which he had fought in every action during his absence, was thrown by Elizabeth into the scale of his merits, and the counterpoise forgotten. Elizabeth admired brave men; and yet it has been observed that when, about this time, Essex, in a sudden fit of jealousy of her favour, had affronted Sir Charles Blount, afterwards Lord Montjoy, because he had decorated his person with a jewel which the Queen had given to him, and had been therefore challenged, and wounded in a duel, by that gentleman, she swore, with great seeming wrath, that "unless some one or other should take him down, there would be no ruling him." There can be little doubt that this speech was meant to disguise her real sentiments. Such a favourite as Essex could not have offended a woman of her character by contending for her good graces. His marriage however, which shortly followed these events, did indeed provoke her resentment to the utmost; but here too the same feelings led her to dissemble : she ascribed he ranger to the alleged inequality of the match, by which she alleged that the honour of the Earl's house was degraded—degraded by his having married the daughter of Sir Francis Walsingham, and relict of Sir Philip Sidney !

In 1591 he was appointed to the command of a force of four

thousand troops, sent by Elizabeth to assist Henry the Fourth of France in the siege of Rouen. The object of this expedition was wholly disconcerted by the tardy co-operation of the French. Essex however distinguished himself by a chivalrous gallantry in many skirmishes, and, after an absence of some months, returned, highly disgusted because the greatest captain of the age had declined his advice on a military question. He was received with unabated kindness by the Queen, who now admitted him into her Privy Council, but it is at this period, as perhaps might naturally be expected, that historians have dated the commencement of his discontents. His captivating talents, his unbounded liberality, his courtesy, and his courage, had rendered him the idol of all warm and generous hearts; while the selfish and the needy crowded round him, and loaded him with adulation, in the hope of sharing the fruits of his unbounded influence over Elizabeth. The younger nobility, and the military, looked up to him with mixed motives of affection and interest, and considered him at once their example and their patron; the Puritans, now becoming a formidable body, arrogantly claimed his protection as a duty which had devolved on him from his father-in-law, Leicester, who had openly favoured their doctrines and their pretensions; and the disaffected of other classes courted him with unceasing assiduity, in the view of, some time, availing themselves of that discord with the Queen or her servants, into which the simplicity of his heart, and the eagerness of his temper, were so likely to betray him. This enormous popularity at length excited in secret the fears of Elizabeth, and increased the jealousy already raised in the breasts of her ministers by the favours that she had bestowed on him. She sought to avert her danger by furnishing incessant employment to his activity and love of glory, and they laboured to drive him to desperation by schemes to render his services abortive.

These passions were beginning to operate when, in June 1596, he undertook, jointly with the High Admiral Howard, the command of the expedition to Cadiz. The particulars of this, and of his excursions in the succeeding year, are so largely given by our historians, that it would be impertinent to repeat them here. It is worthy however of observation, that in the former his opinion was always uniformly rejected, save only as to the proper moment for attacking the Spanish fleet in the harbour, the Admiral's concession to which was so joyfully received by him, that, in an ecstacy, he threw his hat into the sea. The Island voyage, as it was called, of 1597, in which he acted as commander-in-chief both of the army and fleet, was unhappily distinguished by his differences with Raleigh, who served as Rear Admiral, the origin and circumstances of which have been variously and even contradictorily represented by different writers; and yet, amidst this confusion, strong grounds appear to suspect Raleigh of a premeditated design to prevent the success of the enterprise. Essex, on his arrival from Cadiz, had been better received by the Queen than by her ministers, whom he found inclined to censure every part of his conduct in the expedition. He published therefore a narrative of it, more remarkable for sincerity than prudence, in which, as has been well observed, " he set down whatever was omitted in the prosecution of it, and then, by way of answer to those objections, imputed all miscarriages to other men ; by which he raised to himself many implacable enemies, and did not gain one friend." In the mean time his attempts to use his influence for the service of his friends, which indeed seems to have been the end to which he wished always to apply it, were constantly thwarted. He was now deeply mortified, and Elizabeth, who seems to have shared in his chagrin, endeavoured to console him by a gift for life of the post of Master of the Ordnance, to which he was appointed on the nineteenth of March, 1597. New causes, however, of dissatisfaction arose. During his absence on the Island voyage the Admiral, Howard, had been created Earl of Nottingham, and in his patent the reduction of Cadiz was ascribed to his good service. This affront, as Essex, and perhaps rightly, conceived it, together with his vexation at the moderate success of that expedition, produced in him a disgust which became publicly visible. On his return, he retired to the country, and, according to the fashion of that time, pleaded illness to excuse his attendance in Parliament, which was then sitting. Elizabeth again interfered to appease him, and on the twenty-eighth of December, 1597, raised him to the splendid office of Earl Marshal of England.

His services, or rather his endeavours to serve, were now transferred to the Council, and he appeared in the character of a statesman, for which he possessed every qualification but patience. Here he opposed, with equal vehemence and good argument, the proposals offered in May, 1598, for a treaty of amity with Spain. On this great topic he engaged in disputes with the Treasurer, Burghley, which rose to such warmth that Burghley, at the council table, drew a prayer-book from his bosom, and prophetically pointed out to the Earl this passage—" Men of blood shall not live out half their days." Peace was determined on ; and Essex, in his dread of being misrepresented, to the abatement of that popularity his affection to which was his greatest fault and misfortune, immediately composed his " Apology against those which falsely and maliciously take him to be the only hindrance of the peace and quiet of their country, addressed to his friend Anthony Bacon." This exquisite example of his talents and integrity, as well as of the purity and elegance of his style, infinitely valuable too as it exhibits a sketch by his own hand of the circumstances of his public conduct to that period, was soon after printed, doubtless at least with his concurrence, to the great offence of the Queen. Burghley, his ancient guardian, whose power had in some measure warded off the attacks of his enemies, and to the wisdom and kindness of whose advice his impetuosity had frequently submitted, died while Essex was preparing his Apology, and he fell into new errors and excesses. Among these the most remarkable occurred in his memorable and well-known quarrel with Elizabeth on the choice of a Governor for Ireland, which terminated on his part with the grossest personal insult ever offered by a subject to a sovereign, and on hers by manual chastisement. He fled to hide his rage in the most obscure retirement, and it was with the utmost difficulty that he could be prevailed on to acknowledge his fault. The wise and worthy Lord Keeper Egerton, in addressing to him a long letter of gentle remonstrance, uses these persuasions—"If you still hold this course, which hitherto you find to be worse and worse, (and the longer you go, the further you go out of the way) there is little hope or likelihood the end will be better. You are not yet gone so far but that you may well return. The return is safe, but the progress is dangerous and desperate in this course you hold. If you have any enemies, you do that for them which they could never do for themselves; your friends you leave to scorn and contempt. You forsake yourself, and overthrow your fortunes, and ruinate your honour and reputation. You give that comfort and courage to the foreign enemies as greater they cannot have; for what can be more welcome and pleasing news than to hear that her Majesty and the realm are maimed of so worthy a member, who hath so often and so valiantly quailed and daunted them? You forsake your country when it hath most need of your counsel and aid: and, lastly, you fail in your indissoluble duty which you owe unto your most gracious Sovereign; a duty imposed on you, not by nature and policy only, but by the religious and sacred bond wherein the Divine Majesty of Almighty God hath by the rule of Christianity obliged you."

Essex's reply presents perhaps the truest picture extant not only of his natural but of his political character; of the grandeur of his mind, and of the tyranny of his passions; of his habitual loyalty, and his republican inclinations. In this admirable letter we find the following vivacious expressions of defiance—"When the vilest of all indignities are done unto me, doth religion inforce me to sue? Doth God require it? Is it impiety not to do it? Why? Cannot Princes err? Cannot subjects receive wrong? Is an earthly power infinite? Pardon me, pardon me, my Lord; I can never subscribe to these principles. Let Solomon's fool laugh when he is stricken. Let those that mean to make

9

their profit of Princes shew to have no sense of Princes' injuries. Let them acknowledge an infinite absoluteness on earth that do not believe an infinite absoluteness in heaven. As for me, I have received wrong; I feel it: My cause is good; I know it: and, whatsoever comes, all the powers on earth can never shew more strength or constancy in oppressing than I can shew in suffering whatsoever can or shall be imposed on me." He was at length persuaded to make a proud submission, and was again received into Elizabeth's favour, which seemed even yet to have been but little impaired.

The affairs of Ireland appear indeed to have been at that time Essex's favourite political study. He had frequently, in the debates of the council, complained of an unreasonable parsimony with which he charged the Ministers in the government of that country, and of restrictions by which they had long fettered the faculties of the Queen's Deputies. His enemies determined to avail themselves of this disposition and to tempt him by an offer of that important and honourable post, with unusually enlarged authority, and the command of a more numerous army than had ever been sent thither. To conquer rebellious factions; to civilize a people at once barbarous and generous; to administer strict justice through the means of absolute power; were noble objects in the view of one whose character united, with a haughty and courageous spirit, the mildest humanity and the most exalted moral principles. Prudence too, if he ever used it, now perhaps reminded him that anger is best cooled by absence, and that past errors are frequently forgotten in the grateful sense of new services. He accepted the office however with reluctance and disgust, unless we are to consider the following exquisite little epistle to Elizabeth, which is said, I know not on what ground, to have been written between the dates of his appointment and his departure, merely as a general appeal to her feelings, and a strong effort to regain the fulness of her favour, for which he made his commission to Ireland the pretext.

10

" From a mind delighting in sorrow ; from spirits wasted with passion ; from a heart torn in pieces with care, grief, and travel ; from a man that hateth himself, and all things else that keep him alive ; what service can your Majesty expect, since any service past deserves no more than banishment and proscription to the cursedest of all islands ? It is your rebels' pride and success must give me leave to ransom myself out of this hateful prison ; out of my loathed body ; which, if it happen so, your majesty shall have no cause to mislike the fashion of my death, since the course of my life could never please you."

> " Happy he could finish forth his fate
> In some unhaunted desert, most obscure
> From all society, from love and hate
> Of worldly folk ; then should he sleep secure ;
> Then wake again, and yield God ever praise ;
> Content with hips, and haws, and brambleberry,
> In contemplation passing out his days,
> And change of holy thoughts, to make him merry ;
> Who when he dies his tomb may be a bush,
> Where harmless Robin dwells with gentle Thrush."

Your Majesty's exiled servant,

ROBERT ESSEX."

On the twenty-seventh of March, 1599, he left London, on his way towards Ireland, to the great joy of those who had thus freed themselves of his unwelcome presence to place him amidst perils which they well knew how to increase. Their efforts however were needless. The short term of his government was a tissue of imprudence, confusion, and misfortune. He passed the first two months in making journeys of observation, and plans for action, and laid the fruits of those labours before the Queen at large in a letter of consummate ability. Elizabeth slighted his opinions, and blamed his conduct in the very first military enter-prize which he undertook. During the irritation produced by these crosses, a large body of his troops was worsted by the Irish,

11

and he punished the remainder of the detachment, contrary to his nature, with a frightful severity. He undertook an unsuccessful expedition, contrary to the Queen's express order to march his army into another province, and afterwards, in obeying that order, was yet more unfortunate. He demanded reinforcements, and obtained them; marched in person, at the head of his main army, to attack the rebels, under the command of Tir-oen; and, without striking a blow, concluded a disgraceful treaty with that chieftain. His incessant reflection at that period on the designs of his enemies in England, seems to have been either the cause or the consequence of a degree of actual insanity which never after left him. He formed a serious resolution to return with his army, and to employ it in subduing them, and it was with much difficulty that some of his dearest friends succeeded in dissuading him from that monstrous attempt. Shortly after, on receiving a reproachful letter from the Queen, he suddenly quitted Ireland, almost alone, and travelling with the utmost speed, appeared most unexpectedly in her presence at Nonsuch, on the twenty-eighth of September, 1599, and implored her to listen to his apology.

Elizabeth was touched by the singular character of this appeal, which once more excited in some degree her tenderness, while it flattered her pride. Essex, once so beloved; whose disobedience she had threatened with condign punishment; whose rebellious resistance she had been taught to anticipate; instead of persisting in his contumacy; or standing aloof to treat for pardon; or employing friends to intercede on his behalf; had fled from an army which adored him, and crossed the sea, to throw himself singly on her mercy and her wisdom. She received him with complacency, and admitted him to a long conference, in the conclusion of which she commanded him not to quit his apartment in the Court, and soon after committed him to an honourable, though close, confinement in the house of the Lord Keeper. It is more than probable that, had matters been left wholly to her undisturbed decision, he might even now have escaped with very light penalties, but another powerful passion had been awakened in her breast, and, terrified at the representations which were every hour laid before her of the dangers to be apprehended from his popularity and his violence, she consented at length to leave his case to the Privy Council, before which it had been somewhat agitated immediately after his arrival. He had remained long a prisoner, still occasionally encouraged, and with Elizabeth's connivance, to hope that no more was intended than to humble his spirit, and that he might be again restored to her grace ; till, on the fifth of June, 1600, he was brought publicly before the Council, and, after an examination of eleven hours, for the most part of which he was kept kneeling, it was determined that he should be deprived of his seat in that body, and of all his offices, except that of Master of the Horse, and should remain in custody during the Queen's pleasure. He was finally enlarged on the twenty-seventh of the following August, and retired to one of his seats in the country.

The die was now cast. Essex considered his situation to be desperate, and that conceit effectually rendered it so. In the beginning of the winter he returned to London, and his house became not only the resort but the residence of the idle, the profligate, and the disaffected of all ranks. Cuffe, who had been his secretary in Ireland, a man of considerable talents, rendered useless, or worse, like his own, by an impetuous temper, undertook to execute his plans, if they deserved to be so called. Few circumstances of our history are better known than those which compose the sad sequel of Essex's story. He seems to have conceived the extravagant, and indeed utterly impracticable, design of working simultaneously on the affection and the fears of Elizabeth. Declaring his profound loyalty, and the most earnest personal regard, he armed his little band professedly to force her to hear his grievances, and to dismiss her servants. Terrified perhaps, but still interested in his favour, instead of employing the ample means to reduce him which were in her power, she ordered that he should be summoned before her

Council, and he disobeyed. The next morning she sent the Lord Keeper, the Lord Chief Justice, and others of the Council, to his house, to receive his complaints, and he imprisoned them. He then sallied forth, at the head of his adherents, and sought ineffectually for volunteers in the city; returned by the river, and fortified his house; and, when no means remained to save him from the perdition to which he seemed to have devoted himself, was at length proclaimed a traitor, besieged, and taken prisoner. These strange circumstances occurred on the seventh and eighth of February, 1601, N. S.; and on the nineteenth, he was brought to his trial before the Peers, and condemned to die. Of his treason there could be no doubt, for it had been committed in the sight of thousands; but for his motives, saving the simple impulses of a most fiery and imprudent spirit, we can look only to his own declaration, that his first object was to gain access to the Queen's person, and his final view, to the establishment of the succession in the King of Scots, for the charge preferred against him of a secret design to set up a claim to the crown on his own part, in right of a remote maternal descent from the House of York, is utterly incredible. The Queen was anxious to the last to spare his life. Of the well known, but weakly authenticated, tale of the Countess of Nottingham, and the ring, with which many writers have been fond of amplifying the last scene of this tragedy, I will say nothing; we have otherwise sufficient proof that Elizabeth at length gave way to the importunities of her ministers with the utmost reluctance, and signed the warrant for his execution amidst a dreadful conflict of tenderness, resentment, and terror. He suffered death on the sixth day after his trial, with a piety not less modest than fervid, and a magnanimity at once calm and heroic.

Of all eminent historical characters, that of Essex has generally been deemed the most difficult to be justly estimated. Rare and singular indeed was its construction, but surely not mysterious. The faults of those who deserve to be called good and great usually spring from an exuberance of fine qualities. All the errors

14

of this extraordinary person may be traced to the warmth of his heart, or the noble simplicity of his mind; to his courage, to his friendships, to his exact sense of honour, or his exalted love of truth. With these virtues, joined to admirable talents, he was perhaps the most unfit man living to be trusted with the direction of important affairs, either civil or military, for his candour disqualified him for the cabinet, and his rashness for the field. He weighed the purity of his intentions against the motives of other public servants with accuracy and justice, and the disdain with which he proclaimed the result rendered them his mortal enemies; but he rated his services, and perhaps his powers, too highly; and hence his frequent quarrels with Elizabeth, the enormous extent of whose favour and bounty he seems never to have considered as commensurate to his deserts: his occasional insolence to that Princess was therefore the issue of pride, and not of ingratitude. His resentments were marked by a petulance somewhat inconsistent with genuine dignity, and his friendships were not always worthily placed; but he was not capricious, for his affections and his aversions were unalterable, and he was incapable of disguising either sentiment: in following the dictates of the one, his liberality knew no bounds; in the gratification of the other, his generosity was never sullied by a single instance of private revenge. His domestic conduct seems to have been unexceptionable. In his hours of retirement his impetuosity was soothed by the consolations of sincere piety, and conscious innocence; by the love of his family, and his dependants, who idolized him; by the temperate charms of refined conversation and reflection. In the humble sincerity of his dying confession, he had no moral offences to avow but certain amorous frailties of his youth.

His understanding was of the sort which usually accompanies acute feelings; quick, penetrating, and versatile; admirable in its conceptions, but of uncertain execution; sometimes approaching, sometimes out-reaching, but seldom resting at, that sober and wary point of judgment which in worldly affairs is dignified by

15

the title of wisdom. His acquirements were infinitely varied and extended. It will appear, on an examination of those of his writings which have been fortunately left to us, that his studies, or rather his perceptions, had embraced every usual object of human science. His powers of expression were equal to the measure of his knowledge : indeed he was incomparably the first English prose writer of his time, and it has been lately discovered that in Latin composition he fell nothing short of the best classical models. The present age too, busy in such researches, has brought to light several poems, of various characters, which reflect a new and unexpected lustre on his genius. Such was the man, and so designed by nature to inform, to improve, and to delight society, whom his own ambition, and Elizabeth's folly, misplaced in the characters of a statesman, a general, and a courtier.

On the extravagance of the Queen's attachment to this nobleman, and the motives by which it was dictated, it is unnecessary here to dilate. Lord Orford, in his " Royal and Noble Authors," has treated at large of those matters, with such acuteness of reasoning, and such extent of historical knowledge, that any further endeavour to elucidate that singular subject would be vain and presumptuous. I shall therefore only add that the Earl of Essex married, as has been before stated, Frances, daughter and heir of Sir Francis Walsingham, and widow of Sir Philip Sidney, by whom he had an only son, Robert, who was the last Earl of the family of Devereux ; and two daughters ; Frances, married to William Seymour, Earl of Hertford, afterwards Duke of Somerset ; and Dorothy, wife, first to Sir Henry Shirley, of Stanton Harold, in Leicestershire, Bart., secondly, to William Stafford, of Blatherwick, in the county of Northampton.

NON SINE SOLE
IRIS

Engraved by W.T. Fry.

QUEEN ELIZABETH.

OB. 1603.

FROM THE ORIGINAL OF ZUCCHERO, IN THE COLLECTION OF

THE MOST NOBLE THE MARQUIS OF SALISBURY.

PROOF

London, Published Dec.ʳ 1,1836 by Harding & Lepard, Pall Mall East.

QUEEN ELIZABETH.

It has been an inveterate fashion to place this Princess in the class of wise monarchs. Whether this has been founded on an impartial and judicious examination of her character, or on the report of certain great authorities, to whose sincerity as well as judgment a ready credit has been given, may be, however, fairly questioned. Henry the Fourth of France, who, it should be recollected, anxiously sought her friendship, professed a high respect for her talents, and took care to make it known to her; and the acute but eccentric Sixtus the Fifth regretted that his vow of celibacy excluded him from the possibility of an union with her, the issue of which he said would have been naturally qualified to govern the world. Another great person, of equal fame with these, and I think of equal rank, answered to one who was inclined to depreciate the powers of her mind, and to ascribe the success and glory of her reign to the sagacity of her counsellors, by asking " whether he ever heard of a weak Prince who chose wise ministers;" a remark, by the way, not very applicable to her, who had but the negative merit of retaining in office those who had been chosen by her father and brother. A few such testimonies and smart sayings from such sources would be at all times sufficient to fix the opinions of those who read history for amusement, that is to say of nearly the whole of mankind. It may seem bold to declare that the history of Elizabeth's reign furnishes no substantial evidence that she possessed remarkable talents, either solid or brilliant. She had however violent passions, and the sudden bursts of these will frequently be mistaken by

1

the multitude for proofs of exalted talent. Hers were all of the unamiable order, but their baleful effects were generally neutralized by counteraction on each other. Thus it was her timidity that prevented her from emulating the horrible tyranny of her father, and her pride that saved her from the disgrace of open profligacy. We seek in vain through the whole of her life for instances of generosity, benevolence, or gratitude, those bright jewels of a crown which Princes to whom nature has denied them have generally been prudent enough to counterfeit.—But we must hasten to our brief compilation, and leave these few remarks to the censure which may await them. They will not be popular, but it will be difficult to contradict them.

Elizabeth, the daughter of Henry the Eighth and Anne Bullen, was born at Greenwich on the seventh of September, 1533. The frantic despotism of her father surrounded her very cradle with terrors, and planted with thorns her path to womanhood. The imperfect divorce of Catherine of Arragon, and the vote of a servile Parliament, had invested her with a factitious and doubtful right to the inheritance of the crown, of which the speedily succeeding alleged infidelity and attainder of her mother, followed by another specific act of the same body, legally deprived her. Mary, her paternal sister, was living, with pretensions which, although they had been in a great measure similarly annulled, furnished ample ground for discord and competition. The birth of a Prince, afterwards Edward the Sixth, as it seemed to settle, though to their mutual prejudice, the succession to the Throne, gave them a chance of safety; but Henry and his obedient Parliament soon after that event replaced them in the order of inheritance, and he specially recognised their right in his will. These dispositions however, powerful as they may seem, were insufficient to remove the prejudices which had arisen out of the confusion that he had previously created, and the premature death of Edward produced a jealousy between the sisters, in which Elizabeth, though too young to appear an active party, was old enough to become an object of persecution.

She had been placed after the decease of her father under the care and in the mansion of his widow, Catherine Par, who presently, with unbecoming haste, took the Lord Admiral Seymour, brother to the Protector Duke of Somerset, for her fourth husband. The extravagant ambition of this nobleman undoubtedly suggested to him the idea of gaining Elizabeth's hand, and the means through which he endeavoured to accomplish his purpose were such as might have been expected from his impetuous and unprincipled character. He sought by the baseness of personal seduction to gain that absolute control over her mind with which her fears of discovery, or her affection, or both, could scarcely have failed to invest him. Of his success in this detestable part of his plan we are of course ignorant, but it appears that Elizabeth regarded him at least with complacency. The singular circumstances of their intercourse were at length made known to Edward's ministers; the young Princess was hastily removed; and a careful inquiry was instituted, many curious documents relative to which are preserved in Haynes's fine collection of Cecil Papers.

The uncertainties and vicissitudes of her youth had not interrupted the regularity of her education. Her surprising facility in the acquisition of languages is commemorated in terms even of rapture in the Latin epistles of her tutor, Ascham. This faculty, and her regular profession of the reformed faith, increased the favour which the tender nature of her brother, the admirable Edward, had always extended to her, and they seem to have been much together after she left the Queen Dowager, and are said to have derived mutual improvement from the joint prosecution of their studies. Edward however was prevailed on, in the feebleness of his last hours, to dispose of the crown to the exclusion of both the Princesses; and in the short contest, if it deserve that name, between Mary and Jane Grey, we are told that Elizabeth raised, we are not informed how, nor is it easy to conceive, a thousand horse for the aid of her sister's cause. She was received therefore with distinction and smiles at the new court; but a secret jealousy lurked in the bosom of Mary. She saw in Elizabeth, a rival, not only in regal claim, but in love, for the Queen had certainly meditated to marry the unfortunate Edward Courtenay, Earl of Devon, who on his part was enamoured, with what return we know not, of her sister. The first act of Mary's first parliament, by decreeing the validity of the marriage of her father and mother, and annulling the sentence of their divorce, virtually reduced Elizabeth again to the condition of a bastard; and that she might have no room to doubt that such was the Queen's interpretation of it, she was presently after placed in the court ceremonial beneath the descendants of her father's sisters. This proof of Mary's aversion was followed by numerous slights and affronts, which at length becoming intolerable, Elizabeth obtained permission to retire into the country, where however she is said to have been closely watched by two trusty servants of the crown, whom she had been obliged to accept as principal officers of her household. But the tranquillity of her retreat was of short duration. She was accused, certainly with little probability, of having been privy to Sir Thomas Wyat's insurrection; was recalled to the Court when in a state of severe illness, strictly examined by the Council, and, after several days, permitted to return; again seized on some new suspicions, and conducted to Hampton Court as a state prisoner, and from thence to close confinement in the Tower of London.

It is remarkable that at this seemingly hopeless period two bills brought into Parliament by her bitter enemy, Bishop Gardiner, the one expressly declaring her illegitimacy, and incapacity to inherit the crown, the other to enable the Queen to appoint her successor, should have been rejected by large majorities. Mary became alarmed at this unexpected opposition to her will in so important a quarter; the rigour of the Princess's imprisonment was presently abated, and she was soon after conducted to the palace of Richmond, where she was offered her liberty if she would accept the hand of the Duke of Savoy. It is probable that to this condition was annexed some proposal tending to an abandonment of her claim to the English crown, for she refused it with a magnanimous perseverance. She was now transferred to Woodstock, and again confined with some severity, and thus she remained till the marriage of her sister to Philip of Spain, when that Prince, among other endeavours to gain popularity with his new subjects, procured her release, at least from the rigours of her captivity, but she was yet watched with the closest attention. The resentment and jealousy of the Queen however gradually abated, and the humility of Elizabeth's concessions kept pace with the increase of her sister's complaisance. When she was at length admitted to personal intercourse and intimacy, she attended all the high ceremonies of the Romish church with seeming devotion, and even partook of the sacrament of the altar. The mutual indifference, or rather aversion, of the King and Queen towards each other, which soon after occurred, operated in her favour. Philip, lately her apparent friend, from some political views regarding his continental interests now reiterated with vehemence the suit of the Duke of Savoy, and Mary, whose favourite measure it had lately been, as earnestly supported Elizabeth in the rejection of it. The Princess presently returned this service by refusing the hand of the heir-apparent to the crown of Sweden, on the alleged ground of the indignity which the King, his father, had offered to Mary by directing his ambassador to propose it in the first instance to herself. The carriage of the sisters towards each other was assuming the appearance of affection, when the Queen died, on the seventeenth of November, 1558.

Elizabeth mounted the Throne amid an extravagance of approbation, flowing from the revived hopes of a people who had been long strangers to the regular protection of laws, and slaves to so many varieties of despotism, civil and religious. They were not disappointed. The first act of her prerogative laid the ground for all her succeeding credit, and fixed the character of her long reign. It was the appointment of William Cecil to the office of Secretary of State, and in effect to that of Prime Minister. That great and good man had been, from the purest motives, her secret correspondent and adviser during the long season of oppression and difficulty through which she had laboured. The strict seclusion in which she had lived, even from her infancy, had rendered her a stranger to all other statesmen, and, without meaning to deny that a sense of obligation to him had its due share in influencing her choice, it may be said that she fell as it were naturally into his hands. He formed her ministry, and presided in it with unparalleled honesty and disinterestedness, and with the rarest combination of wisdom, fortitude, and good temper, that history can produce in the conduct of a public man. The constant activity of these admirable qualities for years averted from his mistress and from the realm the dangers with which her foibles threatened both. From the hour of his appointment those exertions became necessary, for it was almost in the same hour that she chose for her favourite that monster of ambition and profligacy, Robert Dudley, afterwards Earl of Leicester. It would perhaps be too much to ascribe wholly to that unworthy partiality the resolution which she professed already to have taken against matrimony, for it was to her first Parliament, as soon as it had assembled, that she expressed it. Her brother-in-law Philip of Spain, Eric, King of Sweden, and the Archduke Charles of Austria, made their addresses, and were refused accordingly. A few too of the highest of her subjects entertained distant hopes of being chosen by her, and others of them have been mentioned to whom perhaps the thought never occurred. That Dudley however aspired to her hand, and with a boldness unknown to the rest, is certain; and that, to ensure at least the possibility of obtaining it, he connived at the murder of his wife, is scarcely doubtful.

Elizabeth's jealousy of the Queen of Scots commenced with the accession of the one to the English throne, and of the other, as Queen consort to that of France, events nearly simultaneous. The importance that Scotland had derived from the French marriage, which had made it in effect a colony of France, was justly dreaded, and no time was lost in demonstrating the vigilance which it seemed to demand. A fleet sailed to the Frith of Forth, and a powerful army was marched to the borders, and the Regent, Mary of Guise, already perplexed by the insurrectionary spirit of the infant kirk, submitted by the treaty of Edinburgh to terms highly advantageous to the interest of England. In the political effects of the Reformation in Scotland, and indeed elsewhere, Elizabeth found a useful lesson for her own conduct at home. Unencumbered by conscientious scruples and niceties of faith, she determined to reject, in pursuing the separation from the church of Rome, every novelty in which the most remote tendency might be traced towards the abridgment of temporal dominion. The dismission of those splendid ceremonies, and ardent forms of worship, which biassed the judgment by captivating the imagination, was wrested from her with difficulty by her ministers and prelates. She would indeed willingly have retained the whole of the Catholic system, except its dependence on the see of Rome, but it was impracticable. Recent events had prejudiced against it a vast majority of the nation, and the final establishment of the Anglican Church was more indebted to the headstrong and cruel violence of Mary than to the wisdom, the beneficence, or the piety, of her sister. To Elizabeth however, be her motives what they might, it owes its escape from the baseness of Calvinism.

The death of Francis the Second of France, in the winter of 1560, before he could be said to have reached manhood, was the signal for that well-known breach between Elizabeth and his lovely relict, which terminated in the tragical death of the one, and the endless disgrace of the other. Mary's influence in France had expired with her husband, and she returned to Scotland with regret, though to assume an independent crown. Before her departure from Paris she had been pressed by the English ambassador to ratify the treaty of Edinburgh, which was rendered peculiarly odious to her by a stipulation for her abandonment of the royal title and arms of England, her habit of quartering which had been always sternly and most reasonably resisted by Elizabeth. She evaded the demand by various pretences, and Elizabeth in return refused her request of a safe conduct for her voyage, which she, on her part, resented by a message full of anger and disdain. From this period a bitter enmity, at first rather the result of ordinary passion than of political discord, commenced between them, and was gradually aggravated by mutual injuries and affronts till it produced the purest reciprocal hatred. That Mary however cherished, or rather was persuaded to entertain, a hope that she might effectually dispute Elizabeth's right to a throne to which herself was presumptive heir, is certain. The incessant instances of her father-in-law, Henry the Second, of the haughty family of Lorrain, and at length of Spain, had raised an inclination in her mind to which the measure of her own ambition would have been perhaps incompetent. Philip, who had gladly coalesced with Elizabeth to counterbalance the weight of France, now, on its removal from the scale, espoused the party of Mary. He was justly esteemed the temporal head of the Catholics throughout Europe, and with little difficulty excited in those of England an aversion to their Queen, and a proportionate affection to her rival. Thus Elizabeth became compelled to use those measures of severity against the Catholics which distinguished her reign, while she felt secretly inclined towards them; and to countenance, or rather to endure the Calvinists, or Puritans, as they were here called, whom she detested. To those of Scotland, now in open rebellion, she secretly extended every favour that her own interests, or her anger against Mary, could suggest. The influence of these circumstances, and of the policy founded on them, may be discerned in almost all the important features of more than thirty years of her reign.

The two Queens however soon found it necessary to dissemble. They assumed a dignified decency of conduct towards each other, and entered into negotiations. Mary offered to make the clearest acknowledgment of Elizabeth's present title to the throne, on condition of receiving a recognition of her own right to the succession, which was refused, and the mutual disappointment, though it increased the obstinacy of each, was borne by each with a well-affected patience. Elizabeth's denial arose not more from her enmity to the Queen of Scots than from her general aversion to all, however distant, who might in possibility inherit the throne. She seemed desirous even to extinguish the royal race; and of this almost insane foible the long and horrible persecution, which she commenced about this time, of the Earl of Hertford and the Lady Catherine Grey, for their marriage, affords one remarkable instance.

In consonance with the new policy which Elizabeth had unwillingly adopted, she took up with vigour the cause of the Protestants, who were in arms in France, and, after some ineffectual negotiation in their favour with Charles the Ninth, or rather with his mother, Catherine de Medicis, sent a strong force, and from time to time large supplies of money, into Normandy to aid their General, the Prince of Condé, from whom she received in return the possession of Havre de Grace, which she resolved to keep as an equivalent for Calais. This, however, and all other objects of the plan, were within a few months defeated by the sudden submission of the Protestant leaders to the crown. The large disbursements required by these purposes obliged her, early in 1563, to summon her second Parliament, which, like its predecessor, commenced its proceedings by beseeching her to marry, and was answered ambiguously. The Queen of Scots, in the mean time, encouraged the proposals which she was continually receiving through her uncles, the Duke and Cardinal of Guise, for a second marriage, an event which Elizabeth contemplated with terror, not only for the strong probability of its increasing the line of inheritors of the English crown, but for the power which Mary could not but at once acquire by a matrimonial alliance with one of the great royal Houses of Europe. To endeavour to prevent the one was hopeless, but she sought to avoid the danger of the other by at length proposing to acknowledge implicitly Mary's right to succeed to the throne of England, on the condition that she should take a husband from among the English nobility. The Queen of Scots received the motion with affected complacency, and, after long hesitation, Elizabeth availed herself of the opportunity of dissembling her own passion for him by naming Leicester, who she knew would be in the end rejected, while Mary, with equal artifice, concealed the indignation with which so unworthy an offer justly inspired her.

Elizabeth's main purposes were however answered for the time. By this negotiation, and others equally extravagant, she prevented Mary for nearly two years from hearkening to any becoming proposals of marriage, and postponed any definitive answer on the grand question of the succession. Mary's patience was at length subdued. She despatched a letter to Elizabeth in terms so wrathful that her ministers, dreading lest their private quarrel might produce a breach between the two countries, prevailed on her to conciliate, and for that purpose Sir James Melvil was sent to the English court. Those who would contemplate the utmost extravagance of female vanity, envy, and folly, may find it in that minister's memoirs, in his recitals of Elizabeth's conversations with him. She now recommended Darnley for Mary's hand, and sent him to her court, and privately entreated her to restore the honours and estates of his father, the Earl of Lennox, who laboured under an attainder. Mary was at once captivated by his fine person, and made preparations for the marriage, when Elizabeth despatched an order for Darnley's instant return, imprisoned his mother and brother in the Tower, and seized his father's English estates; and even in this miserable faithlessness and caprice some historians have affected to discern a profound policy. Mary, impelled by various passions, now hastened her nuptials with the catholic Darnley amidst the outcries of the reformers, whose leaders Elizabeth, after having seized the opportunity to incite to an unsuccessful rebellion, loaded with reproaches for their treason, and spurned from her presence, when they fled to her court from the vengeance of their mistress. The strange and horrible circumstances which followed this marriage in rapid succession are so well known that to do more than name them here would seem scornful of historical recollection. Mary's partiality to Rizzio, and his assassination ; the murder of Darnley ; her detestable union with Bothwell ; the league against her of her chief nobility, and their subsequent capture of her person ; her imprisonment, escape, and fatal flight into England ; all occurred within little more than two years. In the midst of these distractions, to Elizabeth's infinite chagrin, Mary brought forth her only child, afterwards our James the First.

The conduct adopted by Elizabeth towards Scotland and its miserable monarch during this momentous crisis, was wholly unexpected. She who had been the bitterest foe to Mary when her youth, beauty, innocence, and power, made her the favourite of Europe, now, when worn with care, stripped of dominion, and more than suspected of horrible crimes, suddenly adopted her cause, offered her every aid, and threatened her enemies with summary vengeance. Those who in seeking for refined political causes so frequently overlook obvious motives, have ascribed this anomaly to an insidious design to tempt Mary to the step which she afterwards unhappily took ; while others who judged under the honest dictates of natural feeling, aiming as much beneath the mark, have placed it to the account of pity and generosity, virtues equally strangers to Elizabeth's breast. The truth is that her dread of an example of rebellion in a land divided only by an imaginary line from her own exceeded her hatred to Mary, and that the circumstances of the time prevented her from maintaining a posture of neutrality between that Princess and her insurgent subjects. Mary, however, confided in the sincerity of her professions ; unexpectedly fled to her for protection ; and found herself a prisoner ; and in the mean time her infant son was declared King of Scotland. It became necessary for Elizabeth to decide as suddenly on the part that she was now to act, and her determination involved questions of high policy ; her ministers therefore were obliged to share with her in the iniquities which followed. She commenced them by assuming a jurisdic-

tion wholly illegitimate. Mary was induced, partly by the necessity of her critical situation, and partly by a promise that the
leaders of the party which had deposed her should be called on
for a justification of that act, to submit to the judgment of Elizabeth not only the trial of such their conduct, but also the awful
question of her own respecting the murder of Darnley. Commissioners were forthwith appointed for the cognizance of these great
causes, and the rebel Lords were cited to London ; not, as it
presently appeared, to apologize for their delinquencies, but to
assume the characters of prosecutors or witnesses against their
captive Sovereign. By a series of the most profound artifices the
Regent Murray was induced to give the fullest proof of Mary's
guilt by the production of her letters to Bothwell, and she was
instantly placed in that close confinement from which a violent
death released her at the end of nineteen years.

If Elizabeth sought security or tranquillity in the prosecution
of these unwarrantable measures, she was indeed sorely disappointed. Even while they were in progress the Duke of Norfolk
formed a design to marry the Queen of Scots; imparted it in
confidence to several of the nobility of both nations, and was
betrayed by Leicester; was excused for the time, and three years
after, having reiterated his scheme, with aggravated circumstances, was put to death. In the mean time a hasty and ill-
concerted insurrection, professing for its object the restoration
of the ancient faith, and headed by the Earls of Northumberland
and Westmoreland, broke forth in the North, the suppression of
which was speedily followed by another yet more imprudent.
Mary, from the first hour of her unjust restraint, became the head
of the English Catholics by their tacit and unpremeditated consent,
while she, in like manner, beheld in them her only efficient friends.
Under the influence of a temper naturally sanguine, she seems to
have been ever ready to suggest, or to adopt, any plan, however
visionary, by which she might possibly regain her liberty, and
replace herself on a throne which she had disgraced, and envi-
roned with difficulty and danger. Elizabeth, on her part, equally

dreading to restore, on any terms, an enemy whom she had offended beyond all hope of reconciliation, or to make common cause with rebellious subjects, amused each party with professions never to be verified, and with treaties instituted but to be broken up without effect. Amidst all these causes for just alarm, Pius the Fifth in 1571 excommunicated her in due form, and by the same Bull declared her title to the crown wholly void, and absolved her subjects of their oath of allegiance.

The consolation which she derived from the reformers was very inadequate to this accumulation of evils. She flattered them on all occasions with expressions of more than maternal tenderness, and received in return the most abject professions of devotion, or rather worship; but they who had overthrown the ancient Church were of course not long before they turned their attention to the correction of the State. A freedom of speech hitherto unknown began to distinguish the House of Commons; privileges were sometimes talked of there; and her prerogatives were not unfrequently questioned. As the heat of her temper ebbed and flowed, she sometimes blustered, and sometimes conceded, and occasionally, which was the worst of all, retracted her specific threats in the very hour in which she had uttered them. The die however was cast, and she had assumed the character of patroness of the Protestant persuasion throughout Europe. To maintain that reputation, she again succoured about this period the Huguenots, as they were called, now in formidable array against Charles the Ninth, but was induced to withdraw her aid by insidious proposals from that Prince, and to endure with a sullen patience even that consummation of wickedness, the massacre of St. Bartholomew. At this very period she undertook the friendly office of sponsor to his infant daughter, and listened with an affected complacency to another, but still fruitless offer of the hand of the Duke of Alençon, whom, as well as his elder brother, the Duke of Anjou, soon after Henry the Third, she had formerly rejected. The public anxiety regarding the succession to the crown, repeatedly expressed by her Parliaments, prevented the unpopularity which her seeming apathy towards the Protestant cause might have provoked, while her utter aversion to their remonstrances on the subject of marriage tempted her as frequently to amuse them by engaging in negotiations to that effect, always insincere.

The death of Charles, and the formation, by the talents and boldness of the family of Guise, of the League, altered most of these relations. Philip, from whose interest she had hoped to detach France, now openly declared himself protector of that celebrated combination, and avowed, with more frankness than was usually found in his policy, his determination to extirpate the reformed religion. Elizabeth's safety, as well as her reputation, demanded an undisguised resistance on her part, and the sudden revolt of that Monarch's oppressed subjects in the Low Countries, together with the horrible vengeance inflicted on them by the Duke of Alva, rendered her interference not less popular than politic. The States of Holland and Zealand offered to swear allegiance to her, and were refused. She supplied them liberally however from time to time with arms and money, and her ministers were already occupied in preparations for that warfare with Spain, the triumphant event of which is yet so grateful to English minds. Meanwhile the Catholics at home were watched and pursued with renewed severity; in proof of which the Queen herself, in one of her progresses, imprisoned, by her own special authority, a gentleman who was in the very act of sumptuously entertaining her at his mansion, because some of her attendants had found an image of the Virgin concealed in one of his outhouses. Of such absurd extravagance and injustice could she be capable, when left to the unadvised exercise of her own will!

For several years past Elizabeth had governed Scotland by her influence over the Regent Morton, who was her creature and pensioner; but James was now emerging from childhood, and a small party, secretly under the direction of the Duke of Guise, persuaded him to assume the administration of the kingdom. Morton, after some struggle, in which she vainly endeavoured to

14

support him, was arrested, tried, and executed; a scheme was formed to associate Mary with her son in the sovereign authority; and the interest of the court of France was fruitlessly exerted to the utmost to that effect. It is somewhat singular that Elizabeth should have chosen at this period to encourage the renewed addresses of Alençon, now Duke of Anjou. The negotiations on this remarkable occasion were intsituted and conducted solely by herself; and her Council, hesitating to answer her appeal to its opinion by an unqualified approbation of the match, was almost reprimanded by her. The nation was struck with astonishment that a woman who from her early youth had always declared even an abhorrence of marriage should, at the age of forty-eight, suddenly determine to give her hand to a Prince more than twenty years younger than herself, and little recommended either by talents, person, or manners. Every part of her conduct relating to this strange affair was marked by the most extravagant caprice; Sir Philip Sidney composed with great freedom a long and laboured argument, or rather invective, against the match, and it was received without disapprobation; while a Mr. Stubbs, a barrister, and a man of considerable merit and unquestionable loyalty, followed the same course, and was punished by the loss of his right hand, and a long imprisonment. Anjou at length arrived privately, and she received him with all the airs of an impassioned damsel of romance. He left England for a short interval, and, on his return, after some secret interviews, she presented him to her court, in the full presence of which, among other amorous fooleries, she took a ring from her finger, and placed it on his, in token, as it seemed, of a confirmation of their contract, and six weeks after they coolly parted to meet no more. These mysterious absurdities, for which no one has hitherto satisfactorily accounted, might have arisen out of a wildness of resentment and jealousy suddenly excited by her recent discovery of Leicester's private marriage to the Countess of Essex. As she had been weak enough to betray publicly the influence of those passions over her by imprisoning him for that fact, it cannot be

15

unreasonable to suppose that she was capable of flattering herself that she might mortify him, in her turn, by an affectation of fondness for another lover.

Elizabeth was now surrounded by enemies. The Puritans menaced her monarchical power, and the Catholics her life, and their hatred to each other was exceeded only by their joint hatred of her. In the various plots of the latter, which at this time followed each other in rapid succession, the captive Mary was always directly or indirectly a party. It was deemed necessary to remove her from the milder custody of the Earl of Shrewsbury, in whose several mansions she had been for many years confined, and to place her in the hands of sterner keepers. A bond of association for the defence of Elizabeth was proposed by the court, and eagerly signed by multitudes of nobles and gentry. This instrument was presently after adopted by a new Parliament, and put into the form of an act, with the addition of a clause, clearly foreboding the ultimate fate of Mary, by which the Queen was empowered to appoint commissioners for the trial of any one who, pretending a right to the crown, might contrive any invasion, insurrection, or assassination, against her, and leaving the punishment of such offender to her discretion. The same Parliament, a majority of which was puritanical, among other awkward strides towards independence, made some resolutions trenching on Elizabeth's ecclesiastical supremacy; attacked the authority of the prelacy; and were reprimanded by her in a speech in which she plainly told them that she considered the Puritans not less dangerous than the Catholics. Those of the Low Countries, a peaceful because a commercial people, worn with warfare and oppression, once more besought her to become their Sovereign, and were again refused. It became however a question whether she should wage offensive war against Spain on their behalf, and Elizabeth, usually indifferent where her passions were not excited, left the decision to her ministers. After long debates, they determined it affirmatively. Drake, whose courage and nautical skill had been abundantly proved in former enterprises, was despatched against the Spanish colonies in America, and was eminently successful, and a strong military force was landed in Holland ; but here the Queen's inveterate partiality towards Leicester interfered ; she named him to the command of the expedition ; it failed, through his ambition and inexperience ; she quarrelled with him, and forgave him ; and he returned, despised by the States, and hated at home by all but his infatuated mistress.

The termination of Mary's sufferings approached. The rage of the persecuted Catholics of England, incessantly fomented by the Pope, the King of Spain, and the heads of the League, concentrated itself in a new plot, involving at once the assassination of the Queen, an insurrection, and a foreign invasion. Mary, whom it was proposed to place on the English throne, had been long in close correspondence with the conspirators, and was acquainted, even to minuteness, with all the details of this awful enterprise, which were at length betrayed by one of the parties, and sifted by Walsingham, a minister who seems to have been born but for such employment, and whose vigilance had previously detected the general design. Fourteen of the leaders were seized and executed, but to dispose of Mary required deliberation ; in the course of which let it be remembered that Leicester, a known poisoner, proposed that she should be so removed, and, with that hypocrisy for which he was little less infamous, sent a clergyman to persuade Walsingham by scriptural argument that in such a case the expedient would be lawful. It was however determined that she should be tried on the act which had been lately passed with the peculiar view, it may be said, of so applying it. Of the catastrophe of the tragedy it is needless to speak. In reflecting on the first treacherous and inhospitable detention of this Princess ; on the various horrors of her tedious imprisonment ; and the final sacrifice of her life ; all equally barbarous and unjust ; we almost forget the crimes and the follies of her earlier time, and are inclined to consider her concluding designs on the throne and the life of her great enemy but as measures of retaliation which may readily find an apology in the infirmity of human passions,

17

however lofty. For the conduct of Elizabeth too may a similar plea be urged in extenuation; but what were the passions which actuated her? vanity, envy, and jealousy, succeeded by grovelling fear, and insatiable malice. The incomparable resignation and heroism which marked the death of the one almost completed the redemption of her fame; the vile dissimulation of the other which followed has plunged her memory into irretrievable infamy. She declared, with oaths and tears, that she had forbidden the delivery of the warrant signed by her for the execution; and to support the deception, doomed to disgrace and poverty her faithful servant, the Secretary Davison, in whose hands she had placed it, directing him to forward it, while she lamented to him that Mary's keepers had not prevented the necessity for it by assassinating their prisoner.

James's resentment of the murder of his mother did not exceed the forms of decency, and presently wholly subsided; while the attention of England was suddenly turned from it to the mighty attack meditated by Spain, which had long been foreseen by Elizabeth's ministers, and was now generally known to the public. It had been repeatedly disappointed by the successful enterprises of Drake, and other nautical adventurers, when at length Europe resounded with the news of the equipment of the Armada which the Spaniards called "invincible," the total discomfiture of which it is scarcely necessary even to mention. Leicester, whom the Queen had appointed to the chief command of the land forces raised to oppose the expected invasion, and for whom she had ordered a commission for the unheard-of office of her "Lieutenant in the kingdoms of England and Ireland," survived that great event but for a few weeks, and she coldly seized and sold his property to reimburse his debts to her—a sufficient proof that the extravagance of her partiality had subsisted merely on motives which could not survive him, not to mention the speedy accession of another, and a more youthful favourite. She seems to have hesitated for a while whom to select from three candidates, each of them remarkably handsome, highly accomplished, and about thirty years younger than herself. The Earl of Essex became the unfortunate object of her choice, and succeeded his father-in-law, Leicester, not only in the full measure of her affection, but as leader of the Puritan faction.

Had Elizabeth abstained from this final folly, the concluding years of her public and private life might have passed in uninterrupted tranquillity. The pride and the power of Spain had received a wound not readily to be healed ; France was worn by intestine commotions, and its monarch was her firm friend, as well from prejudice as from policy ; and in Scotland, which was yet in some measure distracted by the violent factions that had alternately ruled during a long regal minority, James, not less pacific in his nature than helpless from circumstances, obeyed her mandates with almost the submission of a tributary prince. The Catholics, stunned by the blows which had fallen on the Queen of Scots, and on their great patron, Philip, required years to re-inspire them even with hope ; and the Puritans had not yet dreamed of connecting rebellion with their profession of faith ; the power of the Crown was almost absolute, and the great mass of the people contented. The history of the last ten years of this Queen would have been nearly a blank, but for the surprising rise and fall of Essex.

She gave him the Garter, and appointed him Master of the Horse, before he had fully attained the age of twenty-one. From the hour of his first appearance at her court she used towards him a singularity of carriage which at first rather excited secret ridicule than envy, and which seems, naturally enough, to have disgusted himself, for he fled privately from her, and became a volunteer in a foreign expedition. She summoned him home, first by an order from her Privy Council, then by an angry letter from herself, and when he unwillingly returned redoubled her fondness. He married, and she became outrageous, but was presently reconciled. She appointed him to military commands, for which he had no requisite but bravery, and forced him into the character of a statesman, for which the natural impetuosity of his generous temper utterly disqualified him. Under the influence of that foible he frequently treated her with rudeness and contempt, and she bore it patiently. In an argument however on the affairs of Ireland, the freedom of his contradictions provoked her to strike him; he fled furiously from the court; and she drew him with difficulty from the privacy in which he had buried himself to invest him with the government of that very country. His measures there were ill-judged, and worse executed. He received a letter from Elizabeth full of bitter reproaches; anticipated at length her vengeance; and his horror of the consequent triumph of his enemies at home irritated his sensitive mind to the brink of frenzy. In this wretched disposition, he took a sudden reso lution to return secretly, and throw himself at her feet. She received him with kindness, but referred the consideration of his case to her Privy Council. He was deprived of his seat in that assembly, and of his offices, and placed for a short time in a mild imprisonment. He retired into the country, and, could he have waited patiently, would probably have been restored to all his former favour; but his mind had been incurably wounded, and he had lost all reasonable power of guiding his own conduct. He returned to London; shut himself up in his own house with a few imprudent followers: detained as hostages the Lord Keeper, and Chief Justice, who had been sent to hear his complaints; and at length sallied forth, with his little force, in hostile array against he knew not whom. He was presently overpowered, and soon after brought to trial for high treason by his Peers, who ought to have acquitted him on the score of insanity; but they found him guilty, and Elizabeth, under an impression of terror, which for the time had overpowered, but not impaired, her affection for him, consigned him to the scaffold. She survived him for two years, gradually sinking, without disease, under a regular abatement of strength and spirits, the commencement of which is proved to have been observed almost immediately after his death. To those who may be inclined to take the pains to examine carefully the numerous notices which remain, on indubitable authority, of her decay, and the expressions which fell from her during its progress, it will be evident that her life fell a sacrifice to the premature loss of that of her favourite. She died on the twenty-fourth of March, 1603.

Some remark may probably be expected here on the singularities which distinguish the portrait prefixed to this outline of Elizabeth's life ; but little can be said in explanation of them. In an age which delighted in the pictorial riddles of inexhaustible allegory, it is perhaps not very strange that she should have adopted this mode of displaying such devices ; still less that one of the vainest women in the world should have invented, or accepted, such as might attribute to herself the beneficence and splendour of the sun, the wisdom of the serpent, and the vigilance of the most acute and watchful organs of the human frame. Besides, her wardrobe at the time of her death contained more than two thousand dresses, of the fashions of all countries, of all times, and of all contrivance that busy fancy could suggest, and in the gratification of this childish whim variety imparted the main charm. The portrait itself, however, were it a mere head, would be of great curiosity, inasmuch as it represents her much younger than any other extant, and with at least as much beauty as she could at any time have possessed.

Engraved by P. Lightfoot.

JOHN, FIRST MARQUIS OF HAMILTON.

OB. 1604.

FROM THE ORIGINAL OF MARK GERARD, IN THE COLLECTION OF

HIS GRACE THE DUKE OF HAMILTON.

London, Published Dec.1.1836 by Harding & Lepard, Pall Mall East.

JOHN, FIRST MARQUIS OF HAMILTON.

———

JAMES HAMILTON, Earl of Arran, and Duke of Chatelherault, had by his lady, Margaret, eldest daughter of James Douglas, third Earl of Morton, four sons. James, the eldest, who, after his father's advancement to his French Dukedom, bore the title of Earl of Arran, was a young nobleman of the proudest hopes. He had been bred in France, and the influence of Mary, his Queen and near relation, who was the consort of the Dauphin, afterwards Francis the Second, had placed him, though a most earnest protestant, in the post of Colonel of the French King's Scottish Guards. The imprudent activity of his zeal became intolerable to a Court distinguished by its attachment to the Papacy, and he was compelled to fly from the pardonable resentment of a land whose faith and modes of worship he had contemned and insulted; but the Reformers of Scotland received him as an object of persecution who had barely escaped martyrdom, and the political prejudices which were interwoven with their affection to the new discipline fixed on the family of Guise the charge of a deliberate plan to sacrifice this illustrious Scot to their vengeance against the reformation. Thus endeared to them, not less than by that presumptive right to the inheritance of the Throne which has been more than once stated in this work, he was formally recommended by the Scottish Parliament to Elizabeth in 1560, a few months after his

1

flight from France, as a husband, and civilly rejected. A similar proposal was made on his behalf, under the same authority, to his own Sovereign, on her return to Scotland, a widow, in the following year, but without better success. These disappointments, operating on a most impetuous and fiery nature, are said to have gradually overset a mind which seems to have been originally ill-balanced, and he became an incurable lunatic.

John, the second son, will be the subject of the present memoir ; and Claud, the third, was a young nobleman of the most exalted spirit and honour, a steady Roman Catholic, and most enthusiastically devoted to the cause of his royal mistress. With David, the fourth son, this little essay has no concern ; nor should I have detailed these particulars of his brothers James and Claud, were not the few facts which I have been able to obtain of the story of Lord John so frequently connected with theirs that the foregoing short recital respecting them seemed indispensably necessary.

He was born in 1532, and endowed, suitably to his high birth, while yet a child, with several royal grants of estates, particularly of the rich Abbey of Aberbrothock, which had been formerly held by Beatoun, during his progress to the primacy. He received his education in France, whether with a view to the ecclesiastical profession is uncertain, but undoubtedly under teachers of the Roman Catholic persuasion, and in strict conformity to the principles of that church ; which, however, after the example of his father and elder brother, he quitted about the year 1559, and embraced the protestant faith. This change seems to have been dictated neither by party views, nor schemes of aggrandisement, in himself or them. The Duke, his father, who was born to the possession of dignity which could have been increased only by his succession to the Throne, loved that retirement for which the character and measure of his talents had in truth best fitted him ; Arran was known to have recanted through a zeal which savoured of bigotry ; and his own invariable fidelity to the Catholic Mary, in opposition to the politics of those whose creed he had adopted, amply proved the honesty and independence of his motives, since he at once hazarded

2

the loss of her favour by renouncing the doctrines of her church, and incurred the hatred of her opponents by cherishing her temporal interests.

He did in fact offend both. Mary, on her arrival from France to mount the Throne of Scotland, found the Duke and his family not only protestants, but supporters of the cause of the congregation, in which she had been taught to believe that she could find only enemies. Arran, even while he aspired to her hand, endeavoured to prevent her practice of the rights of her religion, and entered a public protestation against it. The whole house of Hamilton fell under her disfavour, and retired from the Court, and the subsequent opposition of the Duke to her imprudent marriage with Darnley sealed his disgrace, and forced him to fly with his family into France. They remained there till her calamities required the aid and consolation of their loyalty. On receiving the news of her imprisonment in Lochleven Castle, the Lords John and Claud Hamilton flew to Scotland, and mustered her scattered friends at their father's seat at Hamilton, where they signed with them, on the twenty-fifth of December, 1567, a bond of association to liberate her. The interesting tale of her escape by other means is well known. She reached Hamilton Palace in safety, where an army of six thousand men was presently raised for her service, at the head of which she marched in person to meet a force hastily led against her by her bastard brother the Regent Murray, which however gained a complete victory in the battle of Langside on the 13th of May, 1568. She now fled to England, never to return, and in the following July, every individual of the name of Hamilton who had fought for her on that day, including in fact nearly the whole of her army, was outlawed by a Parliament called by the Regent for that purpose.

The two succeeding years were distinguished by the violent deaths of the Earl of Murray, and his successor in the Regency, the Earl of Lenox. These assassinations, the first of which had been perpetrated by a Hamilton, were laid by the friends of the deceased noblemen to the charge of the Lords John and Claud.

3

Their illegitimate uncle, the Archbishop of St. Andrews, had been accused of the murder of Murray, and put to death without a trial, and their names had been inserted in a general act of attainder, passed with the characteristic violence and injustice of the time, against all parties concerned in either of those crimes. At the treaty however of Perth, in 1573, which was appointed especially for the establishment of securities and amnesties, it was stipulated, that " all the processes, sentences of forfeiture, and all other prosecutions passed against George Earl of Huntly, the Lord John Hamilton, or any of their party or friends, for any crimes committed by them, or any of their party, since the fifteenth day of June, 1567, should be declared null, and of no effect." Six years had passed, during which the Duke of Chatel-herault had died, and the Lord John, in consequence of the insanity of his elder brother Arran, had been declared heir to his father's estates, and was living on them in a dignified retirement; when Morton, then Regent, determined to crush at one blow the existing members of this illustrious House, and by practising on the fears and jealousies of the young King, made him a party in the iniquitous design.

It was pretended that the pardon conceded by the treaty of Perth did not extend to such as were accessary to the murder of the Regents Murray or Lenox. " Lord John and his brother," says Dr. Robertson, " were suspected of being the authors of both these crimes, and had been included in a general act of attainder on that account. Without summoning them to trial, or examining a single witness to prove the charge, this attainder was now thought sufficient to subject them to all the penalties which they would have incurred by being formally convicted. Morton, with some other noblemen, his creatures, received a commission to seize their persons and estates. On a few hours' warning a considerable body of troops was ready, and marched towards Hamilton in hostile array. Happily the two brothers made their escape, though with great difficulty; but their lands were confiscated; the castles of Hamilton and Draffan besieged, and those who defended them punished. The Earl of Arran, though incapable from his situation of committing any crime, was involved by a shameful abuse of law in the common ruin of his family; and, as if he too could have been guilty of rebellion, he was confined a close prisoner. These proceedings, so contrary to the fundamental principles of justice, were all ratified in the subsequent Parliament."

The Lord John Hamilton fled on foot, in the disguise of a sailor, into England, and from thence to Paris, where his resistance to the importunities of the Duke of Guise, and his brother the Cardinal, that he would return to the Catholic church, gave such offence at Court as obliged him to retire, with scarcely the means of subsistence, into obscurity. After some years' painful residence in France he returned privately to England, where he met his brother Claud, and several Scots of high rank, who had fled from the tyranny of James's first and perhaps worst favourite, James Stewart, on whom he had bestowed the title of Earl of Arran, so basely torn from its unhappy owner. These eminent exiles now concerted a plan not only to re-enter their country, but to drive that unworthy minion from the presence of his abused master. They contrived by secret correspondence to appoint many dependents to meet them, armed, on the borders, and having approached Edinburgh by forced marches, with ten thousand men, before the King was apprised of their design, publicly swore never to separate till he should pardon them, and dismiss Stewart. James, dreading the popularity of their design, more than their numbers, threw himself into the castle of Stirling, rather with the view of gaining time to deliberate than in the hope of making a defence, and found himself suddenly invested by their troops. Incapable, and probably unwilling, to offer a military resistance, he consented to both their demands. Admitted to his presence, the Lord John Hamilton addressed him on the behalf of the party, as we are informed by a respectable Scottish historian, in these words. "Sir, we are come, in the most humble manner, to beg mercy, and your Majesty's favour." The King,

5

continues the same writer, answered, " My Lord, I did never see you before, and must confess that of all the company you have been most wronged. You were a faithful servant to the Queen, my mother, in my minority, and, when I understood not as I do the estate of Kings, hardly used."

These curious circumstances, so highly illustrative at once of the timidity, the vanity, and the caprice, of James, occurred in October, 1585, and were immediately followed by the complete restoration in parliament of this illustrious and persecuted family. Lord John Hamilton was shortly after sworn a Privy Councillor, and appointed Governor of Dunbarton Castle; and, when the King in 1589 sailed to Denmark, to espouse in person the Princess Anne, was complimented with the post of Lieutenant General in the south of Scotland till his master's return : but it was not till 1599 that he received the compensation probably most soothing to his outraged feelings, on the seventeenth of April in which year he was created Marquis of Hamilton. He died on the twelfth of April, 1604.

This nobleman married Margaret, only daughter of John Lyon, eighth Lord Glamis, relict of Gilbert Kennedy, fourth Lord Cassilis, and had issue by her one son, James, his successor, and one daughter, Margaret, married to John, eighth Lord Maxwell.

Engraved by W.T.Fry.

GEORGE CLIFFORD, EARL OF CUMBERLAND.

OB. 1605.

FROM THE ORIGINAL IN THE

BODLEIAN GALLERY, OXFORD.

PROOF

London, Published Dec.r 1.1836, by Harding & Lepard, Pall Mall East.

GEORGE CLIFFORD,

THIRD EARL OF CUMBERLAND.

———◆———

WE might search vainly through the whole circle of the biography of later centuries, and through the almost proverbial varieties of the English character, without meeting with a parallel to the disposition of this Nobleman. He was by nature what the heroes of chivalry were from fashion, and stood alone, therefore, in a time to the manners of which he could not assimilate himself, like a being who having slept for ages, had suddenly awaked amidst the distant posterity of his contemporaries. The history of his singular life must be sought sometimes in the journal of the sailor, and sometimes in the tablets of the courtier: in the rough-hewn narrations of Hakluyt and Purchas, and in the light and elegant notices of Walpole and Pennant.

He was the eldest son of Henry Clifford, second Earl, by his second Countess Anne, daughter of William Lord Dacre, of Gillesland. His father, dying in 1569, left him an infant of the age of eleven years, and his wardship was granted by the Crown to Francis Russell, second Earl of Bedford; but his education seems to have been superintended by the Viscount Montague, who had married his mother's sister, and at whose house, in Sussex, he passed some years of his youth. He went from thence to the University of Cambridge, where he studied in Peterhouse under the care of Whitgift, afterwards Archbishop of Canterbury, or rather devoted his attention so earnestly to the Mathematics as to abstract it wholly from all other studies. Thus it happened

1

that the ardent spirit of adventure, and the boundless activity which afterwards distinguished him, took first a nautical turn, acquired an increased force by assuming a peculiar direction, and enhanced the charm of curiosity by adding to it the interest of science.

Several of the earlier years of his manhood passed, however, in unobserved employment, during which we hear only of him that he was one of the Peers who sat in judgment on Mary Queen of Scots; but immediately after that deplorable proceeding, he fitted out, at his private charge, a little naval force which sailed on an expedition planned by himself, while he, with a party of volunteers of distinguished rank, embarked for Holland, with the view of relieving Sluys, then besieged by the Prince of Parma. Both enterprises were unsuccessful. His fleet, consisting of three ships, and a pinnace, the latter commanded by Sir Walter Raleigh, was destined to a voyage of discovery, but with particular instructions to lose no opportunity of annoying the Spaniards. It sailed from Gravesend on the twenty-sixth of June, 1586, but was repeatedly driven back by contrary winds, and could not finally quit England till the end of August, when it bent its course towards the South Seas, and, having reached, amidst considerable dangers and difficulties, as far as forty-four degrees of southern latitude, returned home, after thirteen months' absence, having captured a few Portuguese vessels, from which little had been gained beyond those supplies of provision of which the crews had been frequently in imminent need.

In 1588 he commanded a ship called the Elizabeth Bonaventure, in the fleet which destroyed the Spanish Armada, and distinguished himself equally by his bravery and his skill in the various engagements by which that great work was accomplished, particularly in the last action, which was fought off Calais. Even during that arduous service, his mind was employed in projecting a second voyage to the South Seas, the command of which he determined to take on himself. Elizabeth now flattered him with the distinction of a royal commission, and lent him one of her own ships, named the Golden Lion, which, however, as well as the rest, was fitted out solely at his charge. This expedition, which sailed in the following October, proved even more unfortunate than the former. Baffled by contrary winds and storms, in one of which he had been obliged to cut the mainmast of his own ship by the board, he returned, having scarcely been able to quit the channel during his absence. In 1589, disappointed but not dispirited, on the eighteenth of June he again left England, with a force of three small ships, equipped by himself, and headed by the Victory, from the royal navy, in which he assumed the command. He now sailed to the West Indies, and was at length in some measure successful. He took the town of Fyal, and stripped it of fifty-eight pieces of iron ordnance, and, in the course of this cruise, sent home twenty-eight ships of various burthen, laden with goods to the value of more than twenty thousand pounds. These advantages were not cheaply purchased. In a desperate engagement between the Victory and a Brasil ship, off St. Michael's, he received several wounds, and was severely scorched; and the sufferings of his men from want of provisions, especially water, on his return to England, are perhaps unparalleled in the multifarious relations of naval misery. A particular narrative of this horrible distress, by Edward Wright, a famous mathematician, who sailed with the Earl, may be found in Hakluyt's collection, and states at the conclusion, that the men who died of thirst, exceeded in number those who had perished otherwise during the whole voyage. This calamity occurred almost within sight of the coast of Ireland, where at length, on the second of December, a change of wind permitted the survivors to land in Bantry Bay.

Hardship and danger, however, were agreeable to this singular man, and his romantic mind delighted in extremities of difficulty. He put to sea again, in May, 1591, with five ships, manned and provisioned, as usual, at his own expense, and having cruised for some months in the Mediterranean with indifferent success, returned but to prepare for a fifth expedition, which left the shores of England, destined to the Azores, in the summer of the following year, and which, on some occasion of disgust, he suddenly declined to accompany. It proved more fortunate than any of his preceding enterprises, but in the end produced a serious mortification to himself. His ships, among inferior successes, captured, on their return, one of the Spanish Caraques, valued at one hundred and fifty thousand pounds ; but, under the pretext of his personal absence, and other allegations, it was adjudged at home that he had no legal claim to any part of the sum. He was thrown therefore on the Queen's generosity for his requital, and in the end reluctantly accepted at her hands, as a boon, thirty-six thousand pounds. Yet, in 1593, he again sailed to the Spanish settlements, with four ships of his own, and the Golden Lion, and Bonaventure, from the navy, hoisting his flag on board the former ; and, after having captured a French convoy of great value, was compelled by a severe illness to quit his command, and return to England, leaving his little fleet under the orders of Monson, afterwards the most celebrated naval officer of his time. Several rich prizes were made after his departure, and this was the most profitable of all his expeditions. The ships anchored at Plymouth on the fifteenth of May, 1594 ; but the Earl, barely risen from his sick bed, had left that port three weeks before their arrival, with a small squadron, fitted out at the charge of himself and some others, and bound to the Azores, from whence, having grievously annoyed the Spaniards, with little profit to himself and his companions, he returned to Portsmouth in the end of August.

His passion for nautical adventure was now at the height. Unable to employ ships of sufficient force to support his hired vessels without borrowing from the Queen, and unwilling to subject himself to the control under which the use of such loans necessarily placed him, he determined to build a man of war of his own, and accomplished the task. It was of the burthen of nine hundred tons ; was launched at Deptford ; and named by Eliza-beth " The Scourge of Malice ;" reputed the best and largest ship

4

that had been built by any English subject. He entered it, in the river, on his eighth enterprise, accompanied by three inferior vessels, and had proceeded to Plymouth, when he received the Queen's command, by Raleigh, for his instant return to London, which he obeyed. His squadron, however, proceeded on its voyage to the Spanish main; made some prizes; and returned to take him on board for another cruise thither; in which his great ship was so shattered in a violent storm, which occurred when he had scarcely reached the distance of forty leagues from England, that he was obliged to retrace his course, and to wait, however impatiently, at home, till the vessel should be rendered again fit for service. At length, on the sixth of March, 1598, he embarked in it, at the head of nineteen others, on his last, and most considerable expedition. His expenses in the preparations for it had been enormous, and the expectations of his sanguine mind had kept pace with them. He sailed on the sixth of March for the West Indies, where, for seven months, he incessantly harassed the Spaniards in their settlements, to the great advantage of the public interests of his country; lost two of his ships, and more than a thousand of his men; and received from the produce of his captures about a tenth part of the sum which he had disbursed for the purposes of his voyage. "His fleet," however, says Lloyd, " was bound to no other harbour but the port of honour, though touching at the port of profit in passage thereunto."

Such is the outline of his maritime story. At home, his politeness, his courage and his magnificence, were, in the strictest sense of the word, inimitable: highly tinctured always by the singularity of his mind, they were solely and distinctly his own. He had good parts, but the warmth of his temper, and the punctilious exactness of his notions of honour, rendered him unfit for any concern in public affairs. Elizabeth, who looked narrowly and judiciously into the characters of men, seems therefore to have employed him but on one short service, for which no one could have been better qualified—the reducing to obedience his eccentric compeer, Essex; but she knew, perhaps admired, his

5

foibles, and certainly flattered them. In 1592 she dignified and decorated him with the Order of the Garter. At an audience, upon his return from one of his voyages, she dropped her glove, which he took up, and presented to her on his knees. She desired him to keep it for her sake, and he adorned it richly with diamonds, and wore it ever after in the front of his hat at public ceremonies. This little characteristic circumstance is commemorated in a very scarce whole-length portrait of the Earl, engraved by Robert White. She constituted him, on the resignation of Sir Henry Lea, Knight of the Garter, disabled by age, her own peculiar champion at all tournaments. Sir William Segar has preserved, in his treatise " of Honour Military and Civil," an exact account of the pomp and parade of his admission into that romantic office, for the insertion of a short extract from which perhaps no apology may be necessary.

"On the seventeenth day of November, anno 1590, this honourable gentleman" (Sir Henry Lea), " together with the Earl of Cumberland, having first performed their service in armes, presented themselves unto her Highnesse at the foot of the staires, under her gallery window, in the Tilt-yard at Westminster, where at that time her Majestie did sit, accompanied with the Viscount Turyn, ambassador of France, many ladies, and the chiefest nobilitie. Her Majestie, beholding these armed knights comming toward her, did suddenly heare a musicke so sweete and secret as every one thereat greatly marvailed. And, hearkening to that excellent melodie, the earth as it were opening, there appeared a pavilion, made of white taffata, containing eight score elles, being in proportion like unto the sacred temple of the virgins vestall. This temple seemed to consist upon pillars of pourferry, arched like unto a church : within it were many lamps burning : also on the one side there stood an altar, covered with cloth of gold, and thereupon two waxe candles, burning in rich candlesticks : upon the altar also were laid certain princely presents, which, after, by three virgins were presented unto her Majestie. Before the doore of this temple stood a crowned pillar, embraced by an eglantine tree, whereon was hanged a table, and therein written, with letters of gold, this prayer following. Elizæ, &c. Piæ, potenti, fœlicissimæ Virgini; fidei, pacis, nobilitatis, Vindici; cui Deus, astra, virtus, summa devoverunt omnia. Post tot annos, tot triumphos, animam ad pedes positurus tuos, sacra senex affixit arma. Vitam quietam, imperium, famam æternam, æternum, precatur tibi, sanguine redempturus suo. Ultra Columnas Herculis Columna moveatur tua. Corona superet Coronas omnes, ut quam Cœlum fœlicissimè nascenti Coronam dedit, beatissima moriens reportes Cœlo. Summe, Sancte, Æterne, audi, exaudi, Deus."

Having related other circumstances, not to the present purpose, the narrative concludes, " These presents and prayer being with great reverence delivered into her Majestie's owne hands, and he himself disarmed, offered up his armour at the foot of her Majestie's crowned pillar; and, kneeling upon his knees, presented the Earle of Cumberland, humbly beseeching she would be pleased to accept him for her Knight, to continue the yeerely exercises aforesaid. Her Majestie, gratiously accepting of that offer, this aged knight armed the Earle, and mounted him upon his horse. That being done, he put upon his owne person a side coat of blacke velvet, pointed under the arme, and covered his head, in liew of an helmet, with a buttoned cap, of the countrey fashion."

The Earl's expenses in discharging the duties, if they may be so called, of this fantastic office; in horse-racing, which had then lately become fashionable; and in feasts, which rivalled the splendor of royalty; added to the aggregate loss on the whole of his maritime career, greatly impaired his estate. He was, to say the least, careless of his family; lived on ill terms with his Countess, Margaret, third daughter of his guardian, Francis Earl of Bedford, a woman of extraordinary merit, but perhaps too high-spirited for such a husband; and neglected the interests, as well as the education, of his only surviving child. Of that child, little less remarkable than her father, Anne, wife first to Richard Sackville, Earl of Dorset, and secondly to Philip Herbert, Earl of

Pembroke and Montgomery, some account, together with her portrait, will presently appear in this work.

George, Earl of Cumberland, died at the Savoy, in London, on the thirtieth of October, 1605, and was buried at Skipton, in Yorkshire, where was the chief seat of his family, on the thirtieth, says Dugdale, of the following March.

Engraved by H.Cochran.

CHARLES BLOUNT, BARON MONTJOY, & EARL OF DEVONSHIRE.

OB. 1606.

FROM THE ORIGINAL OF JUAN PANTOXA, IN THE COLLECTION OF

HIS GRACE THE DUKE OF HAMILTON.

London, Published Dec.r 1.1836 by Harding & Lepard, Pall Mall East.

CHARLES BLOUNT,

EARL OF DEVONSHIRE.

———◆———

THIS accomplished person, an ornament equally to the characters of soldier, statesman, scholar, and courtier, was the second of the two sons of James, fifth Lord Montjoy, by Catherine, daughter of Sir Thomas Leigh, of St. Oswald, in the county of York. He was born in the year 1563, and completed a fine education at Oxford, but in what college the industrious biographer of that University has omitted to inform us. The patrimony of his superb House had been long gradually decaying. His grandfather had burthened it with heavy debts in supporting an unusual magnificence in the romantic splendours of the Court of Henry the Eighth; his father, in the view of repairing the loss, increased it tenfold by endless endeavours to discover the philosopher's stone; and his elder brother nearly annihilated the remnant by various and less creditable prodigality. For himself, without money, and without friends, no choice was left between absolute penury and a profession more or less laborious, and he seems to have been destined accordingly to the study and practice of the law. Of his anxiety to repair the fallen fortunes of his family, as well as of his ready wit, we have a striking instance, from the best authority—His parents wishing in his childhood, to have a portrait of him, he desired that he might be painted with a trowel in his hand, with this inscription: "Ad reædificandam antiquam Domum."

Sir Robert Naunton has given us a sketch of his early manhood

1

with a freshness and vivacity which could not but be injured by alteration. "As he came from Oxford," says Naunton, "he took the Inner Temple in his way to the Court, whither he no sooner came but, without asking, he had a pretty strange kind of admission, which I have heard from a discreet man of his own, and much more of the secrets of those times. He was then much about twenty years of age; of a brown hair, a sweet face, a most neat composure, and tall in his person. The Queen was then at Whitehall, and at dinner, whither he came, to see the fashion of the Court. The Queen had soon found him out, and, with a kind of affected frown, asked the lady carver what he was. She answered she knew him not; insomuch as an enquiry was made from one to another who he might be, till at length it was told the Queen he was brother to the Lord William Montjoy. This inquisition with the eye of Majesty fixed upon him (as she was wont to do, and to daunt men she knew not) stirred the blood of this young gentleman insomuch as his colour came and went, which the Queen observing, called him unto her, and gave him her hand to kiss, encouraging him with gracious words, and new looks; and so diverting her speech to the lords and ladies, she said that she no sooner observed him but that she knew there was in him some noble blood, with some other expressions, of pity towards his house; and then again demanding his name, she said 'fail you not to come to the Court, and I will bethink myself how to do you good.' And this was his inlet, and the beginnings of his grace; where it falls into consideration that, though he wanted not wit and courage, for he had very fine attractions, and being a good piece of a scholar, yet were they accompanied with the retractives of bashfulness, and a natural modesty, which, as the tone of his House, and the ebb of his fortune, then stood, might have hindered his progression, had they not been reinforced by the infusion of sovereign favour, and the Queen's gracious invitation. And, that it may appear how low he was, and how much that heretic necessity will work in the dejection of good spirits, I can deliver it with assurance that his exhibition was very scant until his brother died, which was shortly after his admission to the Court, and then it was no more than a thousand marks per annum, wherewith he lived plentifully, in a fine way and garb, and without any great sustentation, during all her time ; and as there was in his nature a kind of backwardness, which did not befriend him, nor suit with the motion of the Court, so there was in him an inclination to arms, with a humour of travelling and gadding abroad, which had not some wise men about him laboured to remove, and the Queen herself laid in her commands, he would, out of his natural propension, have marred his own market."

It seems however to have been some time before he gratified this disposition, for in 1585 he was elected a burgess for St. Ives, in Cornwall, and in the Parliament which met in the following year was chosen for Berealston, in Devon, which borough he again represented some years after. He was also knighted in 1586, and we first hear of him with certainty in a warlike character as one of the crowd of volunters of quality who hired vessels to join the fleet sent to meet the Spanish Armada. Yet there is no doubt that about this time he had a small command in the Low Countries, for we are again told by Naunton that "he would press the Queen with the pretences of visiting his company there so often, that at length he had a flat denial;" but even this he disregarded, and embarked privately with Sir John Norris, whom he entirely loved, and used to call his father, in the furious expedition made by that great officer to the coast of Bretagne in 1591. "At last," says Naunton, "the Queen began to take his decessions for contempts, and confined his residence to the Court, and her own presence."

In 1594 he was appointed Governor of Portsmouth ; nor was it till this year, contrary to Naunton's report, that he succeeded to the Barony of Montjoy, on the death of William his elder brother. Highly distinguished now by a partiality which Elizabeth could not conceal, he had yet long to wait for those solid proofs of her favour which his qualifications evidently merited. Essex

3

seems to have retarded his preferment, under a general impression of jealousy, perhaps heightened by a somewhat vindictive recollection of a particular personal offence. Montjoy, shortly before he became possessed of that title, had so delighted Elizabeth by his gallantry and dexterity in a tilt at which she was present that she sent him, as a mark of her approbation, a chess-queen of gold, richly enamelled, with which, tied to his arm with a crimson riband, he appeared the next day at Court. Essex, observing it as he passed through the privy chamber, enquired of his friend, Sir Fulke Greville, what it meant? and, on being informed, exclaimed, " Now I perceive that every fool must have a favour," which insulting speech having reached Blount's ears, he challenged the Earl, and they met in Marybone Park, where Essex received a wound in the thigh, and was disarmed. Yet it was to this favourite, whom Elizabeth well knew to be too generous to cherish illiberal resentments, that she joined Montjoy in his first conspicuous public services—she appointed him Lieutenant General of the land forces in Essex's expedition to the Azores in 1597, and, on the breaking out of the Irish rebellion, towards the close of the same year, gave him a similar commission to serve under the Earl in that island, adding to it the dignity of the Garter.

The office of Lord Deputy there becoming vacant in the succeeding year, Elizabeth and the most of her Council were strongly inclined to place Montjoy in it, but were opposed by Essex who secretly coveted it for himself. Camden tells us that he objected against his rival his small experience in military affairs ; the slenderness of his estate and interest ; and to use Camden's words, that " he minded books too much to attend to the government." Essex, though his favour was then in the wane, prevailed, and on the final extinction of it, produced a few months after by the extravagance of his own conduct, was succeeded by Montjoy. " So confident," says Naunton, " was the Queen in her own princely judgement and opinion she had conceived of his worth and conduct, that she would have this worthy gentleman, and none other, to finish and bring the Irish war to a propitious end; for it was a prophetical speech of her own that it would be his fortune and his honour to cut the thread of that fatal rebellion, and to bring her in peace to the grave; where she was not deceived, for he achieved it, but with much pains and carefulness, and many jealousies of the Court and time." Montjoy arrived in Ireland on the fourteenth of February, 1600, N. S. and without an hour's delay, commenced the practice of a system of warfare wholly new to his half civilized, however brave, adversaries, and which he had previously formed on a most judicious consideration of the character and habits of the people, and of the peculiar features of those parts of the island which were the main seats of the war. His plans, the produce of his closet, were executed in the field with all the judgment, bravery, activity, and precision, a union of which is esteemed to constitute the perfection of military command. The following letter, written soon after his arrival, affords curious proof of his vivacity, his high spirit, and the familiarity which it may be presumed it was his habit to use in his private intercourse with his haughty Sovereign. The original is in the Cotton Collection.

"May itt please youre Ma^{tye}

In this greate game, wheare on equall hazarde you venture gollde against led, though you winn more, yett your losses willbe more famus, and the best reconyngs wee can make you will seem shorte till you vouchsafe to looke uppon the whole somme. If since my comminge over I should give you an accounte unto this daye, I will presume to speake itt withe assurance, your Matie hathe woon muche more than you have lost, and you have lost nothing thatt the prudence of your minister coulde prevente. Your army hathe recovered harte and reputacyon, and the estate, hope beyond their owne expectation, wch I esteem so great a degree unto good success as thatt by compassinge so much I have already stepped over the greatest barr to doo you servis. The Earle of Ormond's parley I vowe, on my aleageance to God and you, was wthout my privitye, and so muche have I distasted the

5

lyke in others thatt, before this accidente, I have forbidden itt to private captaynes, and no rebell hathe ever yet spoken to myselfe but upon his knees; but, iff I may presume to yeeld unto your Matie a just excuse for the President of Moonster, as itt was not in his power to hinder the Earle's parley, so his intention to be present was to do you servis by discoveringe in his manner many jelozeys conceaved uppon good grownds, and off great consequence to your Matie; neither was he able to give him any farther answ^{r}. when the Earle's owne men had forsaken him. Your Matie, in youre heavenly nature, may be moved with this great example humanæ fragilitatis, but I hope you shall not heere off any dangerus consequence thereoff to your servis. I feare nott his countrye, though itt wear all oute, for neither the place nor people have any great strengthe; but my mynde doth labor wth the estate off no province more then off Conaught: but God prosper youre armye this sum~er, and theas plantations, nowe, and then, I hope itt, will be in your power, either to bowe or to breake the crooked humors of theas people; and God make me able to do your deere and royal Matie the servis I desyre.

2 April, 1600. Your Matie's truest servant,

E. MOUNTJOYE.

To her sacred Majesté."

A detail of the occurrences of this war, after it fell under the direction of Montjoy, is properly matter for the historian; suffice it therefore to say that, after two campaigns of uninterrupted success he terminated it by a most decisive victory, in the neighbourhood of Kinsale, over the largest army ever brought into the field by the insurgents, aided too by between six and seven thousand Spanish troops. O'Neill, Earl of Tyrone, the great chieftain of the rebellion, soon after surrendered on certain conditions of a distant pardon, one of which, it is curious to observe, was that he should present himself to the Lord Deputy on his knees. Montjoy led him afterwards a prisoner to London, but it was to grace the triumph of a new Sovereign, for Elizabeth, in consonance with her

6

prediction, was on her death-bed when Tyrone made his formal submission in Ireland.

James's first care on his arrival in England was to reward the eminent services of Montjoy. On the twenty-fifth of April, 1603, he was appointed Lord Lieutenant of Ireland; within a few days sworn of the Privy Council; and, on the twenty-first of July, created Earl of Devonshire. The appointments of Master of the Ordnance, and Warden of the New Forest, were soon after conferred on him; and to these were added grants of the estate of Kingston Hall in Dorsetshire; of the county of Lecal, together with a reversion of other valuable lands in Ireland; and of an ample pension from the Crown, to him and his heirs for ever. He came to England not long after the King's accession, for we are told that he was one of the Peers present at the arraignment of Raleigh in the following November: nor does he appear after that period to have resided much in his government, which indeed his late eminent services had rendered in great measure a sinecure. In 1604 he was one of the five commissioners to treat in London of a peace between England and Spain; and here it may be proper to account for some singularity in the appearance of the portrait prefixed to this memoir by observing, that the very curious picture from which it is taken represents those five ministers, in conference with six Spanish noblemen, all seated on armed chairs, and ranged in exact order of rank at the opposite sides of a long table. At the foot of the picture appear the names of the eleven negociators, with marks of reference to their several portraits, which, if we may judge from the success which the artist has displayed in depicting those heads among them which are familiar to us, may be presumed to exhibit the most lively resemblances. The inscription which refers to the portrait of the Earl is " Carlos, C^{de} de Denshier, Vi͞rey de Irlanda."

Apparently endowed now with all the choicest gifts of good fortune, this accomplished man pined secretly under the oppression of a domestic misery which a high sense of honour, and a tone of mind acutely sensitive, combined to render intolerable.

A mutual affection, contracted in early life and in the days of his necessity, with Penelope, eldest daughter of Walter Devereux, Earl of Essex, had gradually ripened into the most ardent love, and was privately sealed by an interchange of marriage vows. It is reasonable to suppose that a discovery produced the contest, too common in such cases, between what the world, with equal injustice, calls youthful folly and parental prudence. The lady was forced into a marriage with the wealthy Robert, Lord Rich, and a guilty connection between the lovers followed, which remained for some years unobserved. Lady Rich at length abandoned her husband, taking with her five children whom she declared to be the issue of the Earl; who, on his part, amidst the fearful conflict of various and even contrary feelings, submitted to the impulse of those which till now had been chief ornaments of his character, and sullied the fair passions of love and pity by rendering them the instruments of insult to society, and of aggravation of the censure which fell on himself. He received her, with what mournful cordiality may easily be supposed; and on her divorce from Lord Rich, which of course immediately followed, was married to her at Wanstead, in Essex, on the twenty-sixth of December, 1605. Laud, who was then a young man and the Earl's domestic chaplain, performed the nuptial ceremony; and a loud outcry was instantly raised against him by the puritans, and by his numerous polemical adversaries. The King also felt, or affected, the highest indignation, and Laud was for a time thought to have blasted all his views of preferment, by having thus sanctioned a connection so scandalous; but a severer fate, as well as the most exalted dignities, were in reserve for him.

The Earl survived this wretched union but for a very few months, and it has been even said that he sunk under the weight of the bitter public reflections which it had excited. He died on the third of April, 1606, and was buried with great pomp in St. Paul's chapel, in Westminster Abbey. Fynes Morrison, who had been his secretary in Ireland, tells us, in his "Travels," a book not much known, to which I am obliged for some of the foregoing particulars, that "grief of unsuccessful love brought him to his last end;" but Mr. Chamberlaine, in a letter to Secretary Winwood, of the fifth of April, 1606, seasoning his news with a severity scarcely reasonable, says—"the Earl of Devonshire left this life on Thursday night last, soon and early for his years, but late enough for himself, and happy had he been if he had gone two or three years since, before the world was weary of him, or that he had left that scandal behind him. He was not long sick past eight or ten days, and died of a burning fever, and putrefaction of his lungs, a defect he never complained of. He hath left his lady, (for so she is now generally held to be,) fifteen hundred pounds a year, and most of his move-ables; and of five children that she fathered upon him at the parting from her former husband, I do not hear that he provided for more than three; leaving to the eldest son, I hear, between three and four thousand pounds a year; and to a daughter six thousand pounds in money."

Whatever might have been the extent of the public resentment of the Earl's private conduct in this unhappy instance, the royal family seem to have not long partaken in it, for the " eldest son," mentioned by Chamberlaine, who was called Montjoy Blount, was created by James, Baron Montjoy, of Montjoy Fort, in Ireland; and was advanced by Charles the First to the English dignity of Earl of Newport, in the Isle of Wight; titles which, having passed successively through his three sons, became extinct in Henry Blount, the youngest, in 1681.

In Dr. Birch's collection, in the British Museum, is a manu-script, of twenty-eight closely penned pages, with the title of " A Discourse of Matrimony, written by the Earle of Devonshire, in defence of his marriage with the Lady Riche." It is composed in the best style of the time; abounds with ingenious argument; and quotes, in addition to numberless passages in Scripture, perhaps every author who ever wrote, either professedly or inci-dentally, on the subjects of marriage and divorce. I recollect to have formerly met, I know not where, with some reference to it, but whether it has ever been printed is at least doubtful.

9

Engraved by T. Fry.

THOMAS SACKVILLE, EARL OF DORSET.

OB. 1608.

FROM THE ORIGINAL IN THE COLLECTION OF

HIS GRACE THE DUKE OF DORSET.

London. Published Dec.ʳ 1.1836, by Harding & Lepard, Pall Mall East.

THOMAS SACKVILLE,

EARL OF DORSET.

THERE is little chance that the story of this eminent person should ever be well told, for the narrator ought to possess the rare advantages of a mind somewhat like his own. The grave and minute annalist, and the sober recorder of family history, are seldom qualified even to discern the lofty track, still less to follow the rapid course, of genius; while those whose happy fancies can create and people new worlds, look down with disdain on the dull round of human affairs. Sackville was the first poet, and one of the first statesmen, of his time, and the biographer who would profess to celebrate his fame with justice should be at once a poet and a historian, a politician and a critic.

He was the only son of Sir Richard Sackville, a lineal descendant of one of the Norman band which accompanied William the Conqueror to England; Chancellor of the Court of Augmentation under Edward the sixth, and in the two following reigns, and a Privy Counsellor to Mary and Elizabeth, the last of whom he served also in the office of Chancellor of the Exchequer. This gentleman was nearly related to Elizabeth, for he was first cousin, by his mother, to Anne Boleyn, and that circumstance, which many years before had introduced him at the court, peculiarly recommended him to the favour of her daughter. His first wife was Winifred, daughter of Sir John Bruges, a wealthy Alderman of London, and Thomas Sackville, the subject of this memoir, was the sole issue of their marriage. He was born in 1536, at Buckhurst, in the parish of Witham, in Sussex, where his family had long been seated, and was educated both at Oxford and Cambridge, in the latter of which Universities he took the degree of Master of Arts. He removed from thence to the Inner Temple, where, according to the custom of young men of rank in his time, he studied the law, with no view of making it his profession, but as a necessary part of a gentleman's breeding, and was called to the bar, soon after which he became a member of the House of Commons. He had been already for some years distinguished as a poet, of which however I shall say little at present, and is supposed to have composed many small pieces in English, as well as in Latin verse, of which, being probably mingled with those of others, or in some instances, totally lost, we are now nearly ignorant. We know that those poems on which his fame so justly rests were written before he had reached the twenty-fifth year of his age, and we know not that he wrote any thing afterwards.

About that period he married, and soon after travelled through France and Italy, from whence he returned in 1566, on receiving at Rome the news of his father's death, and, on the eighth of June in that year, he was advanced by Elizabeth to the peerage, by the title of Lord Buckhurst. His father, in addition to a fine inheritance, was so well known to have amassed immense wealth that it was usual, by a vulgar anagram, to call him " Fill Sack." The son, who had been before very profuse, which probably occasioned his going abroad at an unusual time of life, became now extravagant beyond all bounds, and soon fell into considerable difficulties. He is said to have been reclaimed by Elizabeth's wholesome advice; but Fuller tells us, and there is nothing improbable in the tale, that " happening to call on an Alderman of London, who had gained great pennyworths by former purchases of him, he was made to wait so long, that his generous humour, being sensible of the incivility of such attendance, resolved to be no more beholden to wealthy pride, and presently turned a thrifty improver of the remainder of his estate." Certain it is, whatever might have been the cause, that he suddenly changed his imprudence for a magnificent economy, which never after forsook him. The Queen, who either really loved her kindred, or highly countenanced them from a proud respect to herself, took him into considerable personal favour, though she conferred on him no permanent employment, either in her government or household, for many years. She sent him on an embassy to Paris in 1570, to congratulate Charles the ninth on his nuptials, and to treat of the marriage then proposed between herself and the Duke of Anjou, brother to that Prince, appointed him one of the Commissioners for the trial, and committed to him the miserable office of superintending the execution, of Mary Queen of Scots; and in 1587 intrusted to him, in the character of her Ambassador extraordinary to the United States, the difficult duty of hearing and composing their complaints against the Earl of Leicester, his honesty in the performance of which drew on him the vengeance of that favourite, through whose influence the Queen was induced to recall him, and to place him in confinement in his own house, where he remained a prisoner for nine or ten months, during which he never saw his wife, or children.

If Elizabeth by any act of imprudence ever placed herself in the power of another, Leicester was the man. Haughty, furious, and unfeeling as she was, her submission to his will, even when opposite to her own, was invariable; and her conduct at this time towards Lord Buckhurst affords a curious proof of it. Leicester died in September, 1588: Sackville was immediately released: in the April following he was named, without his knowledge, a Knight of the Garter; and in the course of that and the succeeding year, was employed in several services which required the strictest fidelity, among which the affairs of the United Provinces were peculiarly committed to his charge. In 1591 he was elected Chancellor of the University of Oxford, in opposition to the favoured Essex, and that through the especial interference of the Queen herself, who some months after honoured him with a visit there. In 1598 he was selected to treat of a peace with Spain, and on the fifteenth of May in that year was raised to the office of High Treasurer, on the death of Burghley. On the occasion of Essex's wild insurrection he distinguished

3

himself as much by his humanity as his wisdom; warned the unhappy Earl in time, with the kindness of a private friend, of the danger of his courses; and presided as Lord High Steward on his trial, with the strictest impartiality. The office of Earl Marshal becoming vacant by Essex's death, he was appointed one of the Commissioners for performing the duties of it. Elizabeth died soon after.

His patent for the office of Lord Treasurer was renewed by James, even before that Prince quitted Scotland; the choice of the principal servants of the Crown was in a great measure intrusted to him; and on the thirteenth of the March following the King's accession he was created Earl of Dorset. The faculties of his high office soon became strangely changed. In the late reign the main occupation of the chief Minister of finance was to dispose properly of the means which had arisen from natural and simple resources, well chosen, and well husbanded; in this to devise extraordinary methods to replenish a treasury exhausted by the most absurd profusion. The circumstances of Dorset's private life somewhat qualified him for acting in either situation with more ease than most men, but that he should have possessed in each the unvaried good opinion not only of his Sovereigns, but of his compeers, and of the people, can be ascribed only to a rare perfection both of head and heart. The two following letters, which were placed a few years since by me in a Life of Sir Julius Cæsar, who acted under him as Chancellor of the Exchequer, may be considered as great curiosities, for the lively light which they throw on a part of the character of Sackville's mind, independently of the striking proof afforded by them of the financial distress of that reign; nor are they less estimable as specimens of his epistolary composition, especially since Naunton has informed us that " his secretaries did little for him by the way of inditement, wherein they could seldom please him, he was so facete and choice in his phrase and style." These letters were written to Sir Julius by the Earl's own hand.

" I have just sined your 2 orders, and do gretely thank you for delivering my most humble thankes to his Matie. As for clamors for monies when ther is no meanes to pay, that is news to you, but not to me. I know not, nor no man erthly knows, any other remedy but to aunswer them that they must tary til it come in. As for any ordinaries coming in, Sir Vincent Skinner can alwaies tell you far better than I, for he was alwaies my inforrmer; and as for extraordinaries, I know of none but this of the tinne. That can go neither forward nor backwards by my presens. I have left full ordre with Mr Atturney, and Sir Rich. Smith, to expedite the same; but the delivery of the tinne at London, and in Cornwale, in my opinion will not be done thies 20 daies yet. As to my coming to London, I know not a halfpeny of help that I can give you therby, if I were fit, or able; and I thank humbly his Matie he hath geven me credit to seke to recover my helth, wch I desier to do for his serves; but God doth know that I have yet found a small beginning of recovery, and do leave all to God's mercies, knowing, that only time, aier, and free from business, must help this rooted cold and cough of mine, so fast fixed in me.

So I rest, ever your most assured friend,

T. DORSET."

HORSLEY,
31 May, 1607.

He concludes, a few days after, in the following terms a very long letter on the preemption of tin by the Crown; an unpopular, but not new project, in which James's ministers were then busily employed, and which is alluded to in the preceding. The letter has no date, but is indorsed by Sir Julius Cæsar, " 9 Junii, 1607."

" Now, Mr. Chauncellor, touching your lamentacõn of the clamors and sutes that are daily made to you for money, and how grevous it is unto you, and therefore desier my help and advise what you shold do, I can say but this; that true fortitude is never daunted, and truth ought never to be either afraid or ashamed.

5

You may truly aunswer them that the king's dets, his subsidies, his rents, his revenues, notwithstanding all the meanes for levieng of them that possibly may be devised, ar not paid, but pecemele come in, with grete difficulty; and how can the king's ma^tie pay that wch he owes, when that which is owing to him is unpaied? Besides his ma^tie hath brought wth him an increse of a most comfortable charge; as of a quene, the king's wief; a prince; and other his most royall progeny. Thes ar comfortable charges, and all good subjects must help willinglie to beare the burden therof.—That the King of Spaine himself, that hath so many Indian gold and silver mines to help him, doth yet leave his dets many times unpaied, upon accidents that happen.—That the king's ma^tie, and his counsell, do not neglect to devise all possible meanes and waies to bring in monies and do not dout, within convenient time, though sodenly it cannot be doon, to procure good helpes towards satisfaction of the dettes.—That alredy he hath assined a good part of his subsidy to discharge the same.— That no labours shall be spared to effect the same: in the meane while they must have paciens, and be content.—That as the king's revenues do come in, so they shall have part and part among them; for one must not have all, and the rest nothing. These, and such like, are true aunswers, and ought, and must satisfie, and these you must not be afraid to geve; and such as will not be satisfied with thes ar men without dutie or reson; therefore no great matter though they be unsatisfyed.

" Now, Mr. Chauncellor, if 3 weekes be so grevous unto you, what will you think of my greif that in this kind have indured the greif of 3 yeres? But let this be your last and chiefest comfort—that we have a most roiall, rare, and most gracious king, for whom we can never speke to much, nor do sufficient, though we expend our lieves, lands, and goods, and all that we have, in this servis. I have told you that I will bend all my indevours to bring in monies, which also must have it's due time for sodenly you may not expect it: p~fering you therefore that wch now ap˜taineth to you, and, by the grace of God, you shall se that I will so laboriously, and I hope so effectually, procede in the other, as you shall have comfort, and I my harty contentation, that I may do some acceptable servis to so gracious a soverein.

Yo˜r most assured frend,

T. DORSET."

Such was his vivacity in the seventy-second year of his age, and when labouring under the greatest infirmity of body, which is somewhat singularly confirmed by a passage in his most remarkable will, referring to the very date of the last of these letters. After having ordained, at great length, and with the utmost preciseness of diction that caution could suggest, that four certain jewels should be preserved for ever in his family, as heir looms, he proceeds to state his motives for so highly valuing them ; and, having exactly described the first which he names, adds—" and, to the intent that they (his heirs male) may knowe howe just and great cause both they and I have to hould the sayed rynge with twentie diamonds in so highe esteeme, yt is most requisite that I do here set downe the whole course and circumstance howe, and from whome the same rynge did come to my possession, which was this. In the beginning of the monethe of June, one thousand sixe hundred and seaven, this rynge thus sett with twenty diamondes, as ys aforesaid, was sent unto me from my most gracious sovereigne King James, by that honorable personage the Lord Haye, one of the gentlemen of his highness' bedchamber, the courte then being at Whitehall, in London, and I at that time remayning at Horseley House, in Surrey, twentie miles from London, where I laye in such extremitie of sickness as yt was a common and a constant reporte all over London that I was dead, and the same confidentlie affirmed unto the kinge's highnes himself : upon which occasion yt pleased his most excellent majestie, in token of his gracious goodness and great favoure towards me, to send the saied Lord Haye with the ringe, and this royall message unto me, namelie—that his highness wished a speedie and a perfect recovery of my healthe, with all happie and good successe unto me, and that I might live as long as the dyamonds of that rynge (which therewithall he delivered unto me) did endure; and, in token thereof, required me to weare yt, and keep it for his sake. This most gracious and comfortable message restored a new life unto me, as coming from so renowned and benigne a sovereigne unto a servaunte so farre unworthie of of so great a favour," &c.

He recovered his health sufficiently to return to London, and to attend to the more important concerns of his office, and in August made the will of which I have spoken. He survived, however, till the nineteenth of the following April, when he expired in an instant, as he sat at the council table, surrounded by the chief officers of the state, and in the presence of the king. " On opening his head," says Sir Richard Baker, " they found in it certain little bags of water, which, falling upon his brain, caused his death;" but his constitution had been completely broken by his previous illness, though his mind retained it's pristine vigour to his last moment. Perhaps it may not be too much to affirm of him that he possessed, together with the brightest genius, and an understanding abundantly solid and useful, the highest honour, the strictest integrity, and the most undoubted loyalty, that could be found among the great public men of his time.

Sackville's poetical talents have always been regarded by a few in whom a just feeling has been united to a just judgment, with a degree of respect amounting nearly to reverence : to others they are almost wholly unknown. That fashion, however, if I may presume to use so light a term, which has of late so widely diffused itself, of collecting the scattered and forgotten English poesy of former ages may probably place him in his proper rank in general reputation. Those whom nature has qualified to appreciate truly his genius will express their wonder at the neglect which it has experienced; and ignorant affectation will spread his fame, by repeating the lessons it will catch by rote from legitimate taste. Yet Sackville will not delight the multitude of the present time. His very perfections will prevent it. The truth and simplicity of his designs; his stern and solemn morality, the awful grandeur of his imagery; will have no charms for those who can hang in rapture over the bald and tedious ballad monotonies, and the fierce and mysterious rhapsodies, from which the poets of our day derive the laurel. But the scope of these sketches, especially as I cannot deny myself the pleasure of inserting a specimen of his muse, forbids any lengthened discussion of her merits. Suffice it therefore to say, that Lord Orford thought it probable that " to the boldness of Buckhurst's scenes we might owe Shakespeare ;" and that Wharton has given him the credit of teaching to Spenser the method of designing allegorical personages. His works were the tragedy of Ferrex and Porrex, called in a later edition " Gorboduc ;" the " Induction," (or poetical preface) to the series of legendary tales, by several hands, of unfortunate princes, and other great men, intituled " The Mirror for Magistrates ;" together with the " Complaint of the Duke of Buckingham," which are the chief ornaments to that collection. Gorboduc, in which it has been improbably said that he was assisted by Thomas Norton, a contemporary poet of small distinction, amidst several of the imperfections of a bold experiment, has the merits of being the first attempt made in this country to chase from the stage the devout mummeries of its infancy, and of having introduced into dramatic composition a dignity and perspicuity of style, and a strength of reflection, to which it had before been wholly unaccustomed. His greater work shall speak for itself, in an extract from the Induction, which some may think too long, and which others will wish had been yet further extended.—The poet is led by sorrow, exquisitely personified, to the utmost extent of the infernal regions, where the mighty unfortunates are to pass him in review, and to recount their

9

respective histories. On his way he encounters the following griesly inmates of the vast prison.

> And first, within the porch and jawes of hell,
> Sate deep Remorse of conscience, all besprent
> With teares; and to herself oft would she tell
> Her wretchednesse; and, cursing, never stent
> To sob and sigh; but ever thus lament,
> > With thoughtfull care, as she that all in vaine
> > Would weare and waste continually in paine.
>
> Her eyes, unstedfast rolling here and there,
> Whurl'd on each place, as place that vengeance brought :
> So was her mind continually in feare,
> Tossed and tormented with tedious thought
> Of those detested crimes which she had wrought :
> > With dreadfull cheere, and lookes throwne to the skie,
> > Wishing for death, and yet she could not die.
>
> Next saw we Dread—all trembling how he shooke !
> With foote uncertaine, profered here and there,
> Benum'd of speech, and, with a ghastly looke,
> Searcht every place ; all pale, and dead for feare ;
> His cap borne up with staring of his heare :
> > Soyn'd and amaz'd at his own shade for dreed,
> > And fearing greate dangers then was need.
>
> And next, within the entrie of this lake,
> Sate fell Revenge, gnashing her teeth for ire ;
> Devising meanes how she may vengeance take ;
> Never in rest till she have her desire ;
> But frets within so far forth with the fire
> > Of wreaking flames, that now determines she
> > To die by death, or veng'd by death to be.
>
> When fell Revenge, with bloudie foule pretence,
> Had shew'd herselfe as next in order set,
> With trembling limbes we softly parted thence,
> Till in our eyes another sight we met :
> When from my heart a sigh forthwith I fet,

EARL OF DORSET.

Ruing alas ! upon the wofull plight
Of Miserie, that next appear'd in sight.

His face was leane, and some deale pin'd away ;
And eke his hands consumed to the bone :
But what his body was I cannot say,
For on his carkas raymente had he none,
Save clouts and patches, pieced one by one :
    With staffe in hand, and scrip on shoulder cast,
    His chief defence against the winter's blast.

His food for most was wilde fruits of the tree,
Unlesse sometime some crums fell to his share,
Which in his wallet long, God wot, kept he,
As one the which full daintily would faire :
His drinke the running stream ; his cup the bare
    Of his palm closde ; his bed the hard cold ground :
    To this poore life was Miserie ybound.

Whose wretched state when we had well beheld,
With tender ruth on him, and on his feeres,
In thoughtfull cares forth then our pace we held.
And by and by another shape appeares,
Of greedie Care, still brushing up the breers ;
    His knuckles knob'd, his flesh deepe dented in ;
    With tawed hands, and hard ytanned skin.

The morrow gray no sooner hath begun
To spread his light, even peeping in our eyes,
When he is up, and to his worke yrun.
But let the night's blacke mistie mantles rise,
And with foule darke never so much disguise
    The faire bright day, yet ceaseth he no while,
    But hath his candles to prolong his toile.

By him lay heavie Sleepe, cosin of Death,
Flat on the ground, and still as any stone ;
A very corps, save yeelding forth a breath.
Small keepe tooke he whom Fortune frowned on,
Or whom she lifted up into the throne
    Of high renown ; but, as a living death,
    So, dead alive, of life he drew the breath.

THOMAS SACKVILLE,

The bodies rest ; the quiet of the heart ;
The travailes ease ; the still night's feere was he :
And of our life in earth the better part ;
Rever of sight, and yet in whom we see
Things oft that tide, and oft that never bee.
    Without respect esteeming equally
    King Crœsus' pompe, and Irus' povertie.

And next in order sad Old Age we found :
His beard all hore, his eyes hollow and blind ;
With drouping cheere still poring on the ground,
As on the place where nature him assign'd
To rest, when that the Sisters had untwin'd
    His vital thred, and ended with their knife
    The fleeting course of fast declining life.

There heard we him, with broke and hollow plaint,
Rue with himselfe his end approching fast ;
And all for nought his wretched mind torment
With sweete remembrance of his pleasures past,
And fresh delites of lustie youth forewast :
    Recounting which, how would he sob and shreek
    And to be yong again of Jove beseeke.

But, and the cruel fates so fixed be
That time forepast cannot returne again,
This one request of Jove yet prayed he—
That in such withred plight, and wretched paine,
As eld (accompanied with loathsome traine)
    Had brought on him, all were it woe and griefe,
    He might a while yet linger forth his life ;

And not so soone descend into the pit
Where Death, when he the mortall corps hath slaine,
With wretchlesse hand in grave doth cover it,
Thereafter never to enjoy againe
The gladsome light, but, in the ground ylaine,
    In depth of darknesse, waste, and weare, to nought,
    As he had nere into the world been brought.

But who had seene him, sobbing how he stood
Unto himselfe, and how he would bemone
His youth forepast, as though it wrought him good

12

EARL OF DORSET.

To talke of youth all were his youth forgone,
He would have musde and marvail'd much whereon
  This wretched Age should life desire so faine,
  And knows ful wel life doth but length his paine.

Crookebackt he was, toothshaken, and blere eyde;
Went on three feete, and sometime crept on foure;
With old lame bones that rattled by his side;
His scalpe all pil'd, and he with eld forlore;
His withred fist still knocking at Death's dore;
  Fumbling, and driveling, as he draws his breath,
  For briefe, the shape and messenger of Death.

And fast by him pale Maladie was plaste,
Sore sicke in bed, her colour all forgone;
Bereft of stomacke, savour, and of taste:
Ne could she brooke no meate, but broths alone:
Her breath corrupt; her keepers every one
  Abhorring her; her sicknesse past recure;
  Detesting physicke, and all physicke's cure.

But oh the doleful sight that then we see!
We turn'd our looke, and, on the other side,
A griesly shape of Famine mought we see,
With greedie lookes, and gaping mouth, that cried
And roared for meate as she should there have died.
  Her bodie thin, and bare as any bone,
  Whereto was left nought but the case alone:

And that, alas! was gnawne on every where
All full of holes, that I ne mought refraine
From teares to see how she her arms could teare,
And with her teeth gnash on the bones in vaine,
When all for nought she faine would so sustaine
  Her starven corps, that rather seemed a shade
  Than any substance of a creature made.

Great was her force whom stone wall could not stay:
Her tearing nailes, snatching at all she saw;
With gaping jawes that by no meanes ymay
Be satisfied from hunger of her mawe,
But eates herselfe, as she that hath no law:

13

THOMAS SACKVILLE,

Gnawing alas ! her carcase all in vaine,
Where you may count each sinew, bone, and vaine.

On her while we thus firmely fixt our eyes,
That bled for ruth of such a driery sight,
Loe suddenly she shrunkt *(shriekt)* in so huge wise
As made hell gates to shiver with the might.
Wherewith a dart we saw how it did light
   Right on her brest, and, therewithall, pale Death
   Enthrilling it, to reave her of her breath.

And by and by a dumbe dead corps we saw,
Heavie, and cold, the shape of death aright,
That dants all earthly creatures to his law ;
Against whose force in vaine it is to fight :
Ne Peers, ne Princes, nor no mortall wight,
   No Towne, ne Realmes, Cities, ne strongest Tower,
   But all perforce must yeeld unto his power.

His dart anon out of the corps he tooke,
And in his hand, a dreadfull sight to see !
With triumph eftsoones the same he shooke,
That, most of all my feares, affrayed me :
His bodie dight with nought but bones, per die.
   The naked shape of man then saw I plaine,
   All, save the flesh, the sinow, and the vaine.

Lastly stood Warre ; in glittering arms yclad,
With visage grim, sterne looks, and blackely hewed.
In his right hand a naked sword he had,
That to the hilts was all with blood embrued ;
And in his left that Kings and Kingdomes rued,
   Famine and fire he held, and there withall
   He raced townes, and threw downe towers and all.

Cities he sackt, and Realmes that whilome flowred
In honour, glorie, and rule above the best
He overwhelmed, and all their fame devoured ;
Consumed, destroyed, wasted, and never ceast,
Till he their wealth, their name, and all, opprest.
   His face forehew'd with wounds, and by his side
   There hung his targ, with gashes deepe and wide.

EARL OF DORSET.

In midst of which depainted there we found
Deadly Debate, all full of snakie heare,
That with a bloodie fillet was ybound,
Out breathing nought but discord every where :
And round about were portraid heere and there
    The hugie hosts ; Darius, and his power ;
    His Kings, Princes, his Peeres, and all his flower.

This great man married Cicely, daughter of Sir John Baker, of Sittinghurst Castle, in Kent, by whom he had three sons ; Robert, his successor ; William, who was knighted in France, in 1591, by Henry the great, at the age of nineteen, and fell in battle there two years after ; and Thomas, who was also distinguished as a military man : and three daughters ; Anne, wife of Sir Thomas Glemham, of Glemham, in Suffolk ; Jane, married to Anthony Browne, Viscount Montague ; and Mary, to Sir Henry Neville, son, and successor, to Edward, Lord Abergavenny.

15

Engraved by H.T.Ryall.

SIR THOMAS BODLEY.

OB. 1612.

FROM THE ORIGINAL OF CORNELIUS JANSEN, IN THE

BODLEIAN GALLERY, OXFORD.

London, Published Dec.1,1836, by Harding & Lepard, Pall Mall East.

SIR THOMAS BODLEY.

———◆———

IT is a proud reflection for the lovers of literature that the name of this eminent person should scarcely be known but as that of one of its most zealous cultivators ; that Europe should ring, as it ever will, with the fame of that prodigious treasure which it owes to his learning, his diligence, and his munificence ; and that it should be nearly forgotten, even in his own country, that he was any other-wise distinguished. Such is the triumph of immutable principle over fleeting habit ; of wisdom over cunning ; of the judgment over the passions. In our admiration of the retired collector of a library, we have ceased to remember that his counsels once guided the decisions of Sovereigns, and poised the fate of nations. Sir Thomas Bodley was a statesman of the first order, in merit, if not in place, and it will therefore be the object of these pages rather to recall to memory the circumstances of his political life, than to recapitulate minutely the history of that immortal foundation which is already so closely connected with his very name, that while we remember the one, we cannot forget the other.

He was descended from a respectable family, though of no great antiquity, in Devonshire, and was the eldest of the three sons of John Bodley, of Exeter, in which city he was born on the second of March, 1544, by Joan, daughter of Robert Hone, of Ottery St. Mary, in the same county. The persecution under Queen Mary

1

compelled his father, who was a zealous reformer, to seek refuge in a foreign country; and, after some wandering, he settled his family, about the year 1556, at Geneva, and in the University then newly established there his son Thomas commenced his education under teachers of the highest eminence. In some short notices of his life, written by himself, which, together with a few other matters relative to him, were published in 1703, in an octavo volume, now rather scarce, by the antiquary Thomas Hearne, under the title of " Reliquiæ Bodleianæ," he informs us that he was taught Hebrew by Chevalier, and Greek by Beroald and Constantine; and, in particular, that he studied divinity under Calvin and Beza. He returned to England immediately after the accession of Elizabeth, full of learning, and of affection for the Protestant persuasion, and became a student of Magdalen College, in Oxford, where, in 1563, he took the degree of Bachelor of Arts, and became probationer of Merton College, of which house in the ensuing year he was admitted fellow. In 1565 he read a Greek lecture in the hall of that college; in 1566, obtained the degree of Master of Arts, and read the lecture on natural philosophy in the Schools; and in 1569 was elected one of the Proctors, and undertook the office of University Orator, which he exercised for several years. He remained at Oxford till 1576, when he set out to visit the continent. Thus the first eighteen years of Bodley's manhood were purely academical, and hence that latent affection and gratitude to the university, conceived in the warmth of youth, and matured by the reflection of riper age, which burst forth with renewed vigour towards the conclusion of his life. That those sentiments were for a while suspended is evident from his own account: " In 1576," says he, " I waxed desirous to travel beyond the seas, for attaining to the knowledge of some special modern tongues, and for the increase of my experience in the managing of affairs; being wholly then addicted to employ myself, and all my cares, in the service of the State." He passed nearly four years in a slow and inquisitive journey through France, Germany, and Italy, and returned to his college to connect and systematize his observations

2

by reading the best authors on History and Politics. In 1583 he was introduced, we know not by what means, at the Court, and was appointed a Gentleman Usher, or, according to Antony Wood, an Esquire of the Body, to Queen Elizabeth : he soon after married Anne, daughter of a Mr. Carey, of Bristol, and the rich widow, says the author just now mentioned, for we have it only on his authority, of some person of the name of Ball.

It was Elizabeth's habit to seek for political ability through all ranks of her servants, and to try their talents and their fidelity in minor embassies. Bodley attracted her notice, and she dispatched him in 1586 on a circular mission to Frederick King of Denmark, and to the German Princes of the Protestant persuasion, to urge them to aid her endeavours in favour of the French Huguenots, then headed by the great Henry King of Navarre. He acquitted himself in this employment so much to her satisfaction, that she appointed him, immediately after his return, to another, not only of a nature almost wholly different, but which required a far greater measure of dexterity and delicacy. Henry the Third of France, the declared patron of the Papal interest in his realm, had been driven from his capital by that memorable party led by the Duke of Guise, which had named itself the Holy League, and which, with the usual detestable affectation of faction, had professed to unite for his defence and protection in that character. To him was Bodley sent with such extreme caution and secrecy, that he was not permitted, as he informs us, to take with him even a single servant, nor any other letters than such as were written by the Queen's own hand. " The effect," says he, "of that message it is fit that I should conceal ; but it tended greatly to the advantage of all the Protestants in France, and to the Duke's overthrow, which also followed soon upon it."

Elizabeth, having thus proved his worth, nominated him, in 1588, her resident minister at the Hague, a station then at the head of English diplomacy, the United Provinces being, from well-known historical circumstances, the theatre on which the political combat between her, and her great rival Philip of Spain, might be fought with the best prospect of success. In order to preserve her ascendancy there, he was admitted, according to a stipulation insisted on by Elizabeth before his departure, a member of their Council of State, in the sittings of which he placed himself, by her order, next to Count Maurice of Nassau. He enjoyed in this mission her perfect confidence. " After the Queen," says he, " had had some experience of my conduct there, from that time forward I did never almost receive any set instructions how to govern my proceedings in her Majesty's occasions, but the carriage, in a manner, of all her affairs was left to me and my discretion." Of the zeal, as well as the wisdom, with which he managed those affairs, we have a noble instance in a letter in the Harleian Collection, (No. 278, p. 190,) hitherto unpublished, the great length of which obliges me, though with much reluctance, to content myself with giving a few extracts from it. It is indorsed by himself, " Project of a Letter which I proposed to send to the Emperor's Ambassadors ; Nov. 1591," and affords perhaps the finest example extant of the frank and masculine spirit which then guided the policy of England, not to mention the very singular coincidence of the public circumstances to which it alludes with those of the present time.

" Having lately understood," he begins, " as well by those letters which yow have written to the States, and to your friendes in these contreis, as by divers other meanes of assured intelligence, that yow determine very shortly to addresse yourselves to the forsaide States, and in the name of the Emperor's Majestie to motion some agreement between them and the Spaniard, I have thought it very requisit, for discharge of my dewtie to my Sovereign Lady and Mistresse, the Queene's Majestie of England, who hath bin pleased to honour me with the place of her counsailor in this Counsaile of State, and for those principal respects which I beare, in all humilitie, to the Emperor's Majestie, between whom and my Soveraigne all offices of amitie have bin alwaies intertened, to prevent your comming hither with such advice as this place, and my fonction, will afford." He proceeds to remind the Austrian Ambassadors

4

that the States, ten months before, had addressed to the Emperor, and to other Princes of the Germanic body, their earnest protest against such mediation : and then informs them that in the articles between Elizabeth and the States, " it is a special point agreed that neither the general nor particular States of those provinces shall enter into treatie with the common enemie, the Spaniard, nor with any Prince or Potentat in his behalf, without the privitie or consent of the Queene's Majestie of England ;" and that such article, above all others, was recommended most precisely to the charge of all Elizabeth's ministers, military as well as civil, in the United States, and most effectually set down in their oaths. That the States themselves undoubtedly entertained the same opinion and resolution. " Nevertheles," adds he, " as if we knewe not that intention of the forsaide States, we are thus much of ourselves to signifie from hens : That unless yow come autorised to this treaty of peace with the allowance and warrant of the Queen our mistresse, we must, all in generall, and every one in particular, stand against yow, not only with good arguments of reason and persuasion, but with all the meanes that we can make, by any violence or force, to disturbe your attempts, and that without attending or expecting what the contrey shall resolve." After some apology for the sternness of this declaration, he proceeds to give his reasons why the States cannot hearken to any proposals for peace with Spain. " First, they say it is certaine, whatever is averred by others to the contrary, that the King of Spaine's disposition is wholly opposit to peace ; and this is proved apparently by a common observation which is in every man's discourse—that there is noe warre at this day in any part of Christendome but is directly or indirectly, sturred and maintained by the King of Spaine. What example can be plainer than his present partaking in the kingdome of France ? Where, without a just reason, be pretext of just occasion, he endeavoureth to depose the right owner from his scepter, and all under coller of zele and divotion to the Romishe religion. And, if that be all his cause, as his pretence is no other, would the Emperor's Majestie have this people to ima-

5

gine that the King of Spaine can be pleased to permitte unto them over whom he clameth a right, and absolut autoritie, the use of that religion for the extirpation wherof he poursueth a forraine Prince with all the actes of hostillitie that he can possibly practise? His purpose is too manifest: He mindes to make holyday with the States of these contreis till his maters in France succeede to his minde, and then his hope is undoubtedlie that not onely these Provinces united, but England, and Scotland, and every part of Germany, or of any other contrey that is different from him in religion, or disjoined by faction, shall accept of such lawes as he, for his benefit, shall prescribe unto them."

Having stated much at large the repeated breaches of treaty, and the various deceptions practised by the King of Spain towards the United Provinces, he goes on—" But, besides the examples among themselves, they saw the other day in his dealing with England a most palpable patterne of Spanish falsehoode and deceate: For, even then, and at the same instant that his ministers were emploied to persuade her Majestie to a peace, by proposing unto her verie plausible conditions, he armed a navy to the seas which, in his Lucifer's pride, he termed 'Invincible,' to make a conquest of her kingdome. But howe that wickednes was punished by the mightie hand of God it is knowen 'ere this to all the worlde, and it will be recorded to all posteritie. In effect," adds Bodley, after having cited other instances of treachery, " all his actions are directed by that most unchristian and barbarous maxime, that with an hereticke there is no faith to be observed; which infamous point of doctrine was most wickedly devised by the Pope, and Popish Princes, to serve their worldly turnes; distrusting, as it seemeth, the truth of their owne religion; as if God were not able (their cause being just, as they are persuaded, and their party being greater by many multitudes of people,) to uphold their estate without the breache of common faith. But if this be so maintened against heretickes in general, what application will be made by the King, and his favourers, against the heretickes of this contrey which have taken armes against him, have renounced

6

his religion, solemnly deposed him by way of abjuration, and delivered unto others the possession of his landes?" This very memorable letter concludes with the following expressions— "Unless yow shewe for your comming the liking and permission of her Majestie, my Soveraigne, I must needes forewarne yow, as before, that as many of us as are heere of her Majestie's subjects doe resolve to withstand yow, as perturbers of the amitie betweene her and the contrey; and, in that respect, every man, in his charge, will accomplishe the duties of his faith and obedience by forcing yow from hens: and, though I speake in this sorte very plainely and roundly, being bounde thereto by mine othe and allegeance, yet I rest out of doubt that your singular wisedomes will expounde my meaning to the best; and, being so well preadvertised of the strict alliance and contract between her Majestie and these contreis, will forbeare upon it to goe forward with your voiage intended. But if it so fall out in truth, as in semblance is pretended, that the Kinge of Spaine, ether weried with his warres, or reduced to extremity, or finding in continuance that God doth not prosper his dissembled proceeding, shall be willing now at length to speake as he thinketh, and to stipulate a firme and a durable peace, there is no other meanes to effect his purpose but by causing the like proffers of peace as are made to these provinces to be presented in like sorte to her Majestie of England, to the King in France, and to as many other Princes as sitte complaining at the helme of the common cause, and runne in danger to be drowned in the bottomlesse gulph of the Spanish ambition. To this there is no doubt but the Kinge will condescend, if his minde and meaning be cleere and upright; and this is it which her Majesty, my Soveraigne, the States of these contreis, and every forraigne Potentat, will most willingly helpe forewarde with all the meanes of assistaunce that they can minister unto him."

In this important station Bodley remained for nine years, making some occasional visits to his Court, in one of which, in 1695, he highly offended Elizabeth by some proposals which he

7

brought from the States relative to their debts to her. "I hear," says he, in one of his several letters to Mr. Anthony Bacon, preserved in Dr. Birch's Memoirs, "for my comfort, that the Queen, on Monday last, did at the Court wish I had been hanged." He returned however soon after to the Hague, from whence he was not finally recalled, and then at his own earnest request, till 1597. He never held any other public employment. It was his misfortune, according to his own account, to be equally regarded both by Burghley and Essex, each of whom had frequently recommended him with much earnestness to Elizabeth, for the place of Secretary of State, his appointment to which, through jealousy, was always thwarted by the other. Perhaps Elizabeth's dread of strengthening the party of Essex, who certainly was his warmest friend, was yet a stronger impediment. Be this as it may, he determined to retire from public life, and though frequently solicited by her, and by her successor, to accept of high and important offices in the State, abided by his resolution.

He had undoubtedly long entertained the noble design of restoring, or rather founding, the public library at Oxford, for he had scarcely found himself at home when he began to collect books for it with such zeal and avidity that, even before the end of that year, he had amassed a great treasure of general literature, and had formally communicated his intention to the University. Sensible, however, that the life, as well as the wealth, of any individual must fall far short of the accomplishment of the plan he had laid, he spared no pains in invoking the aid of the rich and the learned, and obtained vast contributions in money as well as in books. Many amusing instances of his anxieties, his doubts, his disappointments, and even his jealousies, with regard to these benefactions, may be found in Reliquiæ Bodleianæ, in a long series of his letters to Dr. William James, who was his chief agent in the collection, and the first person who had the office of keeper of the library after its final establishment. We meet in one of them with a curious proof of blameable vanity. Bodley was solicitous to conceal the assistance which he received from others, and thus

8

betrays that disposition which he awkwardly labours to dissemble
—" I am utterly against it that there should be any mention of
their names and gifts that are the chiefest contributors to the
library, for that few in that case would be willingly omitted, and
the gift of the greatest is hardly worth publishing as a matter of
much moment: besides that the number increaseth continually;
and, as I am persuaded, when those that are to come after shall
see no likelihood of occasion to be honoured, as the former, by
some public monument, it may slacken their devotion. And, as
for myself, I am wholly uncertain how far I shall proceed in my
expense about that work, having hitherto made no determinate
design, but purposing to do as my ability shall afford, which may
increase or diminish, and as God shall spare my life, although unto
myself I do resolve in a general project to do more than I am
willing to publish to the world. It may suffice, in my conceit, if
the party employed in the answer to Weston shall but signify, in
general, to what forwardness that work of so great a public benefit
is already brought by my means, in special, and then by the aid of
such of my honourable friends, and others, as in affection to me,
and for the advancement of learning, have been moved to set their
helping hand to it; so as in time it is like, and perhaps very
shortly, to be a most admirable ornament as well of the state as
of the University; to the effecting whereof though so many men
concur, yet the plotting and ordering of all things, and the bulk
of all the burthen, for matter of cost, and otherwise, both hath and
will be mine; wherein, as I will not assume the deserts to myself
of other men's bounties, so I would not that mine own, in a public
memorial, should be lessened."

Even before the end of the year 1599, the Bodleian Library had
become, with the exception of the Vatican, perhaps the first public
collection in Europe, and very soon after stood wholly unrivalled.
James I., who really loved literature, gave a warrant under the
Privy-seal to the founder for such books as he might choose to
take from any of the Royal libraries, and the fashion set by the
Monarch was eagerly followed by his courtiers. The simple line

of building which had formerly contained Duke Humphrey's Library, and which had already been repaired by Bodley, having been long insufficient to admit even a fourth part of his collection, he proposed to the University to convert it, at his own charge, into that noble quadrangle in which it now remains. The first stone of the new building was laid, with great formalities, on the nineteenth of July, 1610, but the founder did not live to see it completed. He had not neglected however to provide for it by his will, by which also he settled two hundred pounds annually on the library for ever, having previously composed, with great care and judgment, a large body of statutes for its government, the original of which, in his own hand-writing, is preserved there, and has been long published, annexed to the Statutes of the University and otherwise.

Sir Thomas Bodley, for he had been knighted by King James the First, on that Prince's accession, died, without issue, on the twenty-eighth of January, 1612, and lies buried at the head of the choir of Merton College Chapel, under a superb monument executed in the best taste of the time.

Engraved by J. Cochran.

ROBERT CECIL, EARL OF SALISBURY.

OB . 1612.

FROM THE ORIGINAL OF ZUCCHERO, IN THE COLLECTION OF

THE RIGHT HON^{ble} THE EARL OF SALISBURY.

London, Publifhed Decr 1,1836, by Harding & Lepard, Pall Mall East.

ROBERT CECIL,

EARL OF SALISBURY.

If the father of this great man, the celebrated Lord Burghley, had never been a minister, the son might probably, and very justly, have been esteemed the most consummate statesman in Europe of his time. Their qualities however differed materially: the father was the wiser man: he loved to act alone, and the greatest measures of his administration may in most instances be traced to the decisions of his own intellect. A principle of moral right, seldom to be found in any who preceded or followed him, was always more or less discernible in them; and a simplicity of character which remarkably adorned his private life, was generally evident also in his ministerial conduct. In his progress to a very exalted eminence he had few competitors, and his long possession of it excited little jealousy, because the public interest was, or seemed to be, the invariable object of his labours; for envy is seldom provoked but by those who are evidently actuated by the selfish passions. The son was more adroit, not to say cunning. He was the first statesman in this country who practised, with the air of a system, the policy of governing by the opposition and balance of parties. His own hand was seldom to be discovered in his measures, and those by whom they were accomplished were rarely conscious of having been his instruments. He was charged, perhaps often unjustly, with duplicity, and with angry and revengeful partialities; nor was he wholly unsuspected of sharing in the gross venality to which most public

1

ministers of all ranks were tempted by the absurd carelessness and profuseness of the Monarch in whose reign he chiefly flourished. Salisbury was pliant, and served Elizabeth with as high a degree of favour as his father; but the wisdom and stern integrity of Burghley would have disqualified him for the place of High Treasurer to a Prince of James's character.

Robert Cecil was the only son of that exemplary minister by his second wife, Mildred, eldest daughter of Sir Anthony Coke, of Gidea Hall in Essex. Of the date of his birth we have the most discordant accounts, but it seems to have occurred about the year 1560. He received the education usual to persons of his rank at home, and afterwards at St. John's College, Cambridge, and, though he was in fact bred from his very childhood for the Court and the State, became amply accomplished in every branch of polite literature. His constitution was weak and sickly, insomuch that his person became deformed, and it was long before he was able to bear the fatigue of any unusual bodily exertion; but in 1584 he ventured to attach himself to the splendid embassy of Henry Earl of Derby to the Court of Paris, and in 1588 had so far mastered his infirmities as to join the number of young nobility who were witnesses to the defeat of the Spanish Armada. Several years however yet passed before he was specifically appointed to any post in the government, during which he was receiving from his father that last instruction in state affairs which can be derived only from a participation in the management of them. The most advantageous opportunity for this was offered by the death of Walsingham, in 1590, and Burghley instantly seized it. He persuaded Elizabeth, on what grounds is now unknown, to keep the office of Principal Secretary nominally vacant, and for the six succeeding years transacted the business of it himself, with the assistance of his son, who in the summer of 1596 was at length formally appointed to it. From this promotion originated the lasting enmity between Cecil and Essex, who had proposed to the Queen first Davison, and then Bodley, for the Secretaryship, and had on those occasions, says

Camden, before whose report the tales of such writers as Welden and Osborne sink into contempt, " with so much bitterness, and so little reason, disparaged Cecil," that she would not listen to Essex's recommendation, even insomuch as to permit either of the objects of his choice to act as coadjutor to Cecil in the office.

In 1597 Elizabeth conferred on him the Chancellorship of the Duchy of Lancaster, and about the same time gave him the custody of the Privy Seal; and in the following year he was the chief commissioner on the part of England in the negotiation for a peace between the Crowns of France and Spain which is known by the name of the treaty of Vervins. Before his departure, such was his opinion of the honour of his generous adversary, he is said to have earnestly sought, and at length to have obtained, from Essex a promise not to injure him during his absence by promoting any of his enemies. He succeeded his father, who died in the autumn of that year, in the post of Master of the Wards; and in his office of secretary exercised in fact that of prime minister for the remaining five years of the Queen's life, with as full a share of her favour and confidence as she had at any time bestowed on his illustrious natural and political predecessor. He had indeed many of his father's qualifications to recommend him, and some, as has been already observed, which that great statesman never possessed. No one among her ministers but himself could have supplied the loss of Walsingham, who furnished her with the means of controlling foreign powers through intelligence gained in their own courts. Cecil even rivalled him in this dark faculty; and Elizabeth, in whom we find the worst meannesses of the feminine character united to an extravagance in the factitious splendour of royalty, valued him accordingly.

His memory has been highly censured for his having held a secret correspondence with the King of Scots for some of the last years of her life; and apparently without any just cause, for it has never been insinuated that he betrayed her confidence to that

Prince. Those who have blamed him on this score forget that the reciprocal relations of monarch and minister cannot be expected to involve that delicacy of personal regard which belongs to the affections of private life, and is even there not frequently to be found. Cecil, a minister by trade, sought to ensure the favour of the successor to the Throne, and he did it fairly and honestly. It has been said that his efforts to that end were powerfully seconded by Hume, Earl of Dunbar, perhaps the most creditable of James's Scottish ministers; and an incredible tale is told by a pamphleteer of that day of his meeting that nobleman privately at York, immediately after the Queen's decease, to negotiate for his good offices. James's motives for accepting and retaining Cecil in his station of prime minister are obvious. His services were indispensably necessary, for the Council of Elizabeth contained not an individual qualified to supply his place. The King was arbitrary and idle; sudden, extravagant, and versatile, in the choice of his private familiars; and more ambitious of the character of an able polemic, and an acute theoretical politician, than of a powerful Prince: Cecil was subservient and vigilant; too wise and too proud to entertain a jealousy of mere favourites; and willingly encouraged James to waste in reveries the time which would otherwise have been employed in interfering with his minister's measures.

It is needless to say that he was continued in the office of Secretary. Throughout the reign of Elizabeth he had possessed no higher title than that of a Knight Bachelor, but James now amply compensated him for the omission; for on the thirteenth of May, 1603, he was created Baron Cecil, of Essendon, in the county of Rutland; on the twentieth of August in the following year Viscount Cranborne; on the fourth of May, 1605, Earl of Salisbury; and on the twentieth of the same month was installed a Knight of the Garter. He was about that time elected Chancellor of the University of Cambridge; and on the death of Thomas Sackville Earl of Dorset, in April 1608, was appointed on the fourth of the following month to succeed him in the great

4

office of Lord Treasurer. With that nobleman Cecil had long lived in the strictest friendship; and we have the good fortune to possess a character of him, drawn by Dorset's exquisite pen, which leaves no room to doubt of the exaggerations of calumny with which his memory has been loaded. The solemn nature of the document in which it is to be found, and the admirable universality of talent and judgment, as well as the perfect integrity and honour, of the writer, unite to give it every claim to credit; and as Dorset's name has thus occurred, it may as well be inserted in this place.

In his last will he bequeaths to Cecil several jewels of great value, not only as tokens of a most earnest personal affection, which he declares at considerable length, and with the utmost warmth of expression, "but also, and most chiefly," to use the words of the testator, "even in regard of his public merit, both towards his Majesty and this Commonwealth: wherein," continues he, "when I behold the heavy weight of so many grave and great affairs which the special duty of his place as principal Secretary doth daily and necessarily cast upon him; and do note withal what infinite cares, crosses, labours and travels of body and mind, he doth thereby continually sustain and undergo; and, lastly, do see with how great dexterity, sincerity, and judgment, he doth accomplish and perform the painful service of that place; these divine virtues of his, so incessantly exercised and employed for the good of the public, I must confess have made me long since so greatly to love, honour, and esteem him, and so firmly and faithfully fixed my heart unto him, as I do dailie and heartily pray unto Almighty God to continue all strength and ability both of body and mind in him, that he sink not under the weight of so heavy a burthen." After fervently praying at some extent for a continuance of the blessings of Providence on his ministry, Dorset concludes—"Thus I have faithfully set down in some sort the noble parts of this honourable Earl, who, besides such his worthiness and sufficiency for the public service both of his sovereign and country, is also framed of so sweet a nature, so full of mildness, courtesy, honest mirth, bounty, kindness, gratitude, and

5

discourse, so easily reconciled to his foe, and evermore so true unto his friend, as I may justly say that it were one of the chiefest felicities that in this world we can possess, to live, converse, and spend our whole life in mutual love and friendship, with such a one ; of whose excelling virtues, and sweet conditions, so well known to me, in respect of our long communication by so many years in most true love and friendship together, I am desirous to leave some faithful remembrance in this my last Will and Testament ; that since the living speech of my tongue when I am gone from hence must then cease and speak no more, that yet the living speech of my pen, which never dieth, may herein thus for ever truly testify and declare the same."

Cecil's political character, as given by Lord Dorset, is fully justified by the clearest historical evidence. His application to the duties of his several offices was almost incessant, and no object, however minute, which they involved escaped his attention. It appears from an extensive collection of his original papers, which were once my property, that he had not only informed himself, with a correctness which without such proof would have been altogether incredible, of the precise number of acres—of the several buildings and their state of repair—of the woods, and of the timber proper to be felled—comprised in all the estates of the crown ; but that he had applied his mind distinctly to the consideration of every subdivision of each of those several branches of the subject, and had written innumerable notes on them with his own hand, frequently at great length. So too, in his place of Master of the Wards, he wrote himself at the foot of each petition for wardship, even from the meanest persons, his answer, the mode of which always proved that he had carefully considered the merits of each case. It has been said that he procured from James large grants of lands, and made exchanges of estates with that Prince unreasonably to his own advantage. If it were so, he did but imitate the practice of all ministers of that age, and of many which preceded it ; but, on the other hand, he was perhaps the only minister or courtier of that reign who stood even unsuspected of foreign corruption. He has been charged too with abject submission to the will of his master: it is true that he interfered not with the foibles of the man; but he discouraged, sometimes by argument, sometimes by artifice, the prodigality of the monarch; and opposed, vigorously and openly, the Spanish interest, to which James is well known to have been strongly inclined. On the whole, it is surprising that a Prince so careless and so profuse should have had a servant so honest; and under the impression of that candid and impartial opinion some writer of later days has said that "Cecil was the first bad Treasurer, and the last good one since the reign of Elizabeth."

Of Lord Dorset's report of him as a private man, valuable as it is, for no one else has portrayed him in that character, little need be said, because few parts of it have been contradicted. His enmity to Essex, and afterwards to Raleigh, have been frequent themes of historical censure, but neither his motives nor his conduct regarding those unfortunate great men have ever been even slightly examined. His original offence to the former has been already here mentioned, and he aggravated it by opposing the promotion of Bacon to the office of Attorney-General. Essex, the slave of passion, vilified him openly, and the cool prudence with which Cecil endured his attacks was called hypocrisy. The Earl suddenly embraced and headed an imbecile faction to drive Cecil from the ministry: the statesman defended himself, and thwarted his adversary by counteracting his schemes for military glory. To us, who live in the age of party, this will seem but fair collision. When Essex was taken in open rebellion his powerful adversary appears to have made no efforts to forward the impending blow, but he is said to have witnessed the infliction of it, and hence the general impression of his hatred to the unhappy favourite. Some traces of the high generosity as well as of the cruelty of incivilisation were to be yet discerned in that time, and Cecil, if he were a spectator of the death of Essex, prevailed on Elizabeth to spare the life of Southampton, that nobleman's dearest friend, and not less his own enemy. Of the causes of his quarrel with Raleigh, less is known. They had been united against Essex, and disagreed after his overthrow. It is natural to suppose that their ill offices towards each other were mutual; but we have few particulars of the activity of Cecil's resentment, whose station indeed afforded him opportunities of dealing out his vengeance unseen : Raleigh however is known to have presented a memorial to James on his arrival in England, full of bitter reflections on Cecil, charging him with the ruin of Essex, and his father with the death of the Queen of Scots. Forgiveness, or even forbearance, could scarcely be reasonably expected from the infirmity of nature after such an injury.

To endeavour in a work of this nature to digress from these slight notices of this great man's character, into even the most contracted epitome of the history of his ministry, would be idle. To conclude, then, it may be truly said that he sacrificed his life to the public service. His constitution, naturally weak and delicate, had been so fortified by medical care and temperance, that at the time of the death of Elizabeth he seemed to bid fair for long life. Her system, clear, decisive, and regular, suited the character of his mind, and had become engrafted on his habits; but the care and anxiety attendant on the superintendence of an uncertain policy, and an impoverished revenue, gradually undermined his re-established health. In 1611 he showed manifest signs of decay, and at length fell into a pulmonary consumption, in the last stage of which he was advised to use the waters of Bath, and, after a few weeks' ineffectual trial of them, died, on his return from thence, on the twenty-fourth of May, 1612, at Marlborough, and was buried in the parish church of his princely seat of Hatfield in Herts. He married Elizabeth, daughter of William Brook, Lord Cobham, by whom he had one son, William, his successor, lineal ancestor of the present Marquis of Salisbury, and one daughter, Frances, wife of Henry Clifford, fifth Earl of Cumberland.

Engraved by W. Finden.

HENRY, PRINCE OF WALES.

OB. 1612.

FROM THE ORIGINAL OF MYTENS, IN THE COLLECTION OF

HIS GRACE, THE DUKE OF DORSET.

London, Published Dec. 31, 1836, by Harding & Lepard, Pall Mall East.

HENRY, PRINCE OF WALES

HENRY FREDERICK OF WALES.

HENRY, PRINCE OF WALES.

An attempt was made some years since to write at large the life of this admirable youth in the usual strain of regular biography, but it proved wholly ineffectual. Dr. Birch, with that indefatigable assiduity and accuracy by which he was distinguished, drew together from all authentic sources that he could discover, perhaps every letter extant which the Prince had ever received; every dedication which had ever been addressed to him; every public instrument regarding his government, his establishment, and his revenue; together with long original narratives of the tiltings and dancings in which he had taken a part, and of the entertainments which had been provided for him in his several visits and progresses. All this is useless. The life of Prince Henry was a life of prospects, and not of events; the story of a manly childhood, and a wise puberty, subjected to the customary restraints of youth, and debarred by authority from rising into public action: it is therefore chiefly in those detached sallies of character which vainly promised a splendid future fame that we are to seek for his circumscribed history. Sir Charles Cornwallis, Treasurer of his Household, was sensible of this, and has treated his subject accordingly, in a very small but interesting piece, entitled, "The Life and Death of our late most incomparable and heroique Prince, Henry Prince of Wales;" which Birch, in his passion for biographical mechanism,

1

has ventured, in the preface to his own work, to call "a mere pamphlet, extremely superficial, and unsatisfactory on almost every head."

Henry was born in Stirling Castle, in Scotland, on the nineteenth of February, 1594. The care of his person, and of his early education, was almost immediately committed to John Erskine, Earl of Mar, and the Dowager Countess, his mother, who is said to have been a singularly ill-tempered woman, and from them he was removed, at the age of six years, to the custody of Adam Newton, a very learned Scotsman, on whom James, after his accession to the throne of England, conferred the title of Baronet, and, though a layman, the Deanery of Durham. It was at this very early period of his life that his father printed his "Basilicon Doron, or his Majesty's Instructions to his dearest Son, Henry the Prince," confining the impression to seven copies, and swearing the printer to secrecy; a work which, in the vanity of his heart, he afterwards published to the whole world, under the pretence of correcting erroneous transcripts which he alleged had got abroad, in spite of all his caution. Thus trained, in a half civilised country and court, incessantly under the controul and direction of a pedantic and narrow-minded father, and of a mother lately imported from a land actually barbarous, little might reasonably have been expected from a pupil so situated. A mighty character, however, of nature overcame all these disadvantages. Henry, even from his cradle, gave infallible proofs of the best and greatest qualities. His courage, perhaps the first virtue clearly discernible in infancy, was most undaunted. It is recorded of him, that when he happened to hurt himself, even severely, in the eagerness of his infantine sports, he cried not, but concealed and denied the injury. This disposition soon took a military turn. Looking at a chace which he was too young to be allowed to follow, one of his attendants asked him whether he should like that sport. He answered, "Yes, but I should better like another kind of hunting; the hunting of thieves and rebels, with brave men and horses."

2

La Boderie, ambassador from Henry the Fourth of France to James, in a letter to the French Minister, of the 31st of October, 1606, writes thus of him : " None of his pleasures savour in the least of a child. He is a particular lover of horses, and of what belongs to them, but is not fond of hunting; and when he goes to it, it is rather for the pleasure of galloping than that which the dogs give him. He plays willingly enough at tennis, and at another Scottish diversion very like mall; but always with persons older than himself, as if he despised those of his own age. He studies for two hours every day, and employs the rest in tossing the pike, leaping, shooting with the bow, throwing the bar, vaulting, or some other such exercise, and is never idle. He is very kind and faithful to his dependents; supports their interests against all persons whatsoever; and pushes his endeavours for them, or others, with a zeal which seldom fails of success. He is already feared by those who have the management of affairs, and especially by the Earl of Salisbury, who appears to be greatly apprehensive of the Prince's ascendancy: while the Prince, on the other hand, shews very little esteem for his Lordship." The testimony of this foreigner deserves implicit credit, and, be it remembered, that he is speaking of a child just thirteen years old.

As his reason unfolded itself, all the milder virtues gradually shone forth in him. Such was his entire love of sincerity, that he could not endure even the innocent and usual fallacies of polite intercourse. Sir Charles Cornwallis informs us, that having laid before him, for his signature, a letter to a nobleman of whom he had no good opinion, which ended with some common-place expressions of favour, the Prince commanded him to make another copy, the concluding words of which he himself dictated, saying that his hand should never affirm what his heart did not think. " He was so exact" (says an anonymous Harleian MS. addressed to the Lord and Lady Lumley, and entitled " A Relation of Prince Henry's noble and virtuous Disposition, and of sundry his witty and pleasant Speeches") " in all the duties of filial piety, and bore so true a reverence and respect to the King, his father, that, though sometimes he moved his Majesty in some things relating to the public, or his own particular interests, or those of others, yet on the least word, or look, or sign, given him of his Majesty's disapprobation, he would instantly desist from pursuing the point; and return, either with satisfaction, upon finding it disagreeable to the King, or with such a resolved patience, that he, neither in word nor action, gave any appearance of being displeased or discontented." He was strictly pious, and most exact in the exercise of his public and private devotions, and had such an aversion to the profanation of the name of God that he was never heard to use it but devoutly: indeed he abhorred swearing, which, probably because the King himself was much addicted to it, was the fashion of his time. It happened one day when he was hunting that the stag crossed a road in which a butcher and his dog were passing: the dog fell on the stag, and killed it, and the Prince's attendants endeavouring to incense him against the man, he answered, "If the dog killed the stag, could the butcher help it?" One of them hereupon took the liberty to say that if the King's hunting had been interrupted by such an accident he would have sworn terribly. "Nay," said the Prince, "all the pleasure in the world is not worth an oath."

Cornwallis informs us that he loved and practised justice with the utmost strictness. He manifested this disposition particularly in the government of his own family, which consisted of nearly five hundred of all ranks, in which it is said that a blow was never given, nor a quarrel carried to any height. "Whatever abuses," says that gentleman, "were represented to him he immediately redressed, to the entire satisfaction of the parties aggrieved. In his removal from one of his houses to another, and in his attendance on the King, on the same occasions, or in progresses, he would suffer no provisions or carriages to be taken up for his use, without full contentment given to the parties; and he was so solicitous to prevent any person from being prejudiced or annoyed by himself, or any of his train, that whenever he went out to hunt or hawk before harvest was ended, he would take care that none should pass through the corn, and, to set them an example, would himself ride rather a furlong about."

These admirable moral dispositions ornamented an excellent understanding, and governed a temper naturally very haughty. Never failing in any of the duties of the mere man, Henry, in all he thought, or said, or did, seemed to have constantly in his view the great inheritance which his birth had fallaciously promised to him. His household was a little monarchy, which he ruled with equal power, policy, and benignity. He was master, theoretically, of the art of war, and may indeed be said in some measure to have practised it, for he used the frequent military exercises, for his adroitness in which he was so highly distinguished, in order to qualify himself for the field. Cornwallis informs us that "he performed them with so much dexterity and skill, that he became second to no Prince in Christendom, and superior to most of those persons who practised with him;" and adds that, " he sometimes walked fast and far, to enable himself to make long marches, when they should be required." He was critically versed in all that related to the navy, even to the most minute circumstances of ship-building, and no one was more highly favoured by him than Phineas Pett, a man who had applied to the study and practice of naval architecture talents which would have rendered him eminent in any other to which he might have directed them. " He loved and did mightily strive," says Cornwallis, "to do somewhat of every thing, and to excel in the most excellent. He greatly delighted in all kind of rare inventions and arts, and in all kind of engines belonging to the wars both at land and sea; in shooting and levelling great pieces of ordnance; in the ordering and marshalling of armies; in building and gardening; in all sorts of rare music, chiefly the trumpet and drum; in sculpture, limning, and carving; and in all sorts of excellent and rare pictures, which he had brought unto him from all countries." The same author, and we cannot

5

have a better authority, tells us that " he was extremely courteous and affable to strangers, and easily gained their affections upon a very short acquaintance," but that " he had a certain height of mind, and knew well how to keep his distance; which indeed he did to all, admitting no near approach, either to his power or his secrets."

His fault indeed, and perhaps his only fault, seems to have been a degree of reserve so strict and constant, that it could not but have been the result of a temper naturally cold and distrustful. At a time of life usually marked by the sweet errors of over confidence, and extravagant affections, Henry appears but uncertainly in the character either of friend or lover. In the long list of his companions and attendants, Sir John Harington, son, and for a short time successor, to the first Lord Harington of Exon, a young man of great attainments and the most amiable qualities, seems alone to have enjoyed his intimacy. Among the very few private letters written by the Prince which have been preserved is one to this gentleman, on some subjects of classical criticism, full of sprightliness and ingenuity, but without a single expression of kindness. Still less proof have we of his sacrifices to the tender passion. Cornwallis tells us, in terms which sound oddly enough in our day, that, "having been present at great feasts made in the Prince's house, to which he invited the most beautiful of the ladies of the Court and City, he could not discover by his Highness's behaviour, eyes, or countenance, the least appearance of a particular inclination to any of them, nor was he at any time witness of such words or actions as could justly be a ground of the least suspicion of his virtue." Some historical pamphleteers, on the other hand, insist that he had a successful intrigue with the beautiful and wicked Countess of Essex, to which they ascribe strange consequences, which will presently be mentioned ; but this, if true, was but a solitary amour.

He had certainly formed for himself a line of political conduct which, according to the unhappy fatality, for so it seems, in such cases, was directly opposite to that of his father. His high spirit, and the activity of his nature, had irresistibly inspired him with a warlike inclination; and the strictness of his moral and religious habits and exercises, together with an utter aversion to the Romish church, rendered him the idol of the puritans, to whom, on his part, he gave many indirect proofs of favour. " He was saluted by them," says the severe but sagacious Osborne, "as one prefigured in the Apocalypse for Rome's destruction." He seems to have been determined never to marry a Roman Catholic. James, in 1611, had proposed to him the eldest daughter of the Duke of Savoy, and Raleigh, then a prisoner in the Tower, whom the King feared, and therefore hated, and of whom Henry had said that no one but his father would "keep such a bird in a cage," wrote, doubtless with the Prince's approbation, since they were dedicated to him, two admirable invectives against the match. A princess of Spain was afterwards offered to him; and in the spring of 1612 a negociation was commenced for his marriage to a sister of Louis the Thirteenth of France, which subsisted even at the time of his death, of the probable termination of which we may judge from his own declaration in his last hours, that he believed the Almighty had visited him with his grievous distemper to punish him for having listened to overtures of marriage with Roman Catholics. His discretion, his temperance, his economy, and the severity, as it may be called, of his manners, operated with the effect of satire and reproach on the contrary dispositions in the King, who by degrees became jealous of him, and in the end probably considered him as a formidable rival. Indeed James must have possessed supernatural philosophy to have endured the extent of his son's popularity. "The palpable partiality," says Osborne again, "that descended from the father to the Scots did estate the whole love of the English upon his son Henry, whom they engaged by so much expectation, as it may be doubted, whether it ever lay in the power of any Prince, merely human, to bring so much felicity into a nation as they did all his life propose to themselves at the death of King James."

These extravagant hopes were suddenly blasted in the autumn of 1612. He was then in his nineteenth year. Some change appeared to have taken place in his constitution a few months before: he grew pale and thin, and more serious than usual; had heavy pains in his head, and occasional fainting fits; and generally received a temporary relief from sudden bleedings at the nose, which of late had been wholly suspended, owing, as it was thought, to his imprudent practice of too frequent swimming in the Thames when at his palace at Richmond. In August, and when the weather was uncommonly hot, he rode post in two days to Belvoir Castle, the seat of the Earl of Rutland, to meet the king on his progress, and returned suddenly from the fatiguing ceremonies of that visit to prepare a great feast for the court on his taking possession of the royal house of Woodstock, which his father had lately assigned to him. These violent exertions produced an aggravated attack of his indispositions, which caused at length what his medical attendants conceived to be a fit of ague, but what was in fact the commencement of a fever of the most furious character. His numerous physicians, according to the error of that time, plied him for six days with what they called cordial restoratives, and vehemently increased the malignity of his disease. One only, and his name shall be recorded, Sir Theodore Mayerne, urged the necessity of bleeding, but he was obstinately opposed by the rest of the troop. Two days were suffered to pass before they could be brought to consent, and even then it was deferred till the next morning, though nature had, previously to Mayerne's suggestion, given them the signal for his cure, by one of those sudden discharges of blood from the nose to which he had been accustomed, and which produced an immediate temporary relief. At length only seven or eight ounces were permitted to be drawn, the miserable sufferer, says Cornwallis, "desiring and calling upon them to take more, as they were about to stop the same, finding some ease as it were upon the instant." "This day, after bleeding," adds Sir Charles, "the Prince found great ease, insomuch as since the beginning of his

8

sickness he had not found himself so well; his pulse inclining towards a more gentle motion; missing his former cruel doublings; and his former accidents being less, and more mild:" yet, incredible to tell, the bleeding was never repeated. Delirium and agonizing convulsions soon followed. Still, such was the strength of his constitution, that he lived for some days, displaying in his intervals of reason the most beautiful and affecting example of patience and fortitude. He died on Friday, the sixth of November, 1612, notwithstanding that the sages, as Cornwallis informs us, "had lately applied to the soles of his feet a cock cloven by the back, and had redoubled their cordials in number and quantity." A most exact and lengthened journal of his illness, and of the means resorted to for his cure, may be found in that gentleman's narrative, exhibiting perhaps the most extraordinary and frightful instances extant of medical presumption and imbecility. Rumours were spread that he died by poison, and Carre, Viscount Rochester, then the guilty suitor, and afterwards the more guilty husband, of the Countess of Essex, was for a time suspected as the murderer; but they obtained little credit, and certainly deserved none.

Sir Charles Cornwallis concludes his little book with the following sketch of the person of this extraordinary young man. "He was of a comely tall middle stature, about five feet and eight inches high; of a strong, strait, well made body, as if nature in him had shewed all her cunning; with somewhat broad shoulders, and a small waste; of an amiable majestic countenance; his hair of an auborn colour; long faced, and broad forehead; a piercing grave eye; a most gracious smile, with a terrible frown."

Engraved by H. Robinson.

HENRY HOWARD, EARL OF NORTHAMPTON.

OB. 1614.

FROM THE ORIGINAL OF ZUCCHERO, IN THE COLLECTION OF

THE RIGHT HON.BLE THE EARL OF CARLISLE.

London, Published Dec.r 1 1836 by Harding & Lepard, Pall Mall East.

HENRY HOWARD,

EARL OF NORTHAMPTON.

THE circumstances of this nobleman's life have been made the subjects of discussion more minute than impartial, and of animadversion more severe than just. While his talents and acquirements ornamented the name even of Howard, his conduct perhaps threw some shades on its almost unvaried purity. He was one of the very few of that family who ever condescended to practise the littlenesses of the statesman or courtier, and he has been, if the expression may be allowed, posthumously punished for so forgetting himself; but, as praise or blame, especially the latter, generally outrun the merits which respectively call them forth, his character seems to have been devoted to much undeserved censure.

He was the second son of that prodigy of worth, and talent, and gallantry, Henry, Earl of Surrey, by Frances, third daughter of John de Vere, thirteenth Earl of Oxford. He was born at Shottisham, in Norfolk, in 1539, and was yet an infant when his family was overwhelmed by that persecution of it which terminated the enormities of the reign of Henry the Eighth. As he grew towards manhood, he found himself a younger son, standing alone in the world. His admirable father had been snatched from him by an unjust sentence, and an ignominious execution. His grandfather, Thomas, third Duke of Norfolk, had barely outlived the proscription of his House; and his only brother, the youthful heir to mutilated estates just released from an

1

attainder, was waiting the very uncertain decision of Elizabeth's caprice as to the future fortunes of his family. Cramped and chilled by these untoward circumstances, and avoiding with difficulty the gripe of poverty, Lord Henry Howard became selfish and misanthropic, and suffered his vigorous and sober understanding to degenerate into a mysterious cunning which became habitual, and seems to have influenced his conduct through the whole of a long life.

He received his education first at King's College, and afterwards at Trinity Hall, in Cambridge; and left that university, says Bishop Godwin, with so high a character for erudition, that he was commonly called "the learnedst among the nobility, and the noblest among the learned." Having passed some years in foreign travel, he returned to work his way as well as he could in the most jealous and capricious court then in Europe. Neither his merits nor his misfortunes obtained any consideration from Elizabeth beyond his restoration in blood in her first year; nor was it till towards the conclusion of her long reign that he obtained from her a degree of favour which consisted merely in the empty graces of royal civility, and that he seems to have owed to the influence of Essex, with whom he lived in a strict intimacy. Her distaste to him, however, was not altogether unreasonable, for he was all but a declared Papist, and had been strongly suspected of favouring the cause of the Queen of Scots; that cause for which his elder brother bled on the scaffold.

He was amply compensated by her successor. He had been deeply engaged in the negotiations with that Prince which were carried on by Sir Robert Cecil, with not less activity than secrecy, in the concluding years of Elizabeth's life, and experienced an uncommon share of his gratitude. James, on his accession, summoned him to the Privy Council; on the first of January, in the succeeding year, made him Lord Warden of the Cinque Ports, and Constable of Dover Castle; and on the thirteenth of August following advanced him to the dignities of Baron Howard, of Marnhill, and Earl of Northampton. He was soon after constituted one of the Commissioners for executing the office of Earl Marshal; was installed a Knight of the Garter on the twenty-fourth of February, 1605; and on the twenty-ninth of April, 1608, appointed Lord Privy Seal. He was also Chancellor of the University of Cambridge, and High Steward of Oxford. His conduct in his several public offices stands unimpeached, but his private intercourse with the great men of his time has been charged with treachery. He is said to have alternately played off, as the phrase is, Essex and the two Cecils against each other. Certain it is that letters remain from him to those several parties full of the high-toned and hyperbolical expressions of regard which rendered ridiculous the epistolary correspondence of the great in that time, and which he bestowed on all the three in an equal measure. If flattery of that sort can be deemed treachery, he was treacherous indeed; but if it cannot, he must be held guiltless of the charge till stronger evidence can be produced: at present we know of none.

His memory has been defamed too by an accusation of a far deeper cast, which seems not better proved than the former. He had the misfortune to be great-uncle to Frances, Countess of Essex, the frightful circumstance of whose divorce from her Lord, and subsequent marriage to Robert Carre, Earl of Somerset, have been so largely detailed by the historians and memoir-writers of that time. Whether to salve what might have remained of the Countess's reputation, or to court the good graces of Somerset, the new favourite, it is impossible to say, but he certainly made himself a busy instrument in forwarding the match. Possessed of that fact, a late noble writer who had a remarkable talent for defaming the characters of the illustrious dead with the greatest imaginable neatness and politeness, determined to load it with all the mischief of historical conjecture, and, on the authority of two letters in Winwood's Memorials, roundly accuses Lord North-ampton of the murder of Sir Thomas Overbury, who was said to have been poisoned in the Tower, through the vindictive intrigues of the Earl and Countess of Somerset.

3

The letters in question were copied by the editor of Winwood from the originals in the Cotton Collection, now in the British Museum, where they may be found in the volume marked "Titus B 4, page 479," &c. They were written by the Earl to Sir Gervase Elwes, Lieutenant of the Tower, immediately after Overbury's death in his custody there. In the first of them (that is to say in that which stands first in the book, for they are not dated), the Earl, by Lord Rochester's (afterwards Somerset) request, desires that "the body may be delivered to any friend of the deceased who may wish to do him honour at his funeral;" and then expresses a doubt whether it may not have been already buried, "on account of its unsweetness, the deceased having been afflicted with some issues." In a postscript he desires the Lieutenant to inform himself whether "this grace hath been afforded formerly to close prisoners." This letter has a remarkable indorsement in the hand-writing of the Lieutenant, stating that on Overbury's death he had written to the Earl to know what he should do with the corpse, "acquainting his Lordship with his issues, and other foulness of his body;" and that the Earl, in answer, had desired him to have it viewed by a jury; and that he would "send for Sir John Lidcote, and as many else of his friends to see it as would." Elwes adds, "the body was very noisome, so that, notwithstanding my Lord's direction, I kept it over long, as we all felt."

In the second letter, to which the indorsement just now cited seems to refer, the Earl earnestly desires that the body may be buried with as little delay as possible, "for," says he, "it is time, considering the humours of the damned crew that only desire means to move pity, and raise scandals." In this letter, however, which is very short, he directs, four several times, that the body should be viewed by the friends of the deceased, previously to its interment.

It would have been but honest in the editor of Winwood to have noticed a third letter, in the same volume, written before Overbury's death, which could scarcely have been overlooked by

4

any one who inspected the originals. Had he inserted it, however, it would have deprived him of the opportunity of uttering the malignant hint which we find attached to the others, in one of the very few notes which are scattered on the pages of his collection; and, by omitting it, he has misled the opinions of Lord Orford, and of Sir Egerton Brydges, the candour and accuracy of whose pen are even equal to its elegance. In that third letter, the Earl informs Sir Gervase Elwes that, " in compliance with old Mr. Overbury's petition, it is the King's pleasure that Mr. Doctor Cragg, this bearer, shall presently be admitted to Sir Thomas Overbury, that, during the time of his infirmity, he may take care of him, and as often as in his judgment to this end he shall find reason."

Surely these letters, instead of tending to criminate the Earl, exonerate him : nay, they go much further, for they throw a strong doubt on the received opinion that Overbury did not die a natural death. If he were really murdered, can we believe that the Lieutenant of the Tower, and his officers; the physician who attended Sir Thomas, and by the appointment too of his father, in his last illness; the jury, and his own private friends, who viewed his body after death; could possibly have agreed to conceal so horrible a fact? or, if we could suppose that they did so agree at the time, that not an individual, of so many, should ever have divulged it? With these questions, however, this work has no concern, further than as they may apply to the subject immediately before us, to which, after this apology, we may now turn with more satisfaction.

The Earl of Northampton saved from those revenues which himself had acquired a very considerable sum, without unbecoming parsimony, for he was famous for his scrupulous imitation of the grandeur of the ancient nobility in his public appearance, and in his household; and he built that sumptuous palace at Charing-Cross, which was then called Northampton, afterwards Suffolk, and of late years Northumberland-House, in which he ended his life. He founded also three hospitals; at Greenwich, at Clun in

Shropshire, and at Castlerising in Norfolk. His learning, as I have observed, has been highly celebrated, and his natural talents were little inferior to his learning. He employed himself much in his leisure hours with literary composition, and in 1583 printed, at the Earl of Arundel's Press, a very large work, with the following prolix title, which will sufficiently explain its nature and intention—"A Defensative against the Poyson of supposed Prophesies, not hitherto confuted by the penne of any man; which, being grounded eyther uppon the warrant and authority of old paynted Bookes, Expositions of Dreames, Oracles, Revelations, Invocations of damned Spirits, Judicialls of Astrology, or any other kinde of pretended knowledge whatsoever, de futuris Contingentibus, have been causes of great disorder in the Commonwealth, and cheefely among the simple and unlearned People. Very needfull to be published at this time, considering the late offence, which grew by most palpable and grose errours in Astrologie."

The "late Offence" to which he alludes, and which, as Lord Northampton seldom acted without a particular view, probably furnished the motive to this Treatise, is not to be discovered in history, but the book itself is indeed the result of a prodigious extent of study, equally abundant in scriptural and classical learning, and full of good argument, continually illustrated by curious anecdotes, as well modern as ancient. The rest of his works remain unpublished. Two Treatises to justify female government, the one in the Harleian, the other in the Bodleian Collection: "An Abstract of the frauds of the Officers of the Navy," among the King's MSS. "A Defence of the French Monsieur's desiring Queen Elizabeth in marriage," also in the Harleian; and some devotional pieces in other departments of the library of the Museum. But the great treasure of his remains is a volume of twelve hundred pages, in the Cotton MSS. marked Titus C 6, consisting of private letters, speeches in Parliament, small treatises, prayers, detached maxims and observations, poems, &c. written at all times of his life, and here transcribed almost wholly with his own hand. In the authorities which I have consulted for the present purpose I find no notice taken of this very curious collection, which, even from the cursory inspection which I have been able to bestow on it, appears to contain matters of inestimable importance to the history of his time.

This extraordinary man died, unmarried, on the fifteenth of June, 1614. "The Earl of Northampton," says Sir Henry Wotton, in a letter to Sir Edmund Bacon, " having, after a lingering fever, spent more spirits than a younger body could well have borne, by the incision of a wennish tumour on his thigh, yesternight, between eleven and twelve of the clock, departed out of this world."

In his Will, which is dated only on the day before his death, is this passage—" I recognize, with all the loyallnes of my harte, the exceeding extraordinarie love, favour, and bountie, of my most deare and gracious Soveraigne, whom I have found ever so constant to me his unworthy sarvant as no devises of myne enimyes could ever draw or divert his goodnes from me. I most humbly beseech his excellent Majestie to accept, as a poore remembrance of me his faythefull sarvant, a ewer of golde, of one hundred pounds value, with one hundred jacobine pieces of twenty two shillings a peece therein ; on which ewer my desyer is there should be this inscription :—Detur Dignissimo." He was buried in the church of Dover Castle.

Engraved by J. Cochran.

LADY ARABELLA STUART.

OB. 1615.

FROM THE ORIGINAL OF VAN SOMER IN THE COLLECTION OF

THE MOST NOBLE THE MARQUIS OF BATH.

London, Published Dec. 1. 1835. by Harding & Lepard, Pall Mall East.

LADY ARABELLA STUART.

———

IT is surprising that so little attention should have been hitherto bestowed on the fair subject of this memoir. Not more distinguished by royal lineage than by admirable talents and worth; importantly connected with the history of her time, while her private life was marked by events so strange as to resemble the fictions of romance; a victim to various and almost unceasing calamity, and at length a martyr to the vilest persecution; the circumstances of her story have been hitherto suffered to remain in a great measure uncollected. It is true that her name appears in some works of general biography, and it is true also that the articles to which it is prefixed are always superficial, and in many instances erroneous.

She was the only child of Charles Stuart, fifth Earl of Lenox, by Elizabeth, daughter of Sir William Cavendish, of Hardwick, in Derbyshire, and is supposed to have been born in 1577. Her father, unhappily for her, was of the royal blood both of England and Scotland, for he was a younger brother of King Henry, father of James the Sixth, and great-grandson, through his mother, who was a daughter of Margaret, Queen of Scots, to our Henry the Seventh. This illustrious misfortune, from which she derived no kind of claim to the throne of Scotland, and but a remote chance of inheriting the English crown, rendered her equally obnoxious to the caution of Elizabeth, and the timidity of James, and they secretly dreaded the supposed danger of her leaving a legitimate offspring. Many subordinate circumstances concurred to increase their aver-

1

sion. She had been born in England, where her father died in the twenty-first year of his age, and admirably educated under the care of her grandmother, the old Countess of Lenox, who resided in London. Her manners, her habits, and her attachments, were therefore entirely English, and her character displayed, together with a fine understanding and high accomplishments, a heart so kind, so frank, and so innocent, and such a lively humour, as ensured the admiration and delight of all who knew her. Her exalted rank kept her almost always within the circle of a Court to which she was the chief ornament, and she became there the object of that meaner and more common sort of jealousy which constantly follows superior merit. A disgust of a graver order succeeded; and Princes and Statesmen thought that they discerned in the spontaneous tribute of regard which her perfections demanded the views of a party which had conspired to raise her to the throne. It is true that some of those busy and intriguing spirits, from which no State can ever be entirely free, had occasionally glanced at her presumptive title, and even urged some fantastic arguments in favour of her succession to Elizabeth; and the well known father Persons, in his hatred to that Princess, to whom he was conscious that no theme of disquisition could be more odious, collected their reasonings in a pamphlet of no small extent, which he dedicated to the Earl of Essex, and printed in 1594, under the assumed name of Richard Dolman. This work, although the author had the candour to deny Arabella's claim to the immediate inheritance, published her name and descent in every part of Europe: she became for a time the subject of frequent conversation in all the foreign Courts, and the suspicion in which she was already held at home naturally increased.

James, who beheld her with complacency till he had ascended the throne of England, earnestly desired to marry her to his cousin, Esme Stuart, whom he had created Duke of Lenox, and whom, before the birth of his own children, he had considered as his heir; but this match was prevented by Elizabeth, under the false pretence that Lenox was a papist. A son of the Earl of Northumberland then addressed her, and was favourably received. Their correspondence, which the great Thuanus mistakingly asserts to have proceeded to a marriage, was necessarily carried on in privacy, but was presently discovered, and she was placed for a time in confinement, by the Queen's order, but released without further punishment. Thus injured as she had been by Elizabeth, the death of that Princess increased the measure of her misfortunes. Soon after the accession of James, Raleigh, having ruined his own credit with the King by his endeavours to undermine Cecil's, plunged into that conspiracy with the Brooks, so fatal to himself, of which little is known but that its main object was to place her on a throne to which she had neither inclination nor pretensions, and by means unknown to herself. During his trial, at which she was present, on the first mention of her name in the evidence, Cecil rose, and said, " here hath been a touch of the Lady Arabella Stuart, a near kinswoman of the King's. Let us not scandal the innocent by confusion of speech. She is as innocent of all these things as I, or any man here, only she received a letter from my Lord Cobham to prepare her, which she laughed at, and immediately sent it to the King." The old Earl of Nottingham, who stood by her, added, " the Lady doth here protest upon her salvation that she never dealt in any of these things, and so she wills me to tell the court ;" and Cecil proceeded—" The Lord Cobham wrote to my Lady Arabella to know if he might come and speak with her, and gave her to understand that there were some about the King that laboured to disgrace her : she doubted it was but a trick ; but Brook, Lord Cobham's brother, saith that my Lord moved him to procure the Lady Arabella to write to the King of Spain ; but he affirms that he never did move her as his brother devised." Whether these noblemen seriously meant to exculpate her may perhaps be doubtful ; but we have abundant reason to believe that they spoke the truth, since no trace of historical intelligence is to be found that tends to implicate her as an active party in this most obscure, and even ridiculous design.

Some reflections however had been cast on her by one of the witnesses, for Michael Hickes, reciting some particulars of Raleigh's trial, in a letter to her uncle, Gilbert Talbot, Earl of Shrewsbury, of the sixth of December, 1603, writes—" They say the La. Arbella's name came to be mentioned in the evidence against him, but she was cleared in the opinion of all, and, as I hard, my Ld C. spake very honourably on her behalf; but one that gave in evydence, as it is sayd, spake very grossly and rudely concerninge her La. as I thynk yor L^p hath hard, or shall heare." It is worthy of remark that the passages alluded to by Mr. Hickes do not appear in the printed accounts of Raleigh's trial, in which her name is mentioned only in the indictment; and it should seem that the notes of those parts of the evidence had been suppressed, while the apologetic addresses of the two Lords, to which they had given occasion, were inadvertently suffered to be published. It must be inferred then that James, and his government, not only believed her to be innocent, but were inclined even to favour her, for the trial could not have been published but with their sanction : yet she appears at that time to have lost her credit at Court, where she presently afterwards suffered, together with the mortification of being personally neglected by the royal family, the various vexations of a pecuniary embarrassment extending nearly to poverty. Under all these untoward circumstances, she had no prospect of protection but in marriage, while she durst not openly encourage the addresses of any suitor ; and persons of inferior rank, and with sordid views, availed themselves of her situation to make proposals to her which her terrors and distresses induced her to listen to, at least without the contempt which they deserved. Thus too she was forced into habits of deception and hypocrisy, contrary to her generous and candid nature. Fowler, Secretary and Master of Requests to Anne of Denmark, in a letter to the same Earl of Shrewsbury, of the third of October, in the following year, says—" My Lady Arbella spends her time in lecture, reiding, hearing of service and preaching, and visiting all the Princesses. She will not heare

4

of marriage. Inderectlie ther wer speaches used in the recom-mendation of Count Maurice, who pretendeth to be Duke of Gueldres. I dare not attempte her."

Matters proceeded thus till Christmas 1608, when James appears to have received her into some degree of favour, for he gave her, according to the custom of court presents at that season, one thousand marks, to pay her debts, and plate to the amount of two hundred pounds. About this time he granted her, as will be presently shown by a document which has till now escaped notice, and which contradicts the report of all who have men-tioned this part of her story, his permission to marry, only restricting her choice to his own subjects. She determined on William Seymour, grandson, and afterwards heir to the Earl of Hertford, but a natural timidity, which had been increased by constant ill usage, joined perhaps to some doubt of the King's sincerity, or of his resolution, induced her still to dissemble, and they were married with the utmost privacy in January, or February, 1609. Her apprehensions were but too just. A rumour of unu-sual intimacy between them having been conveyed to the court, they were summoned before the Privy Council, and reprehended with great severity. As they were then suffered to escape without further punishment, it may be presumed that they yet denied their marriage, and were credited; but in the summer of the following year it was by some means fully discovered, and the Lady was committed to the custody of Sir Thomas Parry, in his house at Lambeth, and Mr. Seymour to the Tower of London, where, on his arrival, he was complimented by Melvin, a noncon-formist minister, then confined there, with a distich, the pretty quaintness of which may furnish an excuse for the momentary interruption of this narrative—

" Communis tecum mihi causa est carceris : Ara—
Bella tibi causa est ; araque sacra mihi."

It was probably at this precise period that Arabella addressed to the King the following petition, or letter, which has been pre-served in the Harleian collection, together with some other papers

of less moment relating to her marriage, among which is a declaration to the Privy Council by Sir Edward Rodney, that it was
solemnized in his presence, in her chamber at Greenwich.

May itt please your most excellent Matie.

I doe most hartily lament my hard fortune that I
should offend yor Matie, especiallie in that whereby I have longe
desired to meritt of yor Matie, as appeared before yor Matie was
my Soveraigne : and, thoughe yor Ma^{tie's} neglect of me, my good
likeinge of this gent. that is my husband, & my fortune, drewe me
to a contracte before I acquainted yor Matie, I humblie beseech
yor Matie to consider howe impossible itt was for me to ymagine itt
could be offensive unto yor Matie, havinge fewe days before geven
me your royall consent to bestowe myselfe on anie subject of yor
Ma^{tie's}, wch likewise yor Matie had done longe since. Besides, never
havinge ben either prohibited any, or spoken to for any, in this
land by yor Matie these 7 yeares that I have lived in yor Ma^{tie's}
house, I could not conceave that yor Matie regarded my mariage
att all ; whereas, if yor Matie had vouchsafed to tell me yor mynd,
and accepte the free will offeringe of my obedience, I would not
have offended yor Matie, of whose gratious goodness I presume so
much that, if itt weare as convenient in a worldlie respect as
mallice may make itt seame to seperate us whom God hath
joyned, yor Matie would not doe evill that good might come
thereof ; nor make me, that have the honor to be so neare yor
Matie in bloud, the first presedent that ever was, though our
Princes maie have lefte some as little imitable for so good and
gratious a Kinge as yor Matie as David's dealinge with Uriah. But
I assure myselfe, if it please yor Matie in yor owne wisedome to
consider throughlie of my cause, there will noe solide reason
appeare to debarre me of justice, and yor princelie favor, wch I will
endeavor to deserve whilst I breathe, and, never ceasinge to praie
for yor Ma^{tie's} felicitie in all thinges, remaine,

Your Ma^{tie's} &c.

The rigour with which they were first confined was soon abated.

She was allowed the range of Sir Thomas Parry's grounds, and at length placed under the charge of Sir James Crofts, in the house of a Mr. Conyers, at Highgate; and Mr. Seymour seems to have had nearly the freedom of a prisoner on parole. They took the advantage of this relaxation to correspond by letters; their intercourse was detected; and the King commanded that Arabella should be removed to Durham. Mutually terrified at the prospect of so total a separation, they determined to fly, and found means to concert a plan for their departure, which both effected on the same day, the third of June, 1611, unhappily, however, owing to some error in their appointment, never to meet again. The circumstances of their escape are related in a letter from a Mr. John More to Sir Ralph Winwood, dated on the eighth of that month, with a liveliness and simplicity which could not but be injured by describing them in any other form of words.

"On Monday last, in the afternoon," says Mr. More, "my Lady Arabella, lying at Mr. Conyers's house near Highgate, having induced her keepers and attendants into security by the fair shew of conformity, and willingness to go on her journey towards Durham, which the next day she must have done, and in the mean time disguising herself, by drawing a pair of great French-fashioned hose over her petticoats, pulling on a man's doublet, a man-like peruke, with long locks, over her hair, a black hat, black cloak, russet boots with red tops, and a rapier by her side, walked forth between three and four of the clock with Markham. After they had gone a-foot a mile and a half to a sorry inn, where Crompton attended with horses, she grew very sick and faint, so as the ostler that held the stirrups said that gentleman would hardly hold out to London; yet, being set on a good gelding astride, in an unwonted fashion, the stirring of the horse brought blood enough into her face; and so she rode on towards Blackwall, where arriving about six of the clock, finding there in a readiness two men, a gentlewoman, and a chambermaid, with one boat full of Mr. Seymour's and her trunks, and another boat for their persons. they hasted from thence towards Woolwich. Being

7

come so far, they bade the watermen row on to Gravesend : there the watermen were desirous to land, but for a double freight were contented to go on to Leigh, and by that time the day appeared, and they discovered a ship at anchor a mile beyond them, which was the French bark that waited for them. Here the lady would have lain at anchor, expecting Mr. Seymour, but, through the importunity of her followers, they forthwith hoisted sail seaward. In the mean while Mr Seymour, with a peruke and beard of black hair, and in a tawny cloth suit, walked alone without suspicion from his lodging, out of the great west door of the Tower, following a cart that had brought him billets. From thence he walked along by the Tower wharf, by the warders of the south gate, and so to the iron gate, where Rodney was ready with oars to receive him. When they came to Leigh, and found that the French ship was gone, the billows rising high, they hired a fisherman for twenty shillings to set them aboard a certain ship that they saw under sail. That ship they found not to be it they looked for ; so they made forward to the next under sail, which was a ship of Newcastle. This, with much ado, they hired for forty pounds to carry them to Calais, but whether the collier did perform his bargain or no is not as yet here known. On Tuesday, in the afternoon, my Lord Treasurer being advertised that the Lady Arabella had made an escape, sent forthwith to the Lieutenant of the Tower to set strait guard over Mr. Seymour ; but, coming to the prisoner's lodgings, he found, to his great amazement, that he was gone from thence one whole day before."

Mr. More, having stated some other matters not to our present purpose, adds—" Now the King, and the Lords, being much disturbed with this unexpected accident, my Lord Treasurer sent orders to a pinnace that lay at the Downs to put presently to sea, first to Calais roads, and then to scour up the coast towards Dunkirk. This pinnace, spying the aforesaid bark which lay lingering for Mr. Seymour, made to her, which thereupon offered to fly towards Calais, and endured thirteen shot of the pinnace before she would strike. In this bark is the lady taken, with her followers, and brought back towards the Tower, not so sorry for her own restraint as she would be glad if Mr. Seymour might escape, whose welfare she protesteth to affect much more than her own." He did in fact arrive safely in Flanders, where he remained for many years a voluntary exile.

The unfortunate Arabella was led a prisoner to London, and placed in the closest confinement. A great parade was made of the enormity of her crime, perhaps to maintain some consonance with the terms of a proclamation which had been issued for the apprehension of herself, and her husband, in which they were charged with " divers great and heinous offences." Her aunt, Mary Cavendish, Countess of Shrewsbury, was also committed to the Tower, and the Earl, her husband, confined in his own house. Even the Earl of Hertford, infirm and superannuated as he was, received a summons to repair instantly to the Court from his distant retirement. Arabella, and Lady Shrewsbury, were immediately questioned at great length by the Privy Council. The former, says More, in another letter to Winwood, " answered the Lords at her examination with good judgment and discretion, but the other is said to be utterly without reason, crying out that all is but tricks and giggs: that she will answer nothing in private: and if she have offended in law, she will answer it in public,"—a resolution surely not less reasonable than high-spirited. The same letter informs us that great contrariety of prejudice on the subject of her persecution arose between the English and Scottish parties ; the one averring that it was ridiculous to apprehend any design on the throne from pretensions so remote ; the other comparing the offence, for the perils that it involved, to the gunpowder treason ; " and so," adds More, who appears to have been a man of considerable ability and penetration, " it is said to fill his Majesty with fearful imaginations, and with him, the Prince, who cannot so easily be removed from any settled opinion."

After long-protracted and nice inquiry, no ground could be discovered for any criminal charge against either of them, yet they were suffered to remain close prisoners. Early, however, in the following year, it was suddenly reported to the Court that Arabella was inclined to make extraordinary disclosures, and she was again summoned before the Council, and preferred some strange and incoherent accusations against several persons, among whom was the Countess, her aunt, who was still in confinement: but it presently appeared that the frame of her mind had given way under the pressure of aggravated calamity and unjust seclusion. James and his ministers at length sacrificed to prudence what they had denied to justice and humanity, and all proceedings were dropped; but she was remanded to the Tower, where she soon after sank into helpless idiotcy, and survived in that wretched state till September, 1615, on the twenty-seventh of which month she was buried in Westminster Abbey, near the remains of her kinsman, Henry, Prince of Wales. We find in the poems of Richard Corbet, Bishop of Norwich, the following lines, by way of monumental inscription to her memory, which seem to challenge insertion here.

> " How do I thank ye, death, and bless thy power,
> That I have passed the guard, and 'scap'd the Tower !
> And now my pardon is my epitaph,
> And a small coffin my poor carcase hath ;
> For at thy charge both soul and body were
> Enlarg'd at last, secur'd from hope and fear.
> That amongst saints, this amongst Kings is laid,
> And what my birth did claim my death hath paid."

Nor shall I be blamed for concluding this memoir with one of her letters, which, as it has no relation to any particular part of her foregoing story, may perhaps be most properly placed here. The good sense, the elegancy of expression, the innocent playfulness, and the high politeness, with which she communicates the trifles of which it treats, will tend to prove the truth of the slight view which I have ventured to give of her character, and increase our pity for her sufferings, and our indignation against the memory of her persecutors. It is addressed to the Earl of Shrewsbury, and was written in the year 1603.

" At my returne from Oxford, wheare I have spent this day, whilest my Lo. Cecill, amongst many more weighty affaires, was despatching som of mine, I found my cousin Lacy had disburdened himselfe at my chamber of the charge he had from you, and straight fell to prepare his fraught back, for hindering his back returne to-morrow morning, as he intendeth.

" I writt to you of the reason of the delay of Taxis' audience : it remaineth to tell how jovially he behaveth himselfe in the interim. He hath brought great store of Spanish gloves, hauke's hoods, leather for jerkins, and, moreover, a perfumer. These delicacies he bestoweth amongst our ladies and lords, I will not say wth a hope to effeminate the one sex, but certainly wth a hope to grow gracious wth the other, as he already is. The curiosity of our sex drew many la. and gentlewomen to gaze at him betwixt his landing place and Oxford, his abiding place ; which he desirous to satisfy (I will not say nourish that vice) made his coche stop, and tooke occasion wth petty guiftes and cowrtesies to winne soone wonne affections ; who, comparing his manner wth Monsieur de Ronee's hold him theyr farre wellcomer guest. At Oxford he took som distast about his lodging, and would needes lodge at an inne, because he had not all Christe's Colledge to him selfe, and was not received into the towne by the Vice-chancellour, in pontificalibus, which they never use to do but to the King, or Queene, or Chancellour of the University, as they say ; but those scruples were soon disgested, and he vouchsafeth to lodge in a peece of the college till his repaire to the King at Winchester.

" Count Arimberg was heere wthin these few dayes, and pre-sented to the Queene the Archduke and the Infanta's pictures, most excellently drawne. Yesterday the King and Queene dined at a lodge of Sr Henry Lea's 3 miles hence, and weare accom-panied by the French Imbasadour, and a Dutch Duke. I will not say we weare merry at the Dutchkin, least you complaine of me for telling tales out of the Queene's coch ; but I could finde in my heart to write unto you som of our yesterdaye's adventures, but that it groweth late, and by the shortnesse of your letter, I conjecture you would not have this honest gentleman overladen wth such superfluous relations. My Lo. Admirall is returned from the Prince and Princesse, and either is or wil be my cousin before incredulous you will beleeve such incongruities in a councellour, as love maketh no miracles in his subjectes, of what degree or age whatsoever. His daughter of Kildare is discharged of her office, and as neere a free woman as may be, and have a bad husband. The Dutch Lady my Lo. Wotton spoke of at Basing proved a lady sent by the Dutchess of Holstein, to learne the English fashions. She lodgeth at Oxford, and hath binne heere twice, and thincketh every day long till she be at home, so well she liketh her entertainment, or loveth her owne countrey. In truth she is civill, and thearfore cannot but look for the like which she brings out of a ruder countrey : but if ever there weare such a vertu as curtesy at the Court, I marvell what is become of it, for I protest I see little or none of it but in the Queene, who ever since her coming to Newbury hath spoken to the people as she passeth, and receiveth theyr prayers wth thanckes, and thanckfull countenance, barefaced, to the great contentment of natife and forrein people ; for I would not have you thincke the French Imbassador would leave that attractive vertu of our late Queene El. unremembered or uncommended when he saw it imitated by our most gratious Queene, least you should thinke we infect even our neighbours wth incivility. But what a theame have rude I gotten unawares ! It is your owne vertu I commend by the foile of the contrary vice ; and so, thincking on you, my penne accused myselfe before I was aware ; therefore I will put it to silence for this time, only adding a short but most hearty prayer for your prosperity in all kindes, and so humbly take my leave. From Woodstocke, the 16 of September.

Yo^r Lo'. neece,

ARBELLA STUART."

Engraved by E. Scriven.

THOMAS EGERTON, VISCOUNT BRACKLEY,

LORD HIGH CHANCELLOR.

OB. 1617.

FROM THE ORIGINAL, IN THE COLLECTION OF

THE MOST NOBLE, THE MARQUIS OF STAFFORD.

PROOF

London, Published Jan.ʸ 1. 1829. by Harding & Lepard, Pall Mall East.

THOMAS EGERTON,

VISCOUNT BRACKLEY.

———◆———

THIS admirable person, whose virtues and whose wisdom have shed on his memory a fame which the utmost splendour of ancestry could not render more bright, was the natural son of Sir Richard Egerton, of Ridley, in Cheshire, by Alice, daughter of . . . . . Sparke, and was born in that county about the year 1540. At the age of sixteen he was admitted a commoner of Brazen Nose College, in Oxford, and removed from thence in 1559 to Lincoln's Inn, where he studied the law with equal assiduity and success, and acquired soon after his appearance at the bar, the highest distinction, as well for his eloquence as for his professional learning. Many years elapsed before he became a public officer, for he sought not for patronage, and abhorred intrigue. At length, on the twenty-eighth of June, 1581, Elizabeth appointed him her Solicitor-General, and he remained in that office, without further promotion, till the second of June, 1594, when he was placed in that of Attorney. On the tenth of April, 1596, he was raised to the place of Master of the Rolls, and on the sixth of the following month to that of Lord Keeper, on the sudden death of Sir John Puckering.

We have many testimonies that he owed this elevation to the Queen's sole favour, and that it was beheld by the people with the highest approbation. In a letter to the Earl of Essex, printed in Birch's Memoirs of Elizabeth, the writer, a Mr. Reynolds, says, " the Master of the Rolls has changed his style, and is made Lord Keeper, only by her Majesty's gracious favour and by her own

1

choice. I think no man ever came to this dignity with more applause than this worthy gentleman:" and in another, from Anthony Bacon to a friend at Venice, Mr. Bacon, having spoken of the death of the Lord Keeper, adds—"into whose place, with an extraordinary speed, her Majesty hath, ex proprio motu, et speciali gratiâ, advanced Sir Thomas Egerton, with a general applause, both of court, city, and country, for the reputation he hath of integrity, law, knowledge, and courage. It was his good hap to come to the place freely, without competitor or mediator ; yea, against the desire and endeavour, as it is thought, of the omnipotent couple ;" meaning, no doubt, the Cecils, father and son. Camden too, in his history of that year, says, " Puckering's place was supplied by Thomas Egerton, the Attorney General, of whose fair and equal deportment every one had conceived mighty hopes and expectations."

Nature, which had endowed him with all the grand principles whereon to form a statesman, had given him also dispositions which tended to render him unfit for that character. His perfect integrity, and the frank simplicity of his mind and heart, were ill suited to the practice of those artifices and frauds which exalt the fame of the politician while they ought to degrade that of the man. We hear little of him therefore in diplomatic negotiations, although it was the fashion of his time to entrust them mostly to eminent lawyers. He was a Commissioner in 1598 for treating with the United Provinces, chiefly on the subject of their debts to England ; again in 1600, for the arrangement of some affairs with Denmark ; and once more, towards the conclusion of his life, for the surrendering the cautionary towns into the hands of the States General. It is probable, however, that he was literally the keeper of the Queen's conscience, and that such of her affairs as could be submitted to the regulation of unmixed wisdom and honour were directed solely by his advice. Strictly of that nature was the mediation which Elizabeth secretly intrusted to him, by which she vainly sought to shield the amiable and frantic Essex against his own rage. The Lord Keeper and Essex lived in the strictest friendship and confidence. Their dispositions, to common observers, seemed to be dissimilar almost to opposition, but the perfect honesty of their hearts, that sublime principle, compared to which the petty differences of character among men will be found to be little more than habits, had bound them in a firm union. "They love and join very honourably together," says Anthony Racon, in another of his letters; " out of which correspondency, and noble conjunction, betwixt Mars and Pallas; betwixt justice and valour; I mean betwixt so admirable a nobleman as the Earl, and so worthy a justice as the Lord Keeper; I doubt not but very famous effects will daily spring, to her Majesty's honour, the good of the state, and the comfort of both their lordships' particular true friends." The unhappy circumstances which prevented those results form an interesting feature of our history, and have always been well known; but the kind and wise endeavours of Egerton to cool the fever of his friend's mind, to bring Essex to a just sense of his duty, and the Queen to a dispassionate consideration of his merits and infirmities, have been developed chiefly by the publication in Birch's memoirs of the correspondence which passed between them while Essex was smarting under the blow which he had received from the hand of Elizabeth. His subsequent submission has been ascribed to the arguments, at once mild and firm, of the Lord Keeper. On his hasty and imprudent return in the following year from his unfortunate campaign in Ireland, when it was judged necessary to restrain him from the seditious society into which he had thrown himself, he was committed to the hospitable custody of the same friend, in whose house he remained in an honourable captivity for more than six months. When the charges against him were there examined by a committee of the Privy Council, the Lord Keeper sat as president, and again earnestly endeavoured to save him; and, finally, submitted, with a patience and magnanimity equal to Essex's madness, to the indignity and danger of being locked up by that nobleman in Essex House, which he had visited unprotected, with conciliatory proposals from the Queen, exposed

3

to the fury of an infatuated mob, by which his life was every moment threatened. Their friendship was terminated but by the stroke under which the Earl soon after fell on the scaffold.

The accession of James brought him an increase of favour. On the third of May, 1603, he met the King at Broxborne, in Herts ; tendered his resignation of the Great Seal ; and was, with the most flattering expressions, commanded to retain it. On the nineteenth of July following, James, not by the customary warrant, but by a notice, as is said, in his own hand-writing, bestowed on him the title of Baron Ellesmere, " for his good and faithful services, not only in the administration of justice, but also in council, to the late Queen, and to himself." His patent for that honour was dated on the twenty-first of the same month, and on the twenty-fourth his great office was dignified by the more splendid style of Lord High Chancellor. Towards the end of that year he presided at the trials of the Lords Cobham and Grey, and in the next was one of the Commissioners for the union of Scotland to England, which was then ineffectually attempted. In 1605 he was appointed High Steward of the city, and in 1610 elected Chancellor of the University of Oxford, in which character he opposed his authority, with an earnest but well-tempered zeal, and with the strictest impartiality, against the popish and puritan parties which in his time had attained to a great, though unequal, ascendancy in that body. The Church of England never had a truer son, nor learning a more earnest friend ; those therefore who rose by his means were generally as much distinguished by their orthodoxy as by their erudition. Among the many who shared his favour the most remarkable were Bacon and Williams, the one selected from the law, the other from the church, and each of these filled at length the exalted seat which had been so long and so worthily held by their venerable patron. Bacon, indeed, was his immediate successor—a philosopher but in a narrow sense of the word, he had pressed, it is lamentable to say, with a disgusting and unfeeling eagerness, for the Seal long before the death of his benefactor. The fortunes of Williams were not yet

4

sufficiently ripe to enable him to tread on the heels of his illustrious friend. He was the Chancellor's chosen intimate and companion : lived in his house, and was his chaplain, being the first who had served any Chancellor in that capacity since the reformation. He succeeded to Bacon in the custody of the Seal, and became afterwards Bishop of Lincoln, and, finally, Archbishop of York.

The peace of Lord Ellesmere's latter days was somewhat clouded by an attack on the jurisdiction of his Court, which was indirectly encouraged by the great Chief Justice Coke, rather, as it should seem, from a natural turbulence, and busy restlessness of temper, than from any particular impression of malice or envy. The cause, progress, and termination, of this difference are narrated by Arthur Wilson, in his Life of James, with a clearness and conciseness which no alteration could amend. I shall therefore give his account in his own words.

" A little before this time " (in the autumn of 1615) " there was a breach between the Lord Chief Justice Coke and the Lord Chancellor Ellesmere, which made a passage to both their declines. Sir Edward Coke had heard and determined a cause at the common law, and some report there was juggling in the business. The witness that knew, and should have related, the truth, was wrought upon to be absent, if any man would undertake to excuse his non-appearance. A pragmatical fellow of the party undertook it ; went with the witness to a tavern : called for a gallon pot full of sack ; bade him drink ; and so leaving him, went into the Court. This witness is called for, as the prop of the cause. The undertaker answers, upon oath, that he left him ' in such a condition that if he continues in it but a quarter of an hour he is a dead man.' This evidencing the man's incapability to come, deaded the matter so that it lost the cause. The plaintiffs, that had the injury, bring the business about in chancery. The defendants, having had judgment at common law, refuse to obey the orders of the court ; whereupon the Lord Chancellor, for contempt of the court, commits them to prison ; they petition against him in the Star Chamber : The Lord Chief Justice joins

5

with them; foments the difference; threatening the Chancellor with a præmunire: the Chancellor makes the King acquainted with the business, who sent to Sir Francis Bacon, his Attorney General; Sir Henry Montague, and Sir Randolph Crewe, his Serjeants at law; and Sir Henry Yelverton, his Solicitor; commanded them to search what presidents there have been of late years wherein such as complained in Chancery were relieved, according to equity and conscience, after judgment at common law. These, being men well versed in their profession, after canvassing the matter thoroughly, returned answer to the King that there had been a strong current of practice and proceeding in Chancery after judgment in common law, and, many times, after execution, continued since Henry the seventh's time to the Lord Chancellor that now is, both in the reigns, seriatim, of the several Kings, and the times of the several Chancellors, whereof divers were great learned men in the law; it being in cases where there is no remedy for the subject by the strict course of the common law, unto which the judges are sworn. This," continues Wilson, "satisfied the King; justified the Lord Chancellor; and the Chief Justice received the foil, which was a bitter potion to his spirit."

A larger account of this memorable dispute may be found in a very long letter to the King from Sir Francis Bacon, which is printed in the general collection of his works, and elsewhere. The dexterity with which he avoids giving any decided opinion on a question of law on which James had undoubtedly called for his advice, and the flattery which he indirectly lavishes on that Prince's ruling foible, render it a singular curiosity: of the latter the following passage will be a sufficient specimen. "Two things I wish to be done: the one, that your Majesty take this occasion to redouble unto all your judges your ancient and true charge of rule, that you will endure no innovating the point of jurisdiction, but will have every court impaled within their own precedents, and not assume to themselves new powers, upon conceits and inventions of law: the other, that in these high causes that touch upon state and monarchy, your Majesty give them strait charge that, upon any occasions intervenial hereafter, they do not make the vulgar party to their contestations, by publicly handling them before they have consulted with your Majesty, to whom the reglement of those things only appertaineth." The matter terminated in Coke's utter disgrace. On the third of June, 1616, a commission was issued to the Archbishop of Canterbury, and others of the Council, to enquire who were the authors of calling the Chancellor into question of præmunire; and, on the third of the following October, he was cited, says Camden, in his Annals of King James, before the Chancellor; dismissed from his office of Chief Justice; banished Westminster Hall; and, further, ordered to answer some matters contained in his Reports. The truth is that James the more readily sided with the Chancellor in this affair because Coke had of late spoken too freely of the prerogative. He had said publicly in his court, glancing at some recent instance of royal interference, that "the common law of England would be overthrown, and the light of it obscured." The puisne judges also had indulged in the use of similar censures on different occasions, and the King now summoned them to his presence; reprimanded them severely: and required them to crave his pardon on their knees, to which all of them submitted except the Chief Justice, who stedfastly refused. It is but candid to confess that this humiliation was exacted with the Chancellor's concurrence, and was performed in his presence.

Lord Ellesmere, who had attained to the age of seventy-six, lay in a state of extreme illness during the heat of this contest. The flattering prospect, however, of its issue seems to have revived him, and, on the twenty-fourth of May he presided as Lord High Steward on the trials of the Earl and Countess of Somerset, for poisoning Sir Thomas Overbury. It has been said that he positively refused to affix the Seal to the pardon so unjustly granted to them by James; but it is scarcely credible that he who could advise, or at least silently witness, so undue an exertion of the royal prerogative as has been just now mentioned, would have resisted, as it were in the same hour, that exercise of it which has been in all ages implicitly allowed. Soon after this period he rapidly declined. In the autumn of 1616 he solicited James, by an affecting letter, to accept his resignation, which being kindly refused, he repeated his request by a second. The king and Prince flattered him by intreaties to retain his office, and, on the seventh of November in that year, he was advanced to the dignity of Viscount Brackley. At length, on the third of the following March, James, in a visit to him on his death bed, received the Seal from his hand with tears. He survived only till the fifteenth, when, half an hour before his departure, Sir Francis Bacon, the new Lord Keeper, waited on him to notify the King's intention to create him Earl of Bridgwater. He was buried at Dodleston, in Cheshire.

It may not be too much to say that for purity of reputation this great man's character stands distinguished from those of all other public ministers of this country in all ages; while for wisdom in council, profound knowledge of the laws, and general learning, he has seldom been excelled. Hacket, in his life of Archbishop Williams, says that he was a man " qui nihil in vitâ nisi laudandum aut fecit, aut dixit, aut sensit," for his domestic life was as exemplary as his public conduct. His attention to the extrajudicial duties of his high office was not less sedulous and constant than to the causes in his court. In a speech at the conference of divines at Hampton Court in 1603-4, he uttered these expressions, which deserve to be recorded in letters of gold. " Livings rather want learned men than learned men livings, many in the Universities pining for want of places. I wish therefore some may have single coats before others have doublets; and this method I have observed in bestowing the King's benefices." We have three professional tracts from his pen in print—His speech in the Exchequer Chamber in the case of Colvil of Culross, usually called the case of the Postnati, published in 1609 : " The Privileges and Prerogatives of the High Court of Chancery," in 1641 : and " Certain Observations concerning the Office of Lord Chancellor," in 1651. But his great Work, if it yet exists, remains in manu-script—four treatises on the High Court of Parliament; the Court of Chancery; the Starchamber; and the Council board. These, in his last hours, he gave to his chaplain, Williams, who some years after presented them to the King. He was thrice married; first, to Elizabeth, daughter of Thomas Ravenscroft, of Bretton, in the county of Flint, by whom he had two sons and one daughter; Sir Thomas Egerton, who served bravely under the Earl of Essex at Cadiz, and afterwards in Ireland, where he died unmarried; John, who succeeded his father, and was, within a few weeks after his death, created Earl of Bridgewater; and Mary, wife of Sir Francis Leigh, of Newnham Regis, in Warwickshire, Knight of the Bath. The Chancellor married secondly Elizabeth, sister to Sir George More, of Loseley, in Surrey, widow of Sir John Wolley, of Pitford, in the same county; and, thirdly, Alice, daughter of Sir John Spencer, of Althorpe, in Northamptonshire, and widow of Ferdinando, fifth Earl of Derby; but had no issue by either.

Engraved by H. Robinson.

SIR WALTER RALEIGH.

OB. 1618.

FROM THE ORIGINAL OF ZUCCHERO, IN THE COLLECTION OF

THE MOST NOBLE THE MARQUIS OF BATH.

London, Published June 1, 1829, by Harding & Lepard, Pall Mall East.

SIR WALTER RALEIGH.

———

The history of Raleigh has always been an object of anxious and busy enquiry, and the pains that have been taken to render it complete seem to have been rewarded with the most ample success. This will ever be the case with one who moved in so many spheres of action, and shone so brightly in such various classes of fame. The soldier will cherish the reputation of heroes; the critic, of writers; the politician, of statesmen; but in this individuality of attention, in this unconscious singleness of fellow feeling, how many inestimable notices of general character are overlooked, and irrecoverably lost! The life of Raleigh, on the other hand, was a sort of public property, in which every taste and every profession had an interest, and each therefore has lent a helping hand to raise and perfect the biographical monument which has been erected to his memory. To endeavour to add to such a story would be hopeless labour: to select from it can be little better than dull repetition.

Raleigh was descended from a family of high antiquity in Devonshire. He was a younger son of a gentleman of his names who was seated in a mansion called Fardel, in the parish of Cornwood, near Plymouth, by his third wife, Catherine, daughter of Sir Philip Champernoun, of Modbury, and widow of Otho Gilbert, of Compton, all which parishes are in that county. He was born in 1552, and exactly well educated, first under the care of his father, and afterwards in Oriel College, of which he was entered at about the age of sixteen, and which he left, though his residence there had little exceeded one year, with a high reputation for academical attainments. In the autumn of 1569 he entered into public life in the character of a soldier, in a troop of a hundred gentlemen volunteers, raised by his relation Henry Champernoun, which attached itself to the expedition then fitted out by the order of Elizabeth for the succour of the Huguenots in France. In this service, which was of the most arduous character, he remained for not less than five years, and is supposed to have returned in 1576, in which year it is evident that he resided in chambers in the Middle Temple, a circumstance which has given occasion to some contest among his biographers which might have been effectually set at rest by reference to his trial, on which he took occasion expressly to declare that he had never studied the law. He remained however not long inactive, for in 1577 he made a campaign in the Low Countries under the command of Norris, and in the following year, Sir Humphrey Gilbert, one of the celebrated navigators of that day, who was his uterine brother, having obtained a patent from the Queen to colonize in North America, Raleigh embarked with him in that expedition. It proved unsuccessful. They were met on their voyage by a Spanish fleet of superior force, and defeated; and Raleigh, returning just at the period when a new insurrection, aided by the intrigues and the troops of Spain, had broken out in Ireland, flew to the scene of action, and now proved that he possessed, in addition to the personal bravery for which he was already distinguished, all other qualifications for a military commander. The government of Munster, a post then of the greatest importance, was intrusted to him, jointly with two old officers of established fame; a few months after he was appointed Governor of Cork; and these were his first public employments.

The Irish insurgents having been for the time reduced, he arrived in England towards the end of the year 1581, to seek preferment at the Court. It has been said that he first attracted Elizabeth's notice by a singular sort of compliment: that happening to be near her when she was walking abroad, and met with a marshy spot which she hesitated whether to pass over, he stepped suddenly forward, and taking off his velvet cloak, spread it on the place for her to tread on. The same light authorities inform us that, shortly after he had thus introduced himself, he wrote with a diamond on a window in one of her private apartments, " Fain would I climb, yet fear I to fall ;" which coming to her knowledge, she wrote under it, " If thy heart fail thee, climb not at all." Such gallantries were neither inconsistent with the fashion of the time, nor with Elizabeth's taste : whether they really occurred or not, it is certain that she now took him in some measure under her protection ; and indeed he possessed all the requisites to captivate her weakness, as well as her deliberate opinion. " He had," says Sir Robert Naunton, " in the outward man a good presence, and well compacted person ; a strong natural wit, and a better judgment, with a bold and plausible tongue, whereby he could set out his parts to the best advantage ; and to these he had the adjuncts of some general learning, which by diligence he enforced to a great augmentation and perfection ; for he was an indefatigable reader, whether by sea or land, and none of the least observers, both of men and the times." These powers he found an opportunity soon after of bringing into action with the happiest effect, on the occasion of a difference which, having occurred during his service in Ireland between himself and the Deputy, Lord Grey of Wilton, had been referred by a Council of War in that country to the Privy Council of England, before which it was heard in the spring of 1583. " I am somewhat confident," adds Naunton, " among the second causes of his growth was the variance between him and my Lord General Grey, in his descent into Ireland, which drew them both over to the Council Table, there to plead their own causes ; where what advantage he had in the case in controversy I know not, but he had much the better in the telling of his tale ; insomuch as the Queen and the Lords took no slight mark of the man, and his parts : for from thence he came to be known, and to have access to the Lords, and then we are not to doubt how such a man would comply, and learn the way of progression. And whether or no my Lord of Leicester had then cast in a good word for him to the Queen, which would have done no harm, I do not determine ; but true it is he had gotten the Queen's ear at a trice, and she began to be taken with his elocution, and loved to hear his reasons to her demands ; and the truth is she took him for a kind of oracle, which nettled them all ; yea, those that he relied on began to take this his sudden favour for an alarm, and to be sensible of their own supplantation and to project his."

Whether it was with the view, in one who seems not to have abounded in prudence, of avoiding these jealousies, or to gratify an inclination to project and enterprise which certainly belonged to his nature, it is now perhaps too late to learn, but Raleigh, in this moment of triumphant favour, and for several succeeding years, seems to have devoted his serious attention exclusively to maritime discovery and speculation. In 1583 he sailed towards Newfoundland, as Vice Admiral of a fleet of four ships, commanded by his brother Gilbert, one of which he had manned and victualled at his own charge, and named after himself. The expedition was most unfortunate ; and Gilbert, with two of his ships, was lost in returning to England; yet in the following year Raleigh laid a plan before the Queen and Council for another, and, by a grant, dated the twenty-fifth of March, 1584, was allowed " free liberty to discover such remote heathen and barbarous lands as were not actually possessed by any Christian, nor inhabited by Christian people." He now fitted out two ships for the Gulf of Florida, and the fruit of the voyage was the discovery of Virginia, which is well known to have then received its name from Elizabeth, and where, at his recommendation, she consented to the planting of an English colony, which in the spring of the following year was despatched thither under his direction in a fleet of seven sail, commanded by his kinsman, Sir Richard Granville, who on his return captured a Spanish ship worth fifty thousand pounds. Even during this voyage he was actively engaged with Sir Adrian Gilbert, another of his half brothers, in an

4

enterprise to explore the north-west passage, in which those straits which have been denominated from Davis, the ill-fated commander, were first penetrated. In 1586, he fitted out another squadron to Virginia; sent two ships to cruise against the Spaniards, which returned with considerable wealth; and joined George Clifford, Earl of Cumberland, in a less successful adventure to the South Seas. In 1587, he was still anxiously engaged in the establishment of the new colony, his interests in which he soon after assigned, with certain reservations, to several merchants of London; in the succeeding year distinguished himself in the great overthrow of the Spanish Armada; and in 1589 sailed with Norris and Drake to Portugal on the expedition then undertaken to restore Don Antonio to the throne of that country.

While he was thus engaged, favours and distinctions, whether he courted them or not, were lavishly showered on him. In 1584 he obtained the then envied honour of knighthood; was elected to serve in Parliament for his native county, as he was afterwards for Cornwall; and received in that year a patent for licensing the sale of wines throughout the nation, and in the next a grant of twelve thousand acres in the counties of Cork and Waterford. In 1586 he was appointed Seneschal of the Duchies of Cornwall and Exeter, and Lord Warden of the Stanneries, and, a few months after, Captain, that is to say Commander, of the Queen's guard. Great estates in the western counties were afterwards bestowed on him by Elizabeth, particularly the manor of Sherborne, in Dorsetshire, where he built, says Coker, in his survey of that county, in a park adjoining to the castle, out of the ground, a most fine house, which he beautified with orchards, gardens, and groves, of much variety and delight." In the mean time his public and private conduct seem to have been marked by the most perfect independence: he neither led nor served any party; nor do we discover a single instance of his having used that influence which he certainly possessed over the affections of Elizabeth to any unworthy end, nor of his having endeavoured to increase, or even to maintain it, by adulation or servile compliance. On the contrary, his professions, and indeed his practices, were not unfrequently in opposition to her religious or political notions. In receding contemptuously from the ridiculous complexities of school divinity, he is said to have fallen into contrary errors, and to have become a sceptic, if not a deist. The Queen reasoned with him on these subjects, and censured his opinions with sharpness, but he disdained to disavow them. He defended the learned Puritan Udal, who had libelled the Hierarchy with the most virulent bitterness, and, when that minister was therefore condemned for high treason, interfered successfully to save his life. His interest seems indeed to have been continually exerted in the service of others, and we are told that Elizabeth once said to him, alluding to the frequency of such his requests, " When Sir Walter, will you cease to be a beggar?" to which he answered, " When your Majesty shall cease to be beneficent."

In 1592 he sailed again on an expedition against the Spanish settlements in the West Indies, with a strong force, raised by himself and others, to which Elizabeth added two of her best ships of war. It was prevented by storms from reaching its destination, and he returned, but his shattered fleet after his departure captured a Portuguese carrack, said to have been the richest prize that had ever been brought to England. The discovery of his amour with Elizabeth Throckmorton, one of the Queen's maids of honour, occurred just at this period; an offence, which, though he made the best atonement in his power by marrying the lady, Elizabeth punished by imprisoning them in the Tower for many months. It should seem that this severity was dictated rather by prudence, and a sense of propriety, than by resentment, for he certainly received eminent proofs of the Queen's favour immediately after his liberation, yet it is held by several writers that the umbrage into which he fell on this occasion determined him once more to quit England; while others, with perhaps as little reason, ascribe that resolution to the envy and jealousy by which he was assailed at home. It is highly probable that his motive was simply the acquisition of wealth to support his enormous expenses, for no man of his time surpassed him in magnificence. He tilted in silver armour, wearing a sword and belt set with diamonds, rubies, and pearls; appeared at Court, on solemn occasions, covered with jewels, nearly to the value of seventy thousand pounds; and his retinue and table were maintained with proportionate splendour. It is in perfect agreement with a just notion of Raleigh's character to suppose that he wished to owe these luxuries to his own exertions, and his choice of the country to which he now directed his speculations tends in no small degree to favour that conjecture.

He had long contemplated the full discovery of Guiana, in South America, and in the spring of 1594 dispatched a trusty person thither, on whose favourable report he sailed in the following February, and returning in August 1595, described to Elizabeth in the most glowing colours the inexhaustible riches of the soil, on which he besought her to plant a colony. She refused; but to console him for the disappointment, named him Admiral in the expedition of the next year, which ended in the capture of Cadiz, and also in that of the summer of 1597, which is so largely treated of by most of our historians, under the name of the Island Voyage. In both those enterprises Essex had the chief command, and it was in the latter that an unhappy discord arose between these great men, which perhaps accelerated the fall of the one, and was certainly pregnant with the more distant fate of the other. It was clear that the success of the plan had been sacrificed to their envious rivalry, and their misconduct was discussed at home with unusual freedom. They returned, overflowing with mutual reproaches, to the disgraceful consolations usually sought by men so circumstanced; Essex to become the leader of a senseless mob, and Raleigh to resign his independence into the hands of a minister of state. Tempted by views of gratifying his resentment, this great man became a dupe to the artifices of Cecil, who cherished him for the hour as a willing instrument to thwart the ambition, and undermine the favour, of Essex. Of his willingness we have indeed subsequently too frightful a proof in a letter that has been more than once printed, written by him to the secretary after Essex had been made prisoner, from which, amidst some ambiguity of expression, it may be inferred that he thirsted for the blood of that unhappy favourite. Raleigh was now flattered by moderate favours, and cajoled by splendid hopes. The management in the House of Commons of affairs in which the Crown was peculiarly interested seems to have been committed chiefly to him during the remainder of this reign. He obtained, in 1598, a grant of the pre-emption of Cornish tin, a privilege of great lucre; was sent Ambassador to Flanders, with Lord Cobham, in the summer of 1600; and in the autumn of that year was appointed Governor of Jersey. Meanwhile he was fallaciously encouraged to expect the great and arduous post of Deputy of Ireland and the dignity of a Baron.

But Cecil's sole purpose was at length accomplished. Essex had been finally disposed of, and Raleigh in his turn became an object of jealousy and fear. His fortune now hung on the slender thread that supported the life of Elizabeth, for he was too firmly fixed in her favour to be shaken by any effort of malice or intrigue while he remained her servant; but Cecil had not neglected to infuse bitter prejudices against him into the mean and timid mind of her successor, who on mounting the throne received him with coolness, and soon after dismissed him from his employments. Raleigh, in searching for the motives to this indignity, detected the wicked baseness of the Secretary, and, in the first moments of a generous irritation, presented a memorial against him to the King, in which, among many other heavy accusations, he denounced Cecil as a main instrument in causing the death of the unfortunate Mary. The intelligence was received by James with indifference, but it naturally changed the aversion of Cecil into the deepest hatred; while Raleigh, deceived, persecuted, and threatened, by the minister, and neglected by the King, threw himself into the arms of a small party, headed by two noblemen, distinguished only by their bitterness against

8

James and his countrymen. With these, Brook, Lord Cobham, and Thomas Lord Grey de Wilton, he certainly in some measure engaged in that conspiracy to place Arabella Stuart on the throne, the singular extravagancy of which is familiar to all readers of English history, but how far short his offence fell of treason, his trial, which took place at Winchester, on the seventeenth of November, 1603, will abundantly prove. The utter deficiency of evidence in support of the charge ; the courage, candour, and ready wit and judgment displayed by himself; and the brutal speeches of Coke the attorney-general ; combine to render that document a record of one of the most curious and interesting juridical processes on record. He was however found guilty by a jury more barbarous even than his prosecutors, for when the verdict was communicated to Coke, who happened not to be in the court when it was delivered, he exclaimed to the messenger, "Surely thou art mistaken, for I myself accused him but of misprision of treason." He received sentence, and remained at Winchester in daily expectation of death for about a month, during which he appealed to James's mercy, and on the fifteenth of December received a reprieve, and was removed to the Tower, where he continued a prisoner for twelve years. There it is well known that he became an historian, a philosopher, and a poet, and raised a fame for almost universal science equal to his former reputation for arms and enterprise. The severity of his imprisonment was from time to time slackened, and on the twenty-fifth of March, 1616, he was at length released, on the intercession of the new favourite Villiers, some of whose retainers had been bribed by a large sum to move their master to that end. Stripped of his estates by attainder, the sport of his enemies, and timidly abandoned by his friends, nothing now remained to this great man but his admirable powers of mind and body, and that spirit of boundless activity which had ever distinguished both, and which the severity of his fortune had left wholly unimpaired. He was no sooner at large than he undertook a new voyage to Guiana, and James, tempted by the prospect of boundless wealth, readily granted him, on the twenty-sixth of August following, a commission, under the Great Seal, of Admiral. Raleigh, rendered cautious by injustice and calamity, was desirous to obtain a specific pardon before his departure, and consulted his friend Bacon, then Lord Keeper, who fatally assured him that his commission might always be pleaded fully to that effect. After long preparation, and an expense of more than ten thousand pounds, collected with the utmost difficulty, he sailed on the twenty-eighth of March, 1617. Treachery and cowardice combined to blast, together with the views of his expedition, all his future hopes. Through the vigilance and artifice of Gondamar, Ambassador from Madrid, and the base pusillanimity of James, his design was betrayed to the Spaniards at Guiana before his arrival, and he found a superior force in full array to receive him. He attempted to force a passage, and was defeated. " Never," says he, in a narrative which he published after his return, " was poor man so exposed to the slaughter as I was : for being commanded by my allegiance to set down not only the country, but the very river by which I was to enter it ; to name my ship's number, men, and my artillery ; this was sent by the Spanish Ambassador to his master, the King of Spain :" nor was this the partial complaint of a disappointed and enraged commander, for the history of that time abounds in evidences of the justice of his charge. In this unhappy warfare his eldest son fell, bravely fighting. The news of his discomfiture reached London, and the terrified James instantly issued a proclamation, declaring that he had in his original orders to Raleigh expressly prohibited any act of hostility against the Spaniards, and threatening a severe punishment. Raleigh arrived at Plymouth a few days after ; was arrested on his road to London ; and, after two attempts to escape, was, on the tenth of August, once more closely imprisoned in the Tower. It is unnecessary to stain these pages with a detail of the monstrous perversions of law, and justice, and humanity, under the pretext of which the blood of this admirable person was shed, for it may be found in every general history of his country. After the solemn mockery of a conference held by all the Judges, he was, on the twenty-eighth of October, brought to the King's Bench bar, and required to say why execution of the sentence passed on him fifteen years before should not now be awarded; defended himself with a vigour of argument and beauty of eloquence, which astonished all who heard him; and was the next day, under the authority of a special warrant signed by the King, beheaded in Old Palace Yard, Westminster.

To give an ample and correct view of the infinitely diversified character of Raleigh, would double the extent of these pages. A general idea of the wonderful powers which distinguished it may perhaps be best conveyed by a few words of Anthony Wood, delivered with his usual conciseness and simplicity. " Authors are perplexed," says Wood, " under what topic to place him; whether of statesman, seaman, soldier, chemist, or chronologer, for in all these he did excel; and it still remains a dispute whether the age he lived in was more obliged to his pen or his sword, the one being busy in conquering the new, the other in so bravely describing the old world. The truth is, he was unfortunate in nothing else but the greatness of his wit and advancement. His eminent worth was such, both in domestic polity, foreign expeditions and discoveries, arts and literature, both practive and contemplative, that they seemed at once to conquer both example and imitation. Those that knew him well esteemed him to be a person born to that only which he went about, so dexterous was he in all or most of his undertakings, in court, in camp, by sea, by land, with sword, with pen." For an estimate of the profound learning and exquisite genius which he displayed in various branches of literature, let me appeal to a few pages prefixed to a very late publication of his scattered poems, in which the strictest truth of criticism is adorned by the utmost force and beauty of expression. On the whole, it is not too much to say that Raleigh was the most eminent man of the age in which he lived; an age enlightened by his talents, and perhaps improved by his example, for he descended to the grave with an exactness of moral reputation, not only unstained, but, with the single exception lately referred to, wholly unsuspected.

The printed productions of his pen which we have the good fortune to possess, for some of his works remain yet unpublished, are his celebrated History of the World—A Relation of the Discovery of Guiana, presented to Queen Elizabeth—Notes of Direction for the Defence of the Kingdom in 1588—The Prerogative of Parliament in England, proved in a dialogue between a Counsellor of State and a Justice of Peace—Instructions to his Son, and posterity—The History of Mahomet—The Prince, or Maxims of State; republished, with the title of " Aphorisms of State"—The Sceptic, or Speculations—Observations on the Magnificence and Opulency of Cities—The State of Government—Letters to the King, and others of Quality—A dialogue between a Jesuit and a Recusant—Observations on the inventions of Shipping, and Sea Service—Apology for his last Voyage to Guiana—Observations touching Trade and Commerce with the Hollanders—The Cabinet Council, containing the Chief Arts and Mysteries of State—An Historical and Geographical Description of the Great Country and River of the Amazons—Wars with Foreign Princes dangerous to our Commonwealth, or Reasons for Foreign Wars answered —Speeches and Arguments in several Parliaments towards the end of Elizabeth's reign—The Son's Advice to His Father—and the Collection of his poetical pieces lately referred to. Most of the smaller tracts here mentioned were collected by Dr. Birch, and republished in 1751, in two volumes.

Sir Walter Raleigh, as has been already said, married Elizabeth a daughter of Sir Nicholas Throckmorton, alias Carew, of Beddington in Surrey. He had by her two sons; Walter, unmarried, who was killed, as has been already said, by the Spaniards in South America; and Carew. As the subsequent issue of Raleigh has, I believe, never yet been publicly noticed, some extended account of it here may be desirable. Carew married Philippa, daughter of . . . . . Weston, and relict of Sir Anthony Ashley. By that lady he had three daughters, of whom Elizabeth and Mary died spinsters, and Anne, the youngest, became the wife of Sir Peter Tyrrel, of Castlethorpe, in Bucks; and two sons, of whom Walter, the elder, who was seated at West Horsley, in Surrey, an estate which had been purchased by his father, and was knighted soon after the restoration, married Elizabeth, daughter and heir of William Rogers of Sandwell, in Gloucestershire, and left by her three daughters, his coheirs; Elizabeth, wife of Sir John Elwes, Knt.; Philippa, of Oliver Wicks, of Tortington, in Sussex; and Anne, married to William Knight, of Barrels, in the county of Warwick. Philip, the second son of Carew Raleigh, whom I find styled of London, and of Tenchley Meer, in Surrey, married Frances, daughter of a Mr. Granville, of Foscot in Buckinghamshire, and had by her four sons—Walter, Brudenel, Granville, and Carew; and three daughters—Frances, Anne, and Elizabeth. Most of them were living in 1695, in which year all the daughters were unmarried. At that period our intelligence ceases.